Trauma
Informed
Enlightenment

Trauma Informed Enlightenment

"There are many different paths to healing. Michelle's book beautifully reflects one of those paths. Her work supports the reader in awakening and befriending their inner witness. Through the stories and experiences Michelle shares of the healing journey, readers will find hope that even after experiencing trauma that has separated them from their sense of authentic self, there are always pathways to discover that they were never truly disconnected after all."

— SARAH PEYTON, author of *Your Resonant Self* and *Affirmations for Turbulent Times*

"This book has touched my life deeply. I am entranced! It is a brilliant weaving of the core tenets of what healing really is. When I started reading, I could hardly put it down. Since *The Body Knows the Score* has been on the *New York Times* Best Seller list for over 247 weeks, our collective mind is finally recognizing we are all traumatized and how it affects our lives. This book is a brilliant guide on how to heal from trauma.

"I have read Porges, Mate, Schwarz, Levine, and van der Kolk over the years—what you have done is taken those truths and shown how they can be applied in our lives in a profoundly simple way. This is the way of healing that not only individuals, but the collective is ready for. My gratitude is deep."

— MARY O'MALLEY, author of *That's in the Way Is the Way*

"In *Trauma Informed Enlightenment*, Michelle Holling-Brooks has fashioned a handbook for re- membering the soul and the self. Familiar with the landscape of trauma and well-versed in its neurobiological theory, she also has the literal horse sense of what it means to have personally traversed this territory. A great read and a great resource."

— ANN MITRAKUL, LCSW, MD

"This book resonates 100 percent with my own journey. In fact, while reading it, it acts as a sacred witness itself. I felt seen, heard, understood, and less alone in my own experiences. I love and recommend this book to anyone on a journey of healing."

— SANDY NELMS, student of life

Trauma Informed Enlightenment

AWAKENING TO THE HEALING POWER OF THE SACRED WITNESS

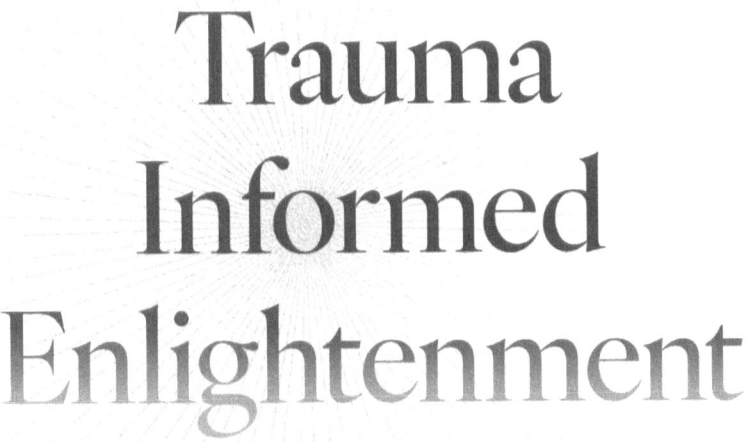

Michelle Holling-Brooks

UNBRIDLED
CHANGE

This book is dedicated to the Sacred Witness within,
through your light and love, we remember who we are—
thank you.

Contents

Foreword

When Michelle first shared her book with me, I was immediately intrigued by the title. Who would ever think that the words *trauma* and *enlightenment* could be coupled together? And yet they are, brilliantly so, in this groundbreaking book on healing trauma.

To understand the heart and soul of this book, it would help to define what trauma is. It was only in 1980 that the psychological wounds from war were given the name PTSD. But for years after, we saw trauma through the narrow lens of war. Slowly, we're beginning to realize that, to some extent, all of us are traumatized, especially when we were little and had little or no control over our situations.

What is the current working definition of trauma? It happens when you are in a situation where you have little or no control and you feel threatened. It is almost impossible to integrate what happens so you either fight, flee, or freeze, stuffing the overwhelming feelings that come from being traumatized deep inside of you. These feelings don't go away. From their hiding place within us, they influence our lives in ways that are too numerous to list.

Other than war, some other experiences that are now understood as traumatic are sexual abuse, neglect, physical abuse, bullying, natural disasters, demanding parents, the sudden loss of a family member, angry relatives, a scary illness, a house burning down, or a major accident. There are also things that we don't perceive at first as traumatic, but for many people they are, such as betrayal, rejection, broken trust, financial loss, divorce, being fired, etc. It is also startling to realize that to one person's nervous system, something is not traumatic, but to another person, it could be.

For many people, their traumas remain invisible, hidden beneath layers of shame, denial, or simply a lack of awareness. Society's collective blindness to certain types of traumas increases this invisibility, leaving many to suffer in silence. But something very exciting is happening. Humanity is beginning to realize how deeply trauma affects us and how it influences our interface with the world. This is indicated by the number of books on trauma that are showing up on the New York Times Best Seller list.

We now comprehend that trauma, rather than something to be hidden or fixed, can be a great healer. How can I say that? Because it is fairly easy for human beings to hide inside of us all the fear shame, and discomfort that come from trauma. We think this makes them go away, but it doesn't. Hidden inside, they can affect our lives without us really understanding what is going on. So the gift of trauma is that it makes it much more difficult to just slide through life. Trauma is an invitation to actually notice what we are experiencing, giving it the healing light of our attention so it can be healed.

The other word in the title is *enlightenment*. For many people this is a much-misunderstood word. They see it as arriving at a particular state that, if you work hard enough, you can stay in forever. For me, that definition totally misses the mark. Enlightenment isn't a fixed state. It is an alive, creative connection with life. Or as one of my teachers once said, "Enlightenment is relaxing into life."

So, I like to use the word *lightenment*. Imagine feeling more ease, peace, and trust in your life. That is what the word *lightenment* is pointing to. It comes when you discover how to free all the traumas you took on that keep you struggling rather than showing up for the amazing adventure that is life. So your traumas, when healed by the sacred witness Michelle introduces you to, can become the doorway to the healing you long for. Hopefully now it makes sense as to why trauma and enlightenment are in the same title.

We are hungry to heal the traumas we all take on that have caused us to be with ourselves, our fellow human beings, and the world in ways that cause harm. Michelle's book is one of the clearest guides I have come across for mending our individual traumas so we can become a healing presence in the world.

Michelle has a PhD in life, having taken on traumas she barely survived. Rather than just surviving, she chose to thrive by learning how to recognize the traumas she carried and how to bring them the heartfelt recognition they needed to let go. Put simply, she made lemonade out of the lemons that life gave her.

I, too, took on a level of trauma that I barely survived. But these traumas put me on the path to healing where I learned you can't change what happened, but you can change its imprint on you. And of all the books I have studied, this book touched me the most deeply. It comes from Michelle's living experience of healing her own traumas and from the thousands of people she has worked with over the years at her non-profit Unbridled Change.

If I could show you my copy of this book, you would see there are almost more underlines than not all the way through. And having had the wonderful grace to spend quality time with Michelle, she is the most skillful guide I have come across for how to recognize and set free the parts of ourselves that keep us cut off from being our authentic self, living a full and rich life.

If this calls to you, this book can become a very good friend. It shows that you don't have to live at the mercy of the frozen energy inside of you that comes from traumatic events. Page by page, chapter by chapter, it can guide you out of chronically struggling with life into the joy of being alive.

—Mary O'Malley,

Author of *What's in the Way IS the Way*, *The Gift of Our Compulsions*, and *The Joy of Being Fully Alive*

Introduction

Why We Need the Sacred Witness Medicine
Now More Than Ever

At the age of twenty-three, I was a shell of a person. I was living a life which I felt no connection to. I felt as if I was stuck watching my life from the outside. This thing called *Michelle* just kept moving, doing, and reacting without any input from Me, as if I was this little balloon following her around but not actually able to interact with life from a felt sense. Anytime I did drop in to actually feel my physical, emotional, mental, or spiritual bodies, all I could access were overwhelming sensations of pain and suffering. Stuck in a shell of a body riddled with pain, trauma, and illness, I could no longer find a good reason to stay on this earth plane. I had no hope—no hope that life could feel different, nor hope or belief that I was worthy of healing. I hated my life. I hated the Michelle that stared back at me in the mirror with hollow empty eyes that felt so separate from me.

One day, at my limit, I took a handful of pills and waited for the pain to stop. At that moment, as I was collapsed unconscious on the bedroom floor, the Divine intervened. My trusty German Shepherd, Baron—one of my amazing soul guardians and companions—licked my mouth to trigger a vomit response. When I woke up after this failed attempt to kill myself, he showed me a vision. Laying there in a puddle of my own vomit, I saw Baron staring at me, pleading with me. In my mind, I heard his voice say, *Why don't you see the amazing Being I see? Why are you hurting yourself and throwing yourself away? Please see what I see. Find her.* Then he showed me an image of my Soul as he witnessed it—a slight outline of a person surrounded by and emanating light from

1

within. The light danced and glimmered with threads of golds, ambers, greens, and blues. It was glorious! As I witnessed what he was showing me, my heart center burst open, and I remembered that Being.

The warmth of my Soul and Baron's Soul bathed through me, thawing out the Parts of me that were shutting down, lost in a frozen tundra of nothingness. I rose off the floor of my basement apartment, hugged Baron, and thanked him for saving me and for helping me remember and find hope again. I got into the shower and washed the vomit and bits of pills from my hair and body. I felt a cellular shift ripple through my whole Body Being. Right then, I knew I had to find my way back to the Being that Baron had shown me. I believed and trusted the vision Baron had given me, even though the current image in the mirror still felt foreign to me. My Mental Being could hardly imagine that this girl staring back at me was the same one Baron showed me. I knew he was showing me my True Self.

Animal Beings don't lie or embellish like Human Beings. This amazing Soul Baron had shown me—with her love, joy, warmth, and light—was *within* me. Now I just had to find her again, uncover her, and embody her. That evening, I made Baron a promise that I was going to try—even though I didn't know how in the world I'd heal or overcome this ocean of pain, suffering, anger, and fear. Just the thought of trying to embody the Soul I'd witnessed felt crazy overwhelming. Nevertheless, he and I set out on a journey to heal—so I could remember and embody the whole Being Baron had shown me. From that moment until now, my daily intention and prayer has been to live, love, and lead a life that is in alignment with my True Self.

This book is a compilation of that journey—of the practices and phases of healing I have walked myself and thousands of clients through over the last twenty-five years, as an equine-partnered mental health practitioner, holistic wellness coach, teacher, and spiritual mentor.

While I have profound transformational concepts and practices to share with you, it's important to note that we're always on the journey and there is no final destination point. This work is more of an infinite spiral than a linear path from A to B. I believe we are always evolving, learning, and uncovering even more of our True Self every day.

I'm definitely still on the journey. Every day, I engage an unfolding *practice,* by setting the intention to see how much of my beautiful, amazing light and Soul can I bring into my daily life. Every day, I hold the space of the Sacred Witness with clients (who are also my teachers) as they traverse that healing spiral. Every day, I tend and deepen my connection with my True Self inside my regular human life, moment to moment.

As I went on my journey, I realized I couldn't heal in isolation. My pain, illnesses, and struggles thrived inside my isolation and disconnection. While I had definitely disconnected myself from others because I didn't trust many humans, I had also disconnected from myself. I needed a path and a guide to walk with me so that I could learn how to heal those disconnections. I needed someone that would hold the space—not just try to *fix* me but *accompany* me as I ventured into the wilderness of my inner world. I needed the power of the Sacred Witness.

Over the next twenty years, the Sacred Witness came forward in various forms—as teachers, friends, co-workers, animal Beings, plant Beings, and other Beings of all shapes, sizes, and types. I followed the breadcrumbs of the universe and my amazing *Wise One Team,* as I now like to call them.

I slowly waded deeper and deeper into my healing and experienced a TON of ups and downs in the process. I got stuck in little eddies and tossed around by whirlpools. I was lured off track by moments of forgetfulness, anger, disease, and complacency. However, somehow my Heart and Soul were always able to break through those moments, wake me up, and invite me into the next part of the journey and exploration.

WHY THIS WORK IS SO NEEDED NOW

I believe more than ever we are being asked, both collectively and individually, to step into the next level of consciousness, and to heal and break free from shadow patterns and ingrained dynamics we all have with the energies of Power and Control. It is time for the Human species to awaken to the levels of pain and suffering that our current ways of being, systems, and shadow wounds are causing to ourselves, each other, and all Beings, including our planet. I believe at the very heart of our human collective, lies a growing call to remember what true empowerment is, dismantling our survival-of-the-fittest-based views of human nature and re-aligning ourselves with our true divine nature.

My own vision quests have shown me that our current way of conception of the Human Being is a result of de-evolution of the species. This de-evolution has landed us in a field of separation, shadow power, control, and domination codes within our system that are overriding our true nature. We are riddled with unresolved trauma and survival programming—which has filled us, collectively, to the brim with hostile tribalism, negative competition, and so on.

In all of this, we've forgotten the truth. These survival paradigms of tribalism, power, and control are not the intended original design for the human experience. That we are meant to run on dominance dynamics where only the "fittest" survive is a massive myth. Humanity was not created to see if we could override and evolve beyond these dominating instincts. We were not meant to hurt ourselves and other Beings to later wake up and prove our worth by evolving into a "new" type of Human Being that is caring, compassionate, capable of honoring life, and able to work together.

Alternative to these original sin-type ideologies, I believe our original and true nature IS one of goodness and love. We were designed as Beings that innately honor life and diversity, have compassion toward other Beings, know how to steward and find balance (within and without), and innately desire and strive to support all beings—via true empowerment, personal agency, and self-responsibility.

We are truly in the transformational re-evolutionary process right now. We have the opportunity to awaken to, remember, and reembody our True Nature. Collectively and individually, we can deconstruct and transmute the destructive inherited burdens and codes passed down for thousands of years and generations. This is not a small task. It is going to take a collective embodiment of the Sacred Witness to root out and repair the full extent of the trapped trauma responses and adaptations passed down from generation to generation.

We need the healing power of the Sacred Witness to break the cycles. We need the healing power of the Sacred Witness to help us discover new ways of being with ourselves and each other that are in alignment with our true nature. Our Souls know that our true nature, in tandem with the Sacred Witness energy, can guide us all back to our True Selves.

When we listen, our hearts feel the deep call to stop vicious trauma cycles and de-perpetuate the experience that hurt people will always hurt people. It is time for a new narrative, prayer, and way of being with ourselves and each other. As I write this, I feel my Heart saying, *I might not know how to do that, or what will come from my own personal journey of healing the unresolved trauma in my own system, but I was sent here now in these times, to reclaim and liberate my body and my life! My legacy is going to be one of empowerment, freedom, and unbridled JOY in living a life that I love, inside and out!* This is what we are up to in this book—liberation, freedom, joy, love, compassion, and the ability to feel at home in our own bodies and lives.

To answer this call, we need courage, compassion, inner wisdom, and strength to illuminate the ways of being that no longer serve us, individually and collectively. We need the same healing power I needed to break free of the wounded cycles of self-destruction and awaken to a totally new way of being, a new level of consciousness. That is the energy of the Sacred Witness. The Sacred Witness is the container and framework I believe can help us compassionately witness that which needs to be seen, felt, and heard within us so that we can truly release the karmic weight of our past and move forward into the next phase of our evolution, both personally and collectively.

WHO THIS BOOK IS FOR

While making the choice to heal and connect more with our True Self seems like an easy choice, actually walking the required path is not always so simple. Many of us experience an ocean of past pains, traumas, and inherited burdens of hopelessness and learned helplessness that cut us off from the ability to fully embody the solutions and options spiritual enlightenment traditions and self-help practices offer us. The struggle isn't because we don't want to free ourselves or because we lack the self-discipline or willpower to liberate ourselves. Rather, it is because past trauma and survival adaptations hinder our ability to match our actions with our Heart and Soul's guidance. As we seek a path of healing, the hidden impact of unresolved trauma can work against us in stealthy ways, leaving us lost adrift storms of inner shame, subtle feelings of worthlessness, and believing that something is truly wrong or broken within us—all of which are not true.

This book is designed to support the spiritual Seeker that has experienced a version of the separation and confusion I was feeling when Baron offered me a lifeline in the storm of unhealed trauma and suffering. It is here to serve as a Soul Companion and a sacred guide for you on your healing and spiritual journey. It invites you to discover for yourself the Soul-Level that we really can free ourselves from shadow survival and trauma adaptations and live our liberation. And we do so by cultivating the healing power of the Sacred Witness.

Whether you are new to Self-Work or a seasoned traveler, this Soul-companion-in-book-form will support you right where you are on your journey of remembering your wholeness and help you embark on the next level of awakening and enlightenment.

Book's Organization

I have designed this book to be a working, living, breathing tool for you. Think of it like a guided vision quest and healing journey. I share different teachings, frameworks, wisdom traditions, and contemplation practices that will help you gain both real-world understanding and embodiment, meaning an inherent felt sense and knowing, of the healing power of the Sacred Witness.

The sections of this book parallel the process I use with clients to holistically support ALL aspects of themselves—physical, mental, emotional, and spiritual. As we journey together, you will open to and befriend the energy of the Sacred Witness as your inner healing companion. You will find that Parts of you awaken easily and sink into the healing embrace of your inner Sacred Witness, releasing their pain and suffering as a welcomed gift. Other Parts of you will struggle, doubt, and at times feel extremely threatened by the power and expansion opportunities our innate healing presence can offer, to our own wounds and to others.

The book builds on itself, each section weaving together foundational invitations, explorations, practices, and skills. When combined, these give you a secure Bridge of Connection™ to your True Self and the Sacred Witness within. More about that Bridge in the chapters to come.

To help immerse us more fully into what we are discovering and exploring, you'll also read many stories and case studies throughout this book—some of which come from my personal healing journey and some from client experiences. For the latter, I have changed names and identifying features to protect their autonomy and confidentiality. All such clients have signed waivers agreeing to share the essence of their stories to help others on their journey. I am so grateful for their willingness and true embodiment of the healing power of the Sacred Witness.

HOW TO WORK WITH THIS BOOK

To help you deeply work with each stage of embodying the Sacred Witness, I suggest keeping a journal to record your reflections, insights, challenges, aha moments, and other impressions as you work with the guided meditations and practices throughout this book. If you are called to go deeper, I offer immersion courses and workshops, and the Sacred Witness Oracle Deck, to help you take this work further.

I suggest two main "ways" you might find helpful in working with this book. First is the Bird's Eye View. In this option, you can read through the book linearly, lingering a little bit here and there with the practices as you feel guided. Once you have completed the book, you can then circle back around for a second pass; taking your time to sink into the different sections and practices, exploring the teachings held within them. The second option is the Immersion Method. This approach allows you to engage deeply and slowly with each teaching, practice, and section as you read, organically moving forward to the next part of the journey as you feel guided. With both options, I encourage you to give yourself the gift of time and be willing to circle back around to anything that calls to you.

You will have moments of ease and grace as you are working with this book. You will feel completely in LOVE with a practice or meditation prompt. AND you will have moments of wanting to throw this book out a window or forget about it. This is completely normal.

If you didn't swing back and forth with this book, I would ask you to read it again and let the material go deeper than surface level.

Right now, give yourself permission to ebb and flow with this journey, to rest when needed, to lean in and dive a little deeper, and to be willing to be a hot mess with it. I also invite you to make a commitment to yourself just like I did with Baron: even though you might not know how, or even want to try on some days, that you commit to showing up and being willing. This is everything you need.

Also, please remember, healing happens in connection. That connection can be internal, as you connect with the inner wisdom from your Heart and Soul Beings. However, we often need outside connection in the form of a spiritual coach or mentor, therapist, medical professionals, and other healing and wellness professionals. Connection may also be creating or joining a circle of fellow travelers to work through the book together.

The thoughts and practices I share within this book are not meant to be used as treatment plans, professional advice, or a replacement for traditional health and wellness professional support. If you need support with what this material is bringing forward, please reach out to a qualified professional of your choice. Trust your Heart and the Sacred Witness within and seek support as you feel guided.

How To Engage The Practices

"Where attention goes, neural firing flows, and neural connections grow."
—Daniel J. Sigel, MD

This book is a combination of teachings and practices, as both understanding and active engagement are required on the path of awakening the Sacred Witness within.

The invitations in this book are designed to meet you exactly where you are at, with no previous experience or skill required. Whether you are new to meditation, contemplative practices, and personal inquiry or are well along your journey of Self-Work, I encourage you to meet this work with fresh eyes and a beginner's mind. Those more experienced readers will get the most out of this book by bringing curiosity and willingness to approaching this work anew, as it will bring new levels of more refined awareness.

In any case, be kind to yourself—these are called *practices* for a reason. You are cultivating new pathways in your system, reshaping your nervous system and expanding its window of tolerance, and reclaiming your original languages of sensation and symbolism. Like any new practice set, your engagement with this book will take repetition and commitment to steadily build new pathways and ways of beingness. I suggest engaging the practices of this book daily, for at least five to ten minutes. This repetition and frequency of engagement makes all the difference. Trust the process—it works!

In the practices that follow, we don't go in with rigid expectations but rather make space to have a deep conversation (sensing, hearing, perceiving, and knowing) with the wisest aspects of our Being—our Soul Being and the Sacred Witness within. The work is designed to facilitate open dialogue with all aspects of ourselves. We come with a deep willingness to see and validate all defensive or wounded Parts of our psyche and ultimately invite them to stand down so insights can come from a more holistic perspective. The work naturally brings us to requests for aligned action based on the insight and guidance we receive—which often ask us to shift our perspectives, thoughts, habits, behaviors, and interaction patterns. Taking these committed actions is how you get the most out of this work.

Further, to get the most out of this work, take your time. Really dwell in sections and on practices for days, weeks, and even months, allowing repetition and consistent engagement to yield benefits. The more you work with the practices and take aligned action, the more you will unwind and release old patterns and perspectives and come into healing and alignment with your True Self.

On a technical note, each practice begins the same, with a Check-In-Process. In the interest of brevity, I will introduce the practice only once, in Chapter Four, which you can reference anytime you need until it becomes second nature.

LANGUAGE USE IN THIS BOOK

Like every teacher, I've developed my own language, verbiage, and use of symbolism to share concepts and insights. I'd like to introduce you to a few of these key terms and concepts here now.

Use of the Term "Being"

Throughout this book, I use the term *Being* in two different ways. One, I often use the term *Being* instead of person. This is because the power of the Sacred Witness energy is not limited to human beings, but includes all Beings (animals, birds, insects, fish, trees, stones, and unseen ones, such as elementals, past loved ones, angels and guides . . . ALL Beings). To me, all Beings have divine sentience. When we learn how to see and hear through the Sacred Witness's point of view, we come to deeply understand and honor that all Beings have their own thoughts, consciousness, needs, and desires (physically, emotionally, mentally, and spiritually), just like humans do.

The second way I use the word *Being* throughout this book is when referring to the different bodies, centers, or aspects of ourselves that have sentience as well. You have most likely heard the terms *emotional body/center*, *mental body/center*, and so on. However, what is missing with the terms *body* or *center* is the recognition of the innate wisdom and intelligence held within these aspects of ourselves. When we hear the terms *body* or *center*, we associate them more with an object—a container or hub that houses our intelligence and not the source of independent thoughts, emotions, wisdom, and ideas.

As you will discover throughout the sections of the book, each center or body of us, which I call a *Being*—our physical, mental, emotional, and spiritual—carry with them their own point of views, ideas, wisdom, and ways of offering support, to help you both survive and thrive in this lifetime. In truth, they each have their own sentience, which often runs independent of your own conscious ego self, especially in our early years of life.

I use the terms *Body Being, Mental Being, Heart Being,* and *Soul Being* to help my clients consciously remember that healing is the process of reclaiming wholeness—gathering the lost fractured pieces of ourselves, bringing them home out of their exile, and reconnecting our consciousness to these *Beings* within ourselves. I invite you to feel into how this language opens pathways within you. It's amazing what changes when you see these different aspects of you as intelligent Beings dedicated to helping you meet life each and every day.

Other Terms in the Book

Additionally, I take the terms *Soul, Spirit, Higher Self, True Self, Sacred Witness,* and the *Divine* and bring them all together under the umbrella of the *Soul Being* for brevity. Many clients ask me what each of these terms means and try to drill down a definition for each one independently. I invite you to release the need to define these individually and instead open to the idea that the act of Sacred Witnessing is a healing function of our Soul Being.

As for the idea of different levels of consciousness within you—*Ego Self, Higher Self, Soul,* and so on—I use the following terms: *True Self* or *Wise One Self* as the representation of the inner wisdom that comes from Soul Being; and *Wise One Team* as a combination of both the wise inner aspects of you, and your external supports, such as Guides, Angels, Guardians, and the Divine.

I'm so grateful that you have taken a leap of faith into the sacred journey of embodying the Sacred Witness. Through this journey, you will learn how to establish and access a safe haven within your own system and life. Life has ups and downs, but once you have gathered the skills, resources, and ways of being offered throughout this book, you will have a calm center to always support you. When we have access to our own Sacred Witness within, there is a safe place to rest, reflect, heal, restore, and renew our connection to our True Self.

This journey allows you to meet life on life's terms and feel capable of living, loving, and leading your authentic life, no matter what. As the ripple expands, this work becomes a truly precious gift that we can offer to our loved ones and the world. You will be able to offer the same safe haven and healing power of the Sacred Witness to the Beings in your life, and the ripples flow out and out and out.

Are you ready to start your own sacred journey of embodying the Sacred Witness? Let's dive in!

Section One
Awakening and Befriending the Sacred Witness

Overview

The first part of our journey to Embodying the Sacred Witness is to explore what the Sacred Witness actually is. This will be our focus in Section One.

We must have access to the Sacred Witness within to experience true healing, liberation, and evolutionary change for the better. When we are being held by a Sacred Witness, we experience a visceral sense of being deeply heard, seen, felt, and understood. This facilitates both internal and external reconciliation and disentangles us from our past pains and hurts. As a result, we gain true freedom and step into a new creation cycle, one that is in alignment with our True Self.

I believe we all have within us the ability to hold the healing presence of the Sacred Witness for others and for ourselves. Yet we may feel cut off from accessing this innate knowledge and wisdom within due to an ocean of past pains, traumas, and survival adaptations that wash out our connections with our Heart and Soul.

In order to awaken and embrace the Sacred Witness within, we must embark on a journey of sacred remembrance, healing, and initiations of our own empowerment. This journey is not one that we can embark on with our minds and intellect alone. Nor can we lead with heart and spirit, forsaking the mind and body, as we seek to remember our own True Self. We must find a way to gather and walk with all aspects, or Beings, within—body, mind, heart, and soul—to truly embody, live, and breathe with our daily life in alignment with our true authentic self.

During Section One, I will be inviting you to:

- Remember the moments in which you have experienced the Sacred Witness on your own journey. This is intended to stir and awaken your own inner knowing of this archetypal pattern and aspect of you once again.
- Explore the basic archetypal patterns or characteristics held within the Sacred Witness and discover the foundational concepts we will explore throughout this whole journey together.
- Gain a road map and basic framework of the stages of developing and befriending the Sacred Witness within as a core part of you.

As we continue throughout the book, I will reference back to the key components and road maps I introduce in this Section so you can always know where we are on the journey of embodying the Sacred Witness energy.

To start our journey of embodying the Sacred Witness within, I would like to share with you the story of my main teachers of the healing power of a Sacred Witness, a horse named Schedule A. Then, I'll help you recall a time in which you were held by a Sacred Witness.

Chapter One

Awakening the Sacred Witness

I'd like to introduce you to the Being who first taught me the healing power of the Sacred Witness. It wasn't a human being, but rather a high-energy thoroughbred horse named Schedule A.[1] As I share about Schedule A, I invite you to think of a Being who has been a similar teacher for you.

At thirteen years old, I suddenly became ill with eastern equine encephalitis, which dominoed into Viral spinal meningitis. Having these two diseases simultaneously made for a very unhappy brain. I ended up in the hospital, slipping into a coma for seven days. When I woke, a few things were different—I was deaf from all the swelling and trapped fluid in my brain. I was so incredibly light sensitive that I was blind. I was paralyzed from the middle of my back down.

However, probably the most impactful side effect of the swelling and damage to my brain and body was that I had lost all sense of self—I didn't remember anything. When I awoke from that coma, I didn't even have a concept left that I was a human being or what that meant. All labeling, language, thought constructs, and logical reasoning were gone. I was a complete blank slate in the body of a thirteen-year-old who was suddenly deaf, blind, and couldn't move.

Paradoxically, I was in a state of sheer survival mode, yet also totally open to the true reality that we are all connected, and no real difference exists between you, me, a tree, an animal, the earth, the cosmos, and so on. The level of confusion I experienced in those first few years post-coma is almost indescribable. I felt completely alone and under constant assault from the outside world. My body was wracked with horrible pain and inner disorganization. My nervous system attuned itself to continual hypervigilance. In those post-coma years, I developed one main belief system—that the human world was not trustworthy or safe, and life was nothing but pure suffering and pain.

I came home from the hospital after three months; and, while my sensitivity to light was reduced to the point that I could make out shadows and outlines, my hearing, the lower half of my body, and my memory were still offline. Because I couldn't fight or flee/run away, my system picked the only option left: total freeze and shutdown. I was a human lump. People could move me around from point to point, but I would not interact with them. I refused to learn how to move on my own. During physical and occupational therapy, I would let people move my body, but I wasn't home. I would leave my body and go into nothingness, into the void. That was my safe haven and my only escape from the human world in a body riddled with pain.

This went on until the day my parents, grasping for anything to bring me back into this world, brought me to the barn where I'd taken riding lessons before I was sick. It was there that I first broke free of the nothingness and willingly entered my body again. It was there that I was able to actually connect to a felt sense of remembering. The Being that brought me back was a horse named Schedule A, whom I met again for the first time post-coma the day that I was brought back to the barn.

As my parents wheeled me around the corner of the barn and into the long center aisle of the large stable, four stalls down on the left, I felt a draw, something pulling me to connect with something outside of me. From that draw, I raised my hands and willingly wheeled myself down the aisle to his stall (a first for me). Schedule A looked like a massive, golden yellow, sparkling, shining Being in front of me. In real life, he was a bay, dark brown horse with a black mane and tail, and had a little white star in the middle of his forehead. (It was a shock when my physical eyesight caught up to the energy I saw and first learned to see and navigate the world post-coma, but that is a story for another book.)

In that moment, this enormous 17-hand horse, a high-strung jumper, didn't mind my wheelchair or the sound it made as it bumped into the stall door. Schedule A put his massive head and neck over the stall door and reached down to touch my shoulder. Then I uttered the first words I'd spoken in six months—*Scheddie*. I knew him and he knew me. His touch was the first touch I welcomed. I melted into it and breathed him in. He reached his head over my shoulder and down to the middle of my back to pull me even closer to him.

We stayed like that for what felt like an eternity. My hands reached as far as they could up his neck. He was holding me in a gentle embrace with his head. In that moment, I felt safe. In that moment, I felt a sensation I hadn't felt since the coma—that I was enough *just as I was*. There was no pressure to be anything else. Do anything else. Answer any questions. He wasn't afraid of me, of catching something from me—a fear I could feel coming off people who came in contact with me. He was just one percent present with me—all the parts of me—even the ones I thought were broken, wrong, and not okay.

That moment ignited spontaneous deep healing within my Heart and Body. There emerged a remembrance of the real me from the darkness I was lost in. In this moment, I became willing to find a way to live in this crazy reality called Earth and try to survive, because there were Beings like him in it.

One of the key aspects of the Sacred Witness is the willingness to truly see the other with a fully present, open heart that allows whatever is being witnessed to be seen, felt, and heard without fear of being judged or condoned, having to brace, or worrying about being pitied. A Sacred Witness is able to see, observe, and be with all the different aspects of you that are up and needing to be shared. When your inner experiences are seen, felt, and heard in this way, they can be released, softened, and healed.

Over the next three years, Schedule A helped me learn how to create a safe haven in a world I didn't understand. His healing presence allowed my body to find its way through the "damaged parts" and bring forward a different pattern within them. Working with him as my teacher, I found, rebuilt, and grew connections and pathways, which facilitated a Body and Soul willingness to heal the lower half of my body, my eyesight, my hearing, and my ability to walk. Schedule A helped lay an additional groundwork within me that would eventually allow my Mental and Heart Beings to find an oasis in the desert of life, as I experienced it.

We ALL have this power of the Sacred Witness innately within us. We don't have to be taught how to support ourselves or others from this space. However, the trick for most humans is working with our wonderful ego mind, protective and survival Parts, and our projections of the various personas we develop throughout our life that often cut us off from this innate wisdom. When we can learn how to work with these aspects of ourselves effectively, compassionately, and consciously, it allows this beautiful innate capacity to observe, be with, believe in, and welcome either the other or ourselves—free from the mental programs, beliefs systems, engrained reactions, thoughts, emotions, and stories (true or not) that muddy up the waters, so to speak.

When we do manage to release our attachments to all those things and show up more like Schedule A, or the teacher Being in your life, we find we truly have an innate ability to compassionately see the ways we've been solely acting on auto pilot, asleep at the wheel of our consciousness. When we connect to the Sacred Witness energy within our True Self, we awaken to a different level of awareness and can step into true consciousness. This allows us to shift gears from simply surviving to living, making choices, and taking committed action to co-create a life in true alignment with our True Self or Soul Being.

Shadow judgments and harsh inner critics have no place within the power of the Sacred Witness. Schedule A didn't judge me for the Parts of me that were angry, scared, or not working "right." Conversely, the Sacred Witness does not give every behavior a "pass" because it is coming from a wounded place either. Schedule A did hold me compassionately accountable for my actions and behaviors. If I reacted from fear and blindly directed my anger and frustration at him, he would walk away from me in the pasture and given me space. If I was riding him, he would refuse to move until I recognized how I was directing my actions and energy at him and waited patiently for me to sense it. Once I was able to sense how I was acting out of alignment and share with him the true source of my anger, he would move forward with me again. When these shifts in awareness came forward (even before I could put words to what I was experiencing), he would come closer or start to gently move with me again, supporting me as I unwound whatever I was stuck with.

The act of Sacred Witnessing is not static but dynamic. It is an energy that invites us into an active loving conversation. The Sacred Witness energy is interactive, clean, clear, compassionate, observes without judgment, brings forward deeper insights, and invites deep exploration of whatever needs or wants to come forward into awareness, understanding, and healing. Sacred Witness energy allows us to cultivate a true sense of inner freedom from old wounds and pains, allowing us to call forward new choices and actions that match our heart and soul. This type of witnessing brings forward healing committed actions that are in UNION with your full self—the you in this moment, your soul, and the divine guidance that is ALWAYS present to help guide you into the present moment.

CHAPTER PRACTICE
Your Sacred Witness Reflection Practice

Before I share with you the basic archetypal patterns of the Sacred Witness, I invite you into a short experiential reflection practice of your own, ideally in a journal.

Can you remember a time when someone, or some Being—it could be a person, animal, plant, tree, or rock Being—really listened to you when you were struggling, hurt, or upset? I mean really deeply listened to you?

If you can, bring up a time when this Being wasn't trying to fix you, or shift you to a different emotion, thought, or perspective. Let yourself take in any sensations, images, thoughts, or feelings that arise from this memory.

At this time, you may feel an inner sense of being held in their undivided attention. You may feel safe because you didn't feel ANY agenda coming from them, other than to let you be seen, felt, and heard.

If you are struggling to find a memory of such an experience, no worries, instead, imagine what this would be like for you. In either scenario, write down answers to the follow questions:

- How did that level of presence and support impact you?
- Did your emotions shift? If so, how?
- Did it open you up to deeper levels of understanding and invite you into deeper questions regarding what unmet needs might be behind the original issue?
- Did it help you become more willing to receive connection and support?
- In turn, could you access greater self-acceptance and compassion instead of only seeing yourself as wounded and wrong?
- What else do you notice about this presence of a Sacred Witness?

Now that you have met my first teacher in the healing power of the Sacred Witness and remembered your own, we are ready to go deeper into exploring the various archetypal patterns and stages of developing the Sacred Witness in the next two chapters.

Chapter Two

The Archetypal Pattern of the Sacred Witness

In this chapter, we will be exploring the characteristics, or archetypal patterns, of a true Sacred Witness when supporting a Being on their healing journey. I will also take you through a guided journey to help you meet a Sacred Witness avatar you can work with as we continue our journey of trauma-informed enlightenment throughout this book.

WHAT IS A SACRED WITNESS

The Sacred Witness is an archetypal pattern that invokes deep listening and space holding in ways that deeply honor the other. The Sacred Witness energy agrees to release any of their own attachments to fixing or healing the other and instead allows the witnessed Being's own innate healing process to lead them.

Some of the characteristics of this archetypal pattern are:

- **True belief in the innate healing power of every Being.** A Sacred Witness does not need to push or "make" anything happen for another. Instead, they are willing to hold space and empower others to activate their own innate healing energy. They know that holding this sacred space invites the other Being to share their truths. The Sacred Witness knows that holding this quality of space invites the other to be fully seen, felt, and heard, which IS the true transformative healing power.

- **A commitment to be free from attachments and expectations of what will come forward as a "result" of the witnessing.** One of the hardest parts of walking with the Sacred Witness pattern is to release our hidden attachments or desires to make or help the other person feel or get "better." Parts of us housed in the wounded or shadow ego structures often need validation that "we" created the healing and/or want to take ownership for what shifts unfold. However, this robs the one being witnessed from a sense of ownership and empowerment. A Sacred Witness knows they are not the primary agent of healing. Any healing that comes forward is a direct result of the witnessed Being's internal process.

- **An ability to be comfortable with the uncomfortable.** A Sacred Witness can hold internal regulation WHILE being open and available to the other. They have cultivated the ability to not take things personally, to be comfortable in the presence of big emotions, and to have compassion and love for that which needs to come forward.

- **An ability to hold Clean Compassion.** The Sacred Witness has what I like to call Clean Compassion (which we'll explore in detail in Chapter Fourteen). They are able to allow the other to be themselves without trying to consciously or subconsciously rescue, take on, over empathize, and/or project their own feelings onto the other. They are able to simply be with and honor the other's truths, while holding their own personal boundaries and commitment to their own Self-Work, which allows them to tend any Parts of them that might awaken in the course of their Sacred Witnessing.

- **An ability to be guided by the other into deeper compassionate, caring invitations, inquiries, and explorations to see what else wants or needs to come forward and unwind during the witnessing.** Remember, the pattern of the Sacred

Witness is not passive; it offers deep, active listening and invites others into deeper inquiries and explorations to see what else wants or needs to come forward and unwind.

To help you feel into this pattern a little more, let's explore a scenario with three different possible outcomes.

Imagine that you have had a really rough day. You've been trying to understand why another's flippant comment is totally throwing you off.

You might be wrestling with anger, internal and external judgment, feelings of being hurt and confused, and thoughts that the other person was intentionally trying to insult or hurt you.

You call your friend and say, "I just need to vent about something silly that happened today, but I can't let go of for some reason. It is really messing me up, can I share it with you?"

Your friend agrees, and you begin to share the story with them.

Once you finish sharing the events and your internal experience your friend may respond in a few different ways. Notice how each of these feels in your system.

Scenario #1

"Wow they are totally wrong and that is crazy! You should be pissed, I would be! I had something like that happen to me a couple of days ago and it was just like this. I'm still pissed at them, and I don't blame you for being pissed too!"

What does that scenario feel like to you?

Do you feel validated? Glossed over? Not really seen? Would Parts of you potentially feel even more angry and puffed up, knowing you have another ally for your point of view of being harmed?

Now try this on in your system:

Scenario #2

"Wow that is not cool, but it really isn't that big of a deal in the grand scheme of things. You should just let it go and not worry about it. By this time tomorrow you are going to laugh at yourself because it will mean nothing. Oh, by the way, let me tell you what happened to me today!"

What does that scenario feel like to you?

Do you feel dismissed, pooh-poohed, or not really heard? Maybe you catch a hint of shaming you for reacting the way you did? This type of response preloads shame and guilt within your own internal system. If by tomorrow you still have a charge in your system over what they said to you, then what, does that make you even more wrong for not letting it go?

How willing do you feel to keep exploring what's behind the reaction you are having in either of these scenarios?

Let's try on a third possibility:

Scenario #3

"Wow, it sounds like this is really causing you a lot of different emotions and reactions in you. Any thoughts or ideas about what might be behind it? I'd love to hold space while you take a moment to explore what's happening inside you in response to this person's comment. Would that feel supportive?"

What does that scenario feel like to you?

Can you see how you might feel validated in a way that honors your experience AND doesn't take a side? Do you feel space to get curious and reflect more on your internal reaction?

Can you feel the difference in the energy behind Scenario #3—the Sacred Witness response—and what it can potentially help elicit for you?

Now imagine being able to work with yourself that way.

In the absence of Sacred Witness energy, our self-talk may sound like this: *Wow, I'm so stupid. I can't believe I'm still losing my center over this. What the hell is wrong with me? Why can I never let things go? I've got to get a grip here . . ."*

With the inner Sacred Witness onboard, your inner narrator might sound like this: *Wow, this is really affecting me. Something more must be happening for me under the surface. I am curious about why this is bringing up such strong feelings for me. What Parts of me are up in arms right now and what is their story?*

The following chart helps you to see the difference between what the harsh inner critic says and what the Sacred Witness invites us into.

Harsh Inner Critic Point of View	Sacred Witness Point of View
I'm stupid and such a waste of people's time.	Wow, I'm having a rough time, What is happening for me right now?
I can never do anything right.	What can I learn about myself from what is happening right now and what might be bringing all this forward?
Everything is all my fault; I just mess everything up.	What patterns might be running that have brought me here?
I fell off my routine and discipline, I can never follow through	I'm human and it's called a practice for a reason. I am going to have moments. I can always start again. Is there a saboteur energy (see Chapter Twelve) awake in me right now? If so, what unseen fears and worries might I have around actually doing my practices and things shifting?

The Sacred Witness takes out shame, blame, judgments, and projections based off past survival and trauma wounds. It opens us up to the grace of understanding, compassion, courage, acknowledgement, awareness, self-acceptance, forgiveness, and the beautiful unconditional love of the Divine (all Medicines of the Soul, explored in Chapter Thirteen). It moves us through stifling inner traps, such as righteous anger and shadow needs for vengeance, and allows the Parts of us that felt unworthy, undervalued, or unacknowledged to be seen, felt, and heard. From the Sacred Witness's point of view, we create a space to help these hidden wounded Parts of ourselves be tended to and unwound. This ultimately guides us into the next right actions we might need to take. The Sacred Witness invites us to step out of victimization and disempowerment. It empowers us to claim our inner agency and make supportive choices. It helps us move forward based on who we truly are rather than versus the karmic weight of our past choices and experiences running the show.

CHAPTER PRACTICES

Practice One: Calling forward your Guide for Embodying the Sacred Witness

During this guided journey, we will be creating a link, or an avatar, to the archetypal power of the Sacred Witness so you can access this innate part of you when you need it.

I love this practice because it consciously connects us to a healthy healing member of our *Wise One Team*. As you might recall, this team includes our supportive inner Parts, our Soul Being, our Sacred Witness, as well as external unseen advisors, guides and other supportive Beings. Our *Wise One Team* is here to support us all the time, especially when we feel cut off from accessing our Wise One Self, or True Self, directly. While our inner council sometimes has team members that critique us out of comparison, shame, blame, protective responses, and internalized conditioning, our *Wise One Team* truly works in alignment with the qualities of the Sacred Witness we've explored in this chapter.

Begin Here

Imagine you are in the presence of a Being with whom you feel truly free to show up just as you are—the good, bad, and ugly Parts, they ALL feel safe and not judged.

You might see the face of a person you knew in the past or know now. You might see the image of a beloved animal or companion who you knew loved you just as you were. You might see an angelic or spirit guide Being coming forward, one that has comforted you in the past. This beloved Being didn't judge the "imperfect" Parts of you.

If an image doesn't come to mind, no worries—we can start to build one out now.

- *What would this Being feel like?*
- *What would their voice sound like?*
- *How would they talk with you?*
- *How would you feel in their presence and when seeking their counsel?*

Take a few moments to imagine, sense, feel, hear, smell, and know the presence of this Being.

What is the name of this team member?

You might also imagine a place where you can meet this amazing healing member of your team anytime you need them. Bring this place alive in your imagination as fully as possible.

What setting helps you feel safe, held, and open?

Now that you have a sacred place to meet this Being, tune back in to them—feel their presence and their willingness to join you.

Ask your new team member:

- Are they willing to be your guide and mentor on this journey?
- Are they willing to help you reconnect with the core aspect of you that knows how to hold space?
- Are they willing to help you learn Sacred Witness self-talk?
- Are they willing to come forward when you're judging yourself or doubling down in righteous shadow victimization and redirect you into the power of the Sacred Witness?
- Are they willing to give you an Exit Ramp[1] from destructive self-talk so you can learn and remember how to be kinder and more compassionate with yourself?
- Are they willing to help you learn and remember healthy ways to tend the Parts of you that are hurt and need support?
- Lastly, open your Heart Being to receive any additional messages your new team member would like to share with you.

Next, ask yourself:
- Are you willing to make a commitment to seek their help and guidance?
- Are you willing to accept their help?

If you need any help imagining the voice of this new team member, read this:

I'm here to help you expand your ability to hear your Heart and Soul, follow their guidance, and allow them to support you. So much has happened in your life, it is no wonder you have lost some of your connection with your Heart, inner wisdom, and Wise One Healer within. You have the ability to hold yourself in a field of grace, love, and compassion. It is not gone, even though at times I know it feels like it is.

Take our hand, allow us to be a part of your team, and together we will go on an adventure to find the missing pieces of you, to uncover the connections you thought were lost forever. I am here, your Soul is here, the Divine is here; together we can bring back your inner connections to love, laughter, and joy through your whole Body Being. And so it is.

Take a few deep breaths in and out. Give thanks to yourself and your new team member for being willing to develop this supportive connection. Wiggle your fingers and toes and become fully present in this moment in time. Come fully back into your body and softly allow your eyes to look around and see the space you are in.

This practice helps open you up to remembering and connecting with the pattern of the Sacred Witness. It is here to support and guide you, both internally and externally as we walk together. I invite you to continue with these meetings and share with this Sacred Witness Guide what wakes up in you throughout the course of your journey through this book.

PRACTICE TWO: REGULAR WISE ONE TEAM STAFF MEETINGS

To build your inner trust that this support can be real, hold "Wise One Team staff meetings" everyday! They can be as short as five minutes or as long as an hour.

Here's an example of how you might dialogue with your new team member and Wise One Team (either via meditation or journaling).

YOU: "I'm having a hard time shifting from the harsh Inner Critic to the Sacred Witness energy in my own self-talk and Self-Work. Can you help me explore what is behind that mistrust and doubt?"

Then open to the Sacred Witness within to illuminate what might be contributing to that belief system.

Don't worry if you don't feel at ease talking to your Wise One Team and this new Sacred Witness Guide right away; this is a practice that gets stronger with time. It's normal to have days where all you can hear is the voice of other inner Parts, which might be angry, shaming, or in pain. You'll have many more opportunities to meet with this Guide throughout the book. Have grace with yourself and be gentle as you navigate a new way forward in your Being.

Chapter Three

Stages of Embodying the Sacred Witness

Next, let us look at the stages every Being goes through as they learn to embody the Sacred Witness energy. These stages will also serve as a road map for the journey we'll take together throughout this book. Understanding these milestones or guideposts is intended to help you get a sense of where you've been, where you are, and where you may be headed. When we have a heads-up on what we can expect, it gives the Mental Being an orientation, as sense of hope, and a lifeline it can use to re-center itself when it feels lost, overwhelmed, or caught up in the snares of confusion and self-doubt.

The framework I'm going to share with you I first discovered while listening to a lecture by Richard Rohr, an amazing spiritual teacher and Franciscan Monk. He presented this model during a conference called "Laughing and Weeping" in 2009 with Russ Hudson, cofounder of the Enneagram Institute.[1]

Below are the stages of developing what he calls the *Inner Witness*, what Buddhism calls the *Stable Witness*, and what I call the *Sacred Witness*. This One within us cultivates the ability to experience and engage the following:

Stage One: To stand back and observe the "me"—what we call the *Observer Self* in meditation practices.

Stage Two: To bring Clean Compassion and a sense of calmness to observing this "me." During this stage, we gain the ability to see any projections, shadow judgements, anger, or other emotions we might be experiencing. And we gain the ability to refrain from directing them toward that which we are observing.

Stage Three: To be able to expand our observations further to include "more-than-me." Here we build the ability to bring clean compassion, curiosity, calmness to observing not only ourselves, but all others involved, and ALL the different threads, stories, projections, and points of view related to an event and that which ripples out from it.

Stage Four: To be able to see "me" and "my" dramas as if they are not me. In this stage, we can observe ourselves without identifying with our attachments and stories about what we are observing. We can see what we see without having to defend ourselves. In shamanism, this stage is related to initiations around the death of the False Self. Once the False Self dies, the Heart Being can open to witness What Is with compassion, love, and truth in alignment with the True Self.

Stage Five: To be able to think and act from the point of view of Non-Attachment and Non-Dual thinking. Okay, those are fancy words, let's break it down. Here, in this stage, we open our ability to be willing to *not know*. We open to whatever we are observing with both curiosity and wonder.

In this stage, we are totally willing to let whatever we are observing inform us, shift us, change us, and transform us. We are also willing to allow that which we are observing to take us to different conclusions then what we think an outcome should be. I like to call this stage *Opening to the Magic of the Divine*. When we are certain what is needed, we are most likely blocking any other insights and truths (big or small) from coming into our awareness.

We often get trapped in dualistic thinking that makes things seem black or white, good or bad, right or wrong, "me" and "not me," and so forth. If we cannot detach from our pure identification with our personalities, knowings, and beliefs, we will remain bound by them and unable to observe our personas, projections, defense strategies, distorted perspectives, and so forth. We'll get locked in by over identifying with and trying to protect and justify old beliefs. Non-dual thinking can relax rigid perceptions to help us see more "truth" and access more of the reality before us. It allows us to observe more and gain the ability to see what is trying to work its way through to co-create a new way of being.

Here, we open to the "yes, and" point of view, where you can allow, and even welcome, opposing truths to be present at the same time. This stage opens us to walking with paradoxes and becoming comfortable with the uncomfortable.

Stage Six: To embody the point of view of the True Self. Here, we begin to allow ourselves to shift away from being emotionally manipulated and blended with the Parts and personas that are wounded, scared, fearful, resentful, or looking to derail us from healing or growing. When we can unblend, we become unbound by these limited points of view and open to the energy and wisdom of our True Self. Our True Self has the innate healing powers of the Sacred Witness—curiosity, understanding, kindness, caring, compassion, and desire to support the whole Self.

Stage Seven: To bring this level of witnessing into our daily reflections, contemplations, and practices. In this stage, we employ practices to help us cultivate a stronger and stronger connection with our True Self as our new "home" and primary Operating Program of consciousness. This gives us more and more space from the old tapes and past programs that used to run our daily actions, thoughts, and attitudes from the shadow.

Stage Eight: To not only be disciplined and devoted to our practices, but also bring this level of awareness into our everyday life activities.[2]

Here, as the Sacred Witness becomes more embodied and integrated within, we come into greater union with the Soul Being as a constant companion. I also like to call this *getting off the cushion* and bringing our practices into motion in our daily life—living and breathing the energy of the Sacred Witness.

Stage Nine: To surrender, trust, and know that we ARE part of the Divine already—period. At this stage, we fully embody the sacred truth that we don't have to earn Divine Love and acceptance. We finally realize we don't have to pledge ourselves to a specific type of practice or religion to be worthy of our own true unique Divine essence and nature. We embrace and know that we and all Beings innately hold the healing power of the Sacred Witness within. We can activate it whenever we need it or are guided to hold that space for another.

At this stage, we willingly accept and receive the support of our Soul Being, the Divine, and other Beings who offer loving support. We walk with this aspect of ourselves through our daily tasks, works, and deeds in alignment with our True Self—living, loving, and leading our TRUE Authentic Life.

You might be thinking right now, *Wow, Michelle. These stages sound great! However, I'm not so sure I can do all those things. I mean, I think I'm pretty good at standing back and trying to get a bigger perspective, but those other stages. Not projecting my beliefs on something? Not getting all wrapped up in my own dramas and stories? I don't know. That feels like a pretty lofty goal.*

Well, I bet you have more qualities of these stages on board than you realize. So often, my clients don't see the amazing strengths, courage, and attributes of the Sacred Witness that are already within them because we have been taught to look for our faults and not our strengths.

Remember when I said road maps are helpful because they give us a big-picture perspective of where we have been, where we are now, and where we are going? This is just what this exploration of the stages is designed to do. It's not a measuring stick with which to beat or judge yourself, but rather an orientation tool so you can see where you want to navigate next.

And this book will help you navigate along your way if you'd like accompaniment. In Section Two, titled "Awakening and Befriending the Body Being," we are focusing on Stages One through Four—cultivating the Observer Self. Section Three, "Awakening and Befriending the Mental Being" will focus on Stage Five, specifically cultivating non-dual thinking and the ability to perceive beyond our attachments. Section Four, "Awakening and Befriending the Heart Being" is all about developing the qualities of Stages Six and Seven—the ability to understand and work with our own personal emotions and Heart Being in clean compassion. Section Five, "Awakening and Befriending our Soul Being" helps us develop into Stages Eight and Nine—cultivating the gifts we'll need to bring daily practices so the Sacred Witness can infuse all aspects of our lives.

Before we dive into the first stages of embodying the Sacred Witness within, let's pause and take a moment to honor where you've been and the wisdom and skills you've developed so far.

CHAPTER PRACTICE
The River of My Life

First, imagine that your life is like a winding, twisting river. Your river has different sections throughout it. In some sections, it may be a slow-moving, lazy river that feels easy and effortless to work with. Other sections are like crazy raging class V rapids or bigger. There may be rocks, surging rapids, big drops, and places that are very tricky to navigate. Some parts might be stagnant and barely moving—waters that cause you to really have to *work* to get through. You may find whirlpools, places where you have to get out and drag your boat through the wilds, places where you encounter and must traverse waterfalls and cliffs. In many different moments, your River of Life converges with another's and they intertwine and move together for sections and then separate back out again.

Keep building out how you imagine your River of Life to be and document how it looks and feels to you. Engage this practice in any way that works for you—you may keep a written chronological list in a journal, rely on mental imagery to guide your way, make doodles and drawings on a page, create an art project, or some combination of these. I personally like to use a big piece of paper (think poster board size or bigger) and use colored pencils and markers to let my inner artist help me with this one.

I invite you to stay big picture here with themes or titles of each section and not zoom in too much into the details of those experiences. Again, we are seeking to remember the journey you have been on up until this point and the jewels you have gathered along the way.

However, as you are engaging this practice, ask yourself:

What are the qualities of each different section, twist, and turn?

What labels or themes would you give to each section?

Examples: Starting College, Living on my own, Start of New Relationship, Ending a Relationship, New job/career, Birth of a Child, addition of new family member, move to new place.

Now, pause and look back at the Sacred Witness stages. Where along your River did you begin to develop or remember being able to embody and express some of those skills? Where along your River did a mentor or guide come along and model the skills of each stage for you? You might notice where you felt you embodied any of the following characteristics of the Sacred Witness: courage, compassion, understanding, self-respect, willingness, ability to see a different perspective, worthiness, hope, empowerment, freedom, liberation, and/ or more choice.

Lastly, take a moment and feel into the part of your River where you are right now. Something called to you to focus on this journey of Embodying the Sacred Witness at this time. Capture a few themes, needs, and desires you have for this journey to help you remember your "why." This will serve as a North Star within you as you explore the different stages of the Sacred Witness to come.

Now that we have a better sense of where we've been, where we are, and where we want to go, let's start at the very beginning—learning how to cultivate the Observer Self. The only way we can truly access the Observer Self is through the present moment, which *must* happen through our Body Being. This brings us to the next essential step on our journey: awakening and befriending the Body Being.

Section Two
Awakening and Befriending the Body Being

Overview

"Before you can hear, much less follow, the voice of your soul [Sacred Witness], you have to win back your body. You have to go on a pilgrimage beneath the skin."

—MEGGAN WATTERSON[1]

THE BODY BEING: OUR FIRST SACRED COMPANION

The next stop on our journey of cultivating the Sacred Witness is to awaken and befriend the Body Being. This opens us up to the question: What exactly IS the wisdom of the Body Being? What is the Body Being trying to share with us? And how do we consciously connect and dialogue with it?

Our body doesn't just serve as a necessary physical vessel for us here on Earth. Our body is also a sacred companion through which our Soul Being can be embodied in during this incarnation. However, in addition to housing our Soul Being, the body still carries its own conscious and innate wisdom, which is why I call it our *Body Being*.

As Watterson expressed in the quote above, the journey of embodying the Sacred Witness must start with winning back our connection to our Body Being. This is because our body is the primary means through which we become present, develop the skills of the Observer Self, and access the first four stages of cultivating the

Sacred Witness within.

The various sensations, emotions, postures, and expressions held within our body and cellular structures serve as sacred messengers for what is happening within our inner worlds, both known and unknown. Within our cellular structure lies the entire record of our life experiences, on every level. Our body literally holds an imprint of EVERY single moment we've experienced throughout our life, from conception to the present.

Over the next three chapters, we will explore how we can begin to:

- Re-establish a dialogue and connection with our Body Being's original language: somatics.
- Understand the hidden impacts of trapped trauma on the nervous system and body as one of the main sources of disconnection from the Body Being.
- Learn how to unwind and release trapped trauma and rebuild our connections with the Body Being as our trusted ally throughout our life.

Throughout this section, I share a few very simple yet foundational somatic experiencing techniques and practices to lay the essential groundwork for our journey of Embodying the Sacred Witness. As we walk through the teachings in this section, you will discover that every experience of life contains both hidden challenges and hidden gifts. Understanding the impact of life's ups and downs on our whole system is super powerful and liberating! Once we call forward the grace of Understanding (which we inherently develop via Stages Two through Four), we get to break up and dissolve insane amounts of self-judgment, self-blame, self-loathing, and self-victimization we experience when we tap into the "now" moment via our body.

BIG PICTURE ROAD MAP CHECK-IN

Once we start healing our relationship with our Body Being via the practices and reflections offered in this section, it naturally opens us to the opportunity to befriend the biggest protector we have, our Mental Being. In order to gain access to our true Heart and Soul Beings, we must develop willingness and capacity—in both the Body Being and Mental Being—to work as allies in our partnership with the Sacred Witness within.

As Watterson says, it all starts with reclaiming our relationship with the Body Being so that we can open to its wisdom as an integral companion on our journey to embodying the Sacred Witness. In order to befriend the Body Being, first we need to rediscover how to dialogue with it through Somatics, our first true language. Let's go there next!

Chapter Four

The Body Being as a Messenger

"The body always leads us home . . . if we can simply learn to trust sensations and stay with it long enough for it to reveal appropriate action, movement, insight, or feeling."

—PAT OGDEN[1]

In this chapter, we'll engage two key foundational Somatic Processing concepts as pathways for developing the Observer Self. First, is learning to stay grounded in the present moment. The second is being able to witness and neutrally observe what is happening in your Body, Mental, and Heart Beings without prejudice, projection, and self-abandonment. However, before we can build the skills of working with the Body Being to develop the Observer Self, we need a solid understand of why and how we stopped listening to the Body Being to begin with.

In order to awaken and befriend the Body Being as a sacred messenger and companion to the Sacred Witness within, we need to remember and reconnect to our first language—somatics. *Somatics* literally means "relating to the body or having to do with the body." Way before we say our first words, our body is talking to us and to our caregivers. In fact, our body is talking to us ALL the time. It is trying to share insights into our needs, wants, fears, and hopes in every moment. In Somatic Experiencing and Processing, we ask our

46

consciousness to "observe" these rich insights and the information offered by the Body Being.

You might be thinking, *Okay Michelle—why do I need to talk to my body to bring greater care and compassion to myself and release self-judgments?*

Great question! Our Body Being holds the programming, a map of sorts, of every belief system we have, conscious or not. It holds the detailed record of every moment you've ever experienced—happy, fearful, grounding, wondrous, safe, and scary. It's important to recognize here that the Body Being holds all the "bad" *and* the "good"—the resources, the skills, the resilience, the wisdom. The Body Being contains the positive pathways and imprints we'll need to heal and release the programs and trapped energies that are not beneficial.

Not only does your Body Being hold imprints of every moment you've lived, it also holds the records of those in your family lineage and their experiences. Spiritual tradition, epigenetics, and neuroscience all confirm that our Body Being holds our ancestral data *and* data from the collective experience in your local area, your country, and the planet itself (collective human consciousness and unconsciousness too).

Even further, the Body Being holds the history of your Soul Being and ALL it has experienced in different incarnations as well. I have personally witnessed how the Body Being holds and expresses Soul memories from lives past, present, and future, as well as your Soul's ancestry and lineage.

Bessel van der Kolk, a leading trauma specialist, said it best with the title of his book—*The Body Keeps the Score.*[2] Everything can be accessed via the Body Being.

The primary ways we will access our Body Being's wisdom is through engaging our sensations—touch, taste, sight, sound, and smell, plus proprioception, interoception, and exteroception—and through the breath. These will all help to bring us into the present and develop the Observer Self.

THE OBSERVER SELF AND THE BODY BEING

The importance of developing the Observer Self is emphasized in every spiritual wisdom tradition and modern-day practices of self-development and mental health. The Observer Self gives us the ability to see beyond our own filters and projections to access the Truth of What Is. Accessing the perspective of the Observer Self through the Body Being requires cultivating some type of inner practice or process to:

- Become aware that we are experiencing different bodily sensations, which serve as messengers to bring our attention to some aspect of our experience.
- Witness and notice that bodily sensations are linked to different internal stories, postures, beliefs, and thoughts.
- Understand how to partner with the body to identify these connections and notice that changing how we meet the body's experience can change the stories themselves.
- Go beyond observing into befriending the Body Being and committing to regularly tune into its wisdom. We don't just notice the body but develop a willingness to become curious about the body and its messages. From this curiosity, we can ally with the Body Being to access more insights into what we are doing and why we are doing it. This permits us more self-agency and choice to respond from our values and who we truly want to be, versus responding from a trauma and survival response.
- Embrace that—when we come from the Sacred Witness perspective—we have the ability to compassionately understand and heal the wounded Parts of ourselves born from trauma and survival responses. We can see that these wounded Parts of ourselves are currently lost and cutting us off from our True Self.
- Willingly and appropriately tend the wounded Parts so they no longer need to drive us to respond to our current relationships and interactions from that woundedness, but rather a

place of being with What Is and responding from a place of connection to our True Self.

The only way to access the Observer Self is by engaging with the present moment. The present moment is the ONLY place where we have the ability to sense, feel, see, hear, and know and interact with anything we are observing. If we are not in the present moment, what we are observing is being filtered through perspectives of the past or some imagined future that hasn't yet arrived.

WHAT REALLY IS THE PRESENT MOMENT?

Well, there is a lot happening in the present moment. It is *full* of sensations, movements, thoughts, feelings, requests, choices, stillness, and so much more.

Here are just a few of the things that are happening in a moment. Based on each Being that you can feel and tap into, you begin to connect with the somatic sensations within the Body Being. While this may feel overwhelming at first, we are going to develop a system to sort through and trust where our awareness is being guided. But first, we have to know all that may be arising in the present-moment field.

Body Being: You have your own internal physical world— breath, circulation, body rhythms, operating organs, movement and interactions of the muscular system, and so on. The body is also constantly sending and receiving signals both, internally and from the external world. The innate wisdom and programing of the Body Being is creating new cells and tissues, shedding old cells, and breaking down the dead cells and waste from the system. The body is transforming and transmuting "food and drink" into energy to feed and produce the fuel needed to run everything in your body. Physical and subtle energy flows are happening too; for example, impulses from the mental body to move toward something go through the nervous system into the muscle, and so on.

Mental Being: The Mental Being is made up of energy signals which are flowing in and around our Body Being to create thoughts and run programs that influence our choices, thus creating a constant karmic wheel of cause and effect throughout our body and life. The mind, our ego consciousness, is constantly working to protect us by projecting into the future based on experiences of the past, and is constantly scanning and inviting you into every moment but the present one.

Heart Being (and its messenger, the emotions): The Heart Being is sending out and receiving a stream of emotions, serving as messengers that link the signals between what our Body Being is sensing and the information held within it, our Mental Being's protective decision-making processes, and the desires of our Personal Heart. The Heart Being is constantly flowing its messages throughout the physical and mental bodies, sharing different emotional frequencies that we sense through our Personal Heart and subtle energy flows that lets us know what we want to move toward and experience more of and what we want to move away from and experience less of. Emotional signals are being activated and vibrating in and through us at all times. This ever-moving stream of emotions creates a shifting tapestry of information for our whole system in what we are sensing and feeling on many different levels and dimensions that are interrelated and interwoven through all aspects of us—physically, mentally, and spiritually. However, sometimes the amount of sensing and information that comes through our Heart Being can overwhelm the system with too many mixed sensations at one time.

Soul Being: Your Soul Being is your constant companion, representing and sharing with you the core aspects of you that are beyond your individual self and into the cosmic immortal facets of you. It is through connection with our Body Being that we gain our ability to access the subtle messages and insights our Soul Being is constantly trying to share with us in every moment. Once we can connect to the Soul Being within ourselves, then we are able to hold that level of connection with another, just like Schedule A did for me.

All of this is a living, breathing orchestra of energy flowing through every single present moment. And all of it can be accessed as needed through the Body Being. The present moment is where we find and have access to our true full Self. The present moment is where we can actively connect and be guided to work with ALL the different dimensions of ourselves in harmony. This is what unlocks the power of our Choice in who and how we want to be in that moment and all it is inviting us to engage in.

COMMON ISSUES WITH
BEFRIENDING THE BODY BEING

Ironically, the biggest block many of us face when trying to connect to the present moment through the body is that we don't know HOW. We are not taught how to listen to the different sensation messengers the Body Being shares with us or how to respond to, interact with, or answer the messages of the body in a kind and compassionate way.

Another HUGE block is that we might be carrying a whole lot of baggage into this relationship with our Body Being. We might experience fear or anger when we drop into the body. We might experience uncomfortable or unfamiliar sensations. Furthermore, cellular memories of past traumas, illnesses, and past programming may be urging us to ignore, push through, numb out, and shut down the very body sensations that are how the body talks with us at first.

When faced with the pain and dysregulation present in our Body Being and the trapped emotions of the Heart Being, most of us have been taught to escape the chaos by retreating into our Mental or Soul Beings. We are further taught that to be successful and survive, we need to value the messenger of the Mental Being and the ego structure above the messages of the Body Being. Especially in Western cultures, the Mental Being is considered the only path to achieving greatness—we even adopt the creed, *mind over matter.*

Unfortunately, to break through the deafening noise of EVERYTHING held in the present moment and get us to truly listen and honor its messages, the Body Being often has to get really loud and almost yell at us to pay attention. Cue the proverbial two-by-four that knocks us out of our mindless, numb daily habits and forces us to look at the past pain and fears that keeps us from connecting with the Body Being as a messenger. Oftentimes, the louder messages from the body are attached to our fears and traumatic events. Therefore, when those messages do break through and get our attention, they often come with intense survival drivers in tow.

When we intend to show up in the energy of the Sacred Witness, for ourselves or others, often our biggest obstacle is actually the Body Being. Why? Because it holds and protects all manners of trapped emotions, events, fears, belief systems, and unresolved traumas. These trapped energies act like land mines waiting for the right scenario to set them off. If we don't know how to sort the Body Being's signals as portals into what is happening in our Mental, Heart, and Soul Beings and learn how to work with them consciously (while holding what I call *center*), we will end up getting lost in the overwhelming sudden flood of conflicting sensations, impulses, and protective mechanisms without knowing what is happening and why.

By learning how to sort through the various levels of information and how to interact with the sacred messenger of the Body Being, we can witness the triggered Parts and the body's survival systems—which will try to override our consciousness and kick in the best automatic survival tactics we have available for ourselves throughout our whole system. I don't know about you, but the defensive "Michelle" that shows up and grabs the wheel from my Heart-Led self when it feels threatened has no sacred ground, so to speak. Having no sacred ground means we don't have any aspects of our life that are "off limits" from our destructive thoughts or behaviors when we are triggered. When the survival Parts kick into gear, they are looking to protect me at all costs. When those Parts of me are triggered, it's nearly impossible to hold the quality of space held by the Sacred Witness. Instead of being in the present moment, my consciousness is strung out all over my timeline and I am literally hemorrhaging my life force energy across space and time.

However, learning how to develop the Observer Self, our first step to embodying the Sacred Witness, helps our overactive Parts step back so we can access the calm inner space in our system, like the eye of a storm. From this place, as the Observer Self, I'm willing to stay centered AND open to the conversation that the Body Being wants to bring forward to support my healing and inner balance.

The Concept of Grounding

Many practitioners stress the importance of being grounded before dropping into any meditation or energy healing work or practice. It is essential for sure. However, it is way more than saying, "I'm grounded great!" Or just working on your kidney and stomach meridians to lock into connecting with the earth. Or "fixing" your polarity with magnetics and other such support.[3]

Truly grounding into the present moment requires the willingness to actually *be* in our body. Being grounded and in our body means that we allow our awareness to willingly drop into sensing, feeling, and being with ALL Parts of ourselves—physically, emotionally, mentally, and spiritually. This is no small feat, especially if you have had any type of adverse experience while you were actually present in your body—which is, unfortunately, pretty much all of us.

As a reminder, I do not support or condone forcing the body, mind, or heart into ANYTHING. It doesn't work in the long run and can cause a TON of added trauma and mistrust in our systems. We will be working on developing true willingness, a foundational concept, throughout the book.

If you think back to my story of Schedule A, you might notice that he was able to hold a compassionate, open healing space for me, which supported my willingness to show up and "be" in my body with him. His beingness and heart created an anchor for me. Because I felt "safe" with him, I was willing to open to the space and connection he was holding for me to connect to myself. During those first moments at the barn with him, I agreed to be with him not only energetically, but physically as well. I was willing to be present even with the pain in my body still being there too. Why? Because I was focusing on what it felt like to be in connection with him and him back to me, and not the pain. Schedule's presence, and the input he gave me, created an anchor point outside my body, allowing me to titrate by checking into my body, then to his, and back and forth. My nervous system had a consistent, safe place to focus outside of me so I didn't get lost or over-whelmed when I tried to go into and start to figure out how to be with this crazy thing called my body.

The practices in this chapter will help you develop a similar practice so that you can experience this same rhythm of being able to pendulate between what is called *exteroception*—orienta-tion/anchoring to an outer object—and *interception*—or an inner felt sense. This foundational practice helps us develop and/or strengthen the pathways needed for embodied grounded reflec-tion—i.e., being open to connecting with your Body Being AND being able to observe what is happening within and outside your-self without disconnecting from your body and floating off into the Mental or Soul Beings—all in a way that feels safe and support-ive to your whole system.

The Concept of Witnessing

Our second foundational concept is the importance of *not* plowing over, changing, disconnecting, and/or trying to numb or edit what the Body Being is bringing forward right off the bat. We want to simply witness and observe *first*, before inserting a "change or adjustment" into the system.

The concept of witnessing is a core component in Somatic Experiencing exercises. Somatic Experiencing, or processing, was pioneered by leaders like Peter Levine and Pat Ogden. As Pat Ogden says, "The body always leads us home . . . if we can simply learn to trust sensations and stay with it long enough for it to reveal appropriate action, movement, insight, or feeling."[1] This means that any actions or support that the body needs to help heal and rebalance itself will come forward innately if we first *witness*.

Additionally, the concept of witnessing before trying to insert any corrections into our system is important because our Body Being and our conscious mind via the Mental Being have disconnected for perfectly exquisite reasons. Reasons that I deeply honor and respect. Remember, I don't support forcing any Parts of us into anything. I don't like to tear down and blow holes in the different protective and defensive ways of being that we have each established. It is not safe nor kind.

We will talk more about Parts in Chapter Six, so I'll leave the details for later. For right now, know that the body doesn't do anything just for giggles. Every behavior, sensation, posture—even down to the way we breathe—is based on an adaptation the Body Being brilliantly chose at some point to help us survive. Therefore, when we tune into the body and witness what it is saying, we sometimes end up with an inner dialogue or storyline like:

My shoulder is aching right now, ugh, whenever I try to do a Body Scan or anything like that my body starts to hurt. Am I ever going to be able to do this meditation thing right? What is wrong with me? Focus. Ugh, what did she just say? See I'll never get it right. I'm going to be this way forever. I might as well just give up and get used to it.

Somatic experiencing and healing work invites us into a different way of being with that type of inner dialogue or storyline. Instead of trying to shift the feeling or sensation of the shoulder hurting, we slow down, let it be there, and get curious about what the aching shoulder is attempting to bring to our attention at this time. The theory is the body will begin to share what is influencing it—what thoughts, beliefs, fears, worries, emotions, and projected responses it thinks it needs to have to survive. Bringing in curiosity, instead of trying to stop the body from talking, will lead us to what is really happening and what it needs to balance itself holistically, across all aspects of us. Like Ogden said, we are not trying to just alleviate symptoms. Instead, the work I'm inviting you into is a willingness to stay with a sensation and open to it. Through Sacred Witnessing, the Body Being itself starts to lead us, through its own inner wisdom, to what needs to be seen, released, and shifted to fully address an unmet need.

Awakening to the wisdom of the Body Being is a process of learning to befriend the body. It is about learning how to witness and see the body as our ally, not an enemy that is constantly betraying us and making our lives miserable—thus needing to be changed, fixed, and/or be bullied back into behaving.

Another part of witnessing is to notice what are often two levels of input happening at the same time: one, your felt sense of touching or feeling into different sensations of your Body Being; and two, a running dialogue that is describing what you are "feeling" and "sensing" via a more mental perspective that I like to call the *Inner Narrator.* The Inner Narrator is a little voice in your head that is giving you a play-by-play description as you are exploring something. This Inner Narrator is likely answering back to any questions as I ask you.

However, what I have found in myself and most of my clients is that the Inner Narrator is doing more than just giving you a running mental record of what is happening. The Inner Narrator often bypasses the physical felt sense and tells you what you are experiencing from its own mental perspective. For example, if I'm feeling an object like a smooth surface, the Inner Narrator would say, "This is a smooth surface." However, when I ask my client to notice if they feel the surface with their fingertips, they are shocked to realize that the answer is no. They have to ask the Inner Narrator to step back a bit so that they can connect directly to their felt sense of touch via their fingertips and then witness what their body feels like, in addition to what this Part of the Mental Being says is happening.

As we move forward with the different guided practices, I invite you to witness your five senses, such as the sensation of touch, and the Inner Narrator as two separate Parts. If it feels good, maybe even try to quiet the Inner Narrator down. See if you can let the Inner Narrator fade to the background, and invite your physical sensations, such as smell, sound, taste, to come forward a little more to share with you directly.

CHAPTER PRACTICES

Since we often move through our day more connected to our mental commentary *about* our experiences instead of registering our body's input, our first practice is designed to help us check in with the Body Being and simply be curious with what it is sensing, saying, or inviting us to feel.

This practice is often called "Orienting and Felt Sense."[4] Instead of going straight into exploring a sensation within the body, I like to guide my clients into learning how to anchor and explore how their senses are interacting with an object outside of them. I also would like to help you explore how to work with the Observer Self through a process called *titration*. Titration is the skill of going into any topic exploration or arising sensation a little bit at a time and then allowing your focus to shift back to a more neutral object, like one outside of us, then leaning back into observing the topic or sensation that you're exploring.

PRACTICE 1: ORIENTING AND FELT SENSE:
ANCHORING TO AN OUTSIDE OBJECT

When you are ready, I invite you to open and explore your felt sense of the surface holding you up right now (e.g., the chair, ground, couch, floor). This will serve as our neutral outside object that you will be pendulating to any time you feel you might be floating away or getting distracted from a felt sense held within your body.

Touch it with your hands. Is it smooth, soft, hard, textured, cool, warm? Take a few moments to really explore it like you are seeing and touching it for the first time. Take in any changes in the surface, such as a temperature change between where your body is touching it and where it is not. Really allow yourself to explore, touch, and sense the surface holding you.

Next, we are going to notice what your body is feeling and doing as it responds to this touching.

How does your body feel about this object holding you up? Notice if your body is tense or relaxed. Is the body allowing the chair or surface to hold you, or is it holding itself up a little bit? What would it feel like to soften the body and allow the surface to hold you a little more, take a little more of your true weight? Does the body feel comfortable with that request? Does it exhale, and have a desire to soften even more? Almost like it is melting into the embrace of the surface? Or, does it get a little nervous and more rigid?

Next, check in to what the breath is doing right now. A gentle reminder: don't shift it or try to force it into a "nice belly breath" or a "meditation" breath. Simply allow the breath to be what it is and notice it.

Presence Check: Is the Mental Being trying to take back over? What is the Inner Narrator up to?

Now let's see if you can tune into the left side of your body. Take some time here to register the sensations. Then do the same on the right side. Are they saying and sensing the same way or differently? If they are sensing differently, in what ways?

Now, bring your awareness to any other aspects of your experience I haven't yet invited you to explore. Allow your attention to flow wherever it wants to direct you.

CORE BEINGS CHECK-IN

Now that we have allowed the body to share how it is interacting with the world around it, we are going to shift into the second part of the conversation—observing what is happening within your different Beings.

Take a moment to notice if your body is inviting you to shift positions or tend it in any way.

Notice how willing are you to answer the body and allow movement to come into your body? Remember there is no right or wrong here. We are getting to know what our body feels comfortable and uncomfortable with. This willingness to notice and answer simple requests is a huge part of building a healthy relationship.

How does your Mental Being respond to the request for movement from the Body Being? Does it flow freely forward or does it react differently to the idea of shifting the body?

To help fill out this picture a little bit more, let's open now to the Heart Being. What is there? Do you sense any emotions with this exercise? Please note that the emotions don't have to justify themselves. Again, it isn't about right or wrong, it is about being with, allowing, and acknowledging what is present with love and compassion.

Notice if the Mental Being offers a storyline or the Inner Narrator is hoping back in. Or is it allowing you simply to be in the present moment—sensing, noticing, asking, receiving, shifting, and then returning to noticing, not attaching to or assigning any storyline that might be running in the background.

If you find yourself disconnecting or floating away from this exercise at any point, simply use the breath to bring your attention back to the Body Being, asking it to share what it needs right now.

When you are ready, bring your attention back fully to the present moment, taking a breath in and out. Call your energy fully into this moment. Maybe even give your body a little stretch, wiggling the toes and or fingers, and come back to center.

How did that go?

This is an adaptation of a Body Scan. I find that having an outside object, like the chair or another object, for the mind to use as a starting point is super helpful, compared to going straight into a full-on

Body Scan of what your body is feeling and sensing in the moment. If you have any chronic pain or anxiety or a history of harsh self-judgment and inner bullying, going straight to an in-depth Body Scan can be a bit of a stressor on the system, compared to this gentler invitation to learn how to connect first to observing something outside of you, then going inward, and titrating back and forth between the outer object and felt sense.

PRACTICE 2: ABBREVIATED VERSION OF ORIENTATING AND FELT SENSE—THE CHECK-IN

Below is a shorter version of the practice we just explored that I call *The Check-In.* Throughout the book in most practices to follow, I will say, "To start, check in with your system." That is a cue to complete this short foundational practice.

Check in by noticing (via your felt sense not your Mental Being):

- What can I see right now?
- What can I smell right now?
- What can I hear right now?
- What can I taste right now?
- What can my body feel or sense right now from the external world?

Next shift to an Internal Check In: Sensing in and noticing what your body is "doing" with each one of the questions above, again, without changing or altering it.

For example, *when I check in with what I am seeing right now, I notice . . .*

 . . . my breath and what it is doing,

 . . . my body posture,

 . . . my heart rate,

 and so on.

Suggestions for Deepening the Practices

- As you rotate through your senses, notice any changes or shifts internally with each "sense" you are observing. For example, when I shift from what am I seeing to what am I hearing right now, does my breath or posture change, or do I notice any tension come to a part of the body.
- I encourage you to bring curiosity to what you are observing. See if there are any Inner Narrator Parts and any old automatic stories that might be present with any shifts. Maybe when you shift to smell, you get a whiff of smoke from a campfire. Your Inner Narrator might remind you that you don't camp enough anymore and Parts of you are upset about that, you might then feel a pit in your stomach or a desire to slump over. Simply notice the different sensations and any messages the Body Being might be sharing at this time.
- If it feels good, you might ask the body if it needs anything to support it.
- You can explore these practices in a more formal sitting meditation or with a mindful walking meditation. You can also do this shorter practice anytime throughout the day, which I call getting off the cushion. Simply bring your intention and attention to checking into what your body is experiencing in that present moment. Noticing what it is doing or saying, be curious, and then see if you are willing to ask what it might need or want support with in that moment.

Healing Tip: I encourage you not to worry too much or be too harsh on yourself if you feel like your body doesn't answer at first. It's common and totally okay if you feel like the body is *trying* to answer you but that the messages are getting lost in translation, or you simply don't understand them. Remember, most of us have had years and years of mis-attunement between our Body Being and our Mental Being. I like the term *befriending* for a reason—just like any relationship, it takes time to build trust and communication. Stick with the Check-Ins and know that consistency is the way to repair and rebuild the lines of communication between you and your Body Being.

We are on our way to strengthening our connection with the Sacred Witness and developing the pathways within our own nervous system, body structures, and emotional, mental, and soul Beings to call forward deep holy listening and the healing presence of the Sacred Witness. Let's turn our attention now to another major roadblock we hit when embodying the Observer Self and Befriending the Body Being—the hidden impact of trauma on the body.

As we dive into exploring how trauma affects our body, it is natural for us to feel a little overwhelmed and perhaps a bit avoidant at the idea of working with old traumas and wounds and witnessing painful experiences held in our Body Being. Over the next two chapters, we'll explore a few concepts that shed light on why and how our internal connection to the Body Being was or is disconnected and how we truly do have the power within us to heal and shift the unresolved trauma held in our system. However, to unlock our Inner Healer within we need to start with awareness and understanding.

Chapter Five

Trauma and the Body Being

In the second Stage of Embodying the Sacred Witness, we develop the ability to shift how we observe, reflect, and interact with the Body Being from shaming and blaming our system to being more curious, compassionate, and open to seeking understanding. We begin to see the Body Being as a Sacred Messenger, helping to give us guidance and insights into what our whole system needs or wants us to know. This shift—from disconnection and harsh self-judgements to understanding and connection—enables us to hold a healing presence. From this non judgmental point of view, healing naturally comes forth to help the unresolved traumas and wounds within unwind, disperse, dissolve, and release their active "stuckness" in the body.

When we bring the Sacred Witness's energy to interact with the trapped trauma in our body (or someone else's), it provides the opportunity for the stuck trauma/wound to resolve. This resolution in the system allows new information to come forward that is based in current time, versus the old tapes, stories, and paradigms from our past experiences blindly running our body, controlling our choices and actions without regard for what is true and present now.

Before we dive into the practices that will help you build/ strengthen the pathways of non judgement and curiosity (thus aiding to shift the hidden impacts of trauma within our Body Being), let's create a common working definition of *trauma* and an understanding of how trapped trauma affects us all.

WHAT IS TRAUMA?

There are TONS of definitions of what trauma is and is not. You will hear people talk about big "T" and little "t" trauma, complex trauma, post-traumatic stress (disorder), secondary trauma, vicarious trauma, and so on. While I'm not undermining the different levels and types of traumas that can be experienced, the bottom line is that your body doesn't really know or care what anyone calls it. Trauma is trauma—period.

I define trauma as anything that overwhelms the system and causes the body to make survival choices and prioritize what to tend to and what to repress in that moment. The process of prioritizing and repressing within the system happens when the body isn't able to tend to a basic need(s) or operations in order to survive. When the Body Being has to prioritize certain survival needs at the expense of other needs, it decides what it will actually respond to, the best it can, and what it will ignore or not tend to in that moment. This repression allows it to redirect resources to what it believes will help meet what is threatening its survival at that moment. The body also has to work with the actual resources available at the time. So while there might be an "ideal" response the body could have made, the body can only respond with the resources that are actually present. Many choices are actually not available to us at the time trauma occurs.

Unfortunately, trauma is an unavoidable aspect of the human experience right now. Functional MRIs, epigenetics, and neuroscience can now track the effects of secondary or vicarious trauma, which are also VERY real in our systems. This is another book and topic within itself: the impact of interpersonal neurobiology and how we can evolve our empathic nature to reclaim and rewire our nervous system.

But for right now, just know that even if your life has felt smooth overall, your body might have what feels like random and often blindsiding different opinions on that perception.

Why? Because both the collective conscious and unconscious Body Beings are a part of you. These collective Body Beings might have very different scripts than what you've directly experienced. However, their influence and impact on your Body Being are very real.

Current findings in interpersonal biology prove that we are constantly sensing and being informed by the collective human experience and the experience of all Beings. For over thousands of years, Beings have experienced trauma in one form or another.

Here is just a SHORT list of traumatic experiences held within our individual and collective consciousness and unconsciousness:

- constriction of the ability to match our choices with our own personal will
- violations of rights and choice
- suppression
- dominance
- war and conflict
- overwhelming trauma of natural disasters, droughts, floods, fires, and earthquakes
- disease
- pressures to succeed
- unworthiness
- perceiving self or others as less than human
- perceiving self or others as "beast of burdens"
- feelings of being owed or owing another human
- effects of being used, abused, taken advantage of, raped, persecuted, and victimized

These experiences are ALL held within both our own DNA and the morphogenetic thought fields that accompany the experience of being on Earth.

Unfortunately, the current reality for almost every human's nervous system and our neurobiology is that WE ARE A TRAUMATIZED COLLECTIVE NERVOUS SYSTEM, consciously and unconsciously.

WHAT IS TRAPPED TRAUMA?

Trauma itself is not the source of disconnection in our system. It is the unresolved and un-met needs that happen in addition to the trauma that cause the often-unseen impact of "trapped" trauma. Therefore, IF a person is able to go back, once the traumatic moment has passed, and tend to the needs that were shelved to the extent that the system now feels it can, it completes the "circuit" and the trauma is resolved. There is no post-traumatic-stress or what I like to call trauma Tic Tacs or shrapnel lodged in the system, acting like landmines scattered throughout your whole body, impeding and influencing it.

What makes something an unresolved or trapped trauma in the system—versus a momentary re-prioritization of needs and redirecting of resources—is IF the body AND the whole system are, for whatever reason, not able to go back and tend to the parts that were repressed or ignored to survive or protect itself.

When the body has to follow a prolonged survival requirement that overrides its preferred prioritization of needs, this creates a new "program" in the system. Our system has programs for everything, from the way we hold ourselves in a posture during different activities, to the way we problem solve an overwhelming situation. When we have to release our preferred programs, or optimal ways of being and tending to ourselves, because of a survival need that outranks some of our personal desires or wants, we form a new survival-based program that runs counter to how we would prefer to respond or tend to our needs, consciously and subconsciously. The impact of trapped trauma and the new survival-based programs, that develop because of the re-prioritization of needs based on any new programming, are called trauma and survival adaptations.

I offer my clients the following metaphor when they are struggling to acknowledge the effects and impacts of trapped trauma in their system, as well as how and why they are directly linked to their health issues—physically, emotionally/mentally, and spiritually.

Imagine your body as a house. This house has all the different rooms in it—a kitchen, a living space, a sleeping place, and so on. You live, breathe, and work in this house. Now imagine that any of the "trash" generated during your normal daily living has to go into the kitchen trash can. Each day, you walk through and tend to any needs and throw out the trash. Every day, you detox or clear from the house what is no longer needed.

Now imagine that one day a massive storm comes into your world. It rips through, blowing out the windows of your house, ripping holes in the roof, and creating tons of excess "trash" to be removed, and requiring many repairs to your house. But, as you go to clean up and make needed repairs after the storm has passed, you find yourself only able to empty out a tiny fraction of the waste because your kitchen trash is always full of bigger objects (debris, or trapped traumas, from the storm) and can only take in a limited amount of refuse now.

Day after day, you are trying to recover from the storm and the ongoing daily trash needs with only half of the trash can's capacity available to you. Plus, now you have holes in your roof and less defenses from the outside elements. All that trash has to go somewhere. It begins to overflow into the other rooms of your house. This process continues day after day, over and over. The same amount of daily trash is being accumulated each day, but only a fraction of it can be completely thrown out and only a fraction of the repairs you need to make to the house are actually being done.

Now imagine you still lived in that house. You still have to function in the kitchen normally while the trash is piling up around you and spilling out into the rest of the house. Notice the trash accumulating in your sitting areas, sleeping areas, recreation areas and so on. Notice what it would feel like to not have any way to control the temperature of the house because there are no windows and roof leaks are letting in the outside elements. The effects of not being able to fully "clear" and/

or repair your house and living with this level of debris each day could create a lot of anxiety, right? It would also create the sense of being overwhelmed, hopelessness, and powerlessness to actually catch up and fully tend to the needs of your house. Anger, frustration, shame, guilt, and other emotions are going to rage every time you try to work your way through the debris overtaking your house. You shift from really loving and thriving in your house to merely surviving. You start to have tons of anxiety and resentment about how to function or not function in a space that is becoming more and more cramped.

Plus, it isn't only filling up with "stuff," it is becoming toxic too. The debris is overwhelming to your senses, and it starts to feel downright miserable in your own house. Eventually, it begins to feel as if there is no way possible to have a functioning house again. You are still trying to empty the trash every day and repair it, but are not able to overcome the fallout.

This trapped trauma's often unseen, but is a real impact on your system. You are trying to function today while the body is still full from yesterday's "trash" and the storm damage hasn't been repaired. Eventually, the body begins to become literally toxic from its own waste and inability to fully detox (physically, emotionally, and mentally).

With this working definition of *trapped trauma,* as unmet needs in the system due to survival re-prioritization and repression, we can start to see how these energies within the Body Being create a WHOLE host of other hidden, unresolved trauma adaptations that compound on themselves over time.

Trauma Responses and Reactions

Let's add another layer that comes with unresolved trauma adaptations and their compounding effect: the phenomenon called a *trauma response* or *reaction.*

69

Remember, because your system is bogged down and overwhelmed in managing daily requests, digging itself out from the past *and* trying to repair and heal your system, it defaults to becoming super reactive to every new request or demand on your system. This reactivity is not because you are too sensitive, but because of the exceedingly profound pressure and demand already present in your system.

Trauma reactions are responses that feel out alignment or proportion with the current situation—these are emotional outbursts and behaviors that don't make sense or match our typical responses. Trauma responses are triggered when the system experiences anything close to the experiences of the wounded Parts of us, which are holding actively trapped and unprocessed trauma. The wounded Parts are desperately trying to get our attention so we will tend to them. Our Body Being doesn't want to hold trapped energy that is working against its original programming. However—remember what I said earlier—that our system had to make a choice, on some level, to re-program itself in order to survive and function therefore, you could NOT attend fully to that wound. Because of this reprogramming, the system has to exile the wounded Parts it views as a threat to our survival and work to keep them at bay so that you can continue to function and survive.

We all have this built-in triaging process. Our survival systems are about self-preservation at all costs. They do not slow down to re-prioritize things that matter to us personally if there is a bigger survival requirement we are facing or have faced in the past that changed our system's wiring.

When we find ourselves experiencing what is called a trauma response/reaction, our behaviors really do match and make sense on some level. However, what they match and how they make sense is often based in the past and the situations that created them, NOT the present moment situation that triggered them. All the unmet needs we were not able to tend in the past literally bleed into the present-time situation that triggered us.

What's noteworthy is that it's almost impossible in the early stages of awakening and healing to stop a trauma response from happening. Think of the house metaphor and ALL the pressure the trash accumulation puts on the system. It is literally bursting at the seams of the house to get out. Once our system is triggered, the wounded Parts of us previously pushed aside burst through all the firewalls we have set up to control or manage ourselves. This is why I see these types of responses, reactions, and sensations in ourselves or in the other as a cry for help from deep within the system and not something that we should take personally or judge harshly (even in ourselves).

Case Study of the Effects of Trapped Trauma

Let's look at an example of the impact of trapped trauma via the story of my client that we'll call Steve. Steve came to me in his mid-30s after years and years of struggling with chronic gut health and digestive issues he was unable to resolve through traditional means. His Functional Medicine physician referred him to me to see if we could add in the holistic approach of subtle energy system work.

As we worked together, Steve's Body Being began to share a story. It showed a picture of him as a young boy sitting at the dinner table. His body should have been cueing itself to relax and start the digestive process, and also to be in open connection with his loved ones. However, the dinner table was not a calm and serene place for him. Instead, it was a place where he typically experienced heated arguments and outbursts from his family members. His Body Being, in its wisdom to protect Steve, began to associate food times with having to be hypervigilant. Instead of sending energy to digestion, his body was chronically redirecting its energy toward reading the subtle non-verbal cues from family members for clues about his safety. Steve's little Body Being had to make the hard call that digestion of food and having open Heart-Led

71

connections with his loved ones were secondary to his being ready to react by running away or becoming invisible and hiding in plain sight. Even after leaving the table, his system blocked digestion, believing it had to remain hypervigilant around meals and after them. Now, as an adult, his system was holding years of trapped trauma, which were over-riding his own natural ways of operating.

Steve had two competing survival needs, each with their own priorities and programs colliding. One, I need to digest my food so I can absorb nutrients and access the fuel sources I need to repair and run my body in top performance; and two, I have to keep my sensory systems on heightened alert so I can respond as quickly as possible to any sudden cues of danger. His Body Being chose protection over digestion, because the system will always prioritize its survival. This program continued operating in his Body Being long after those childhood experiences ceased because he hadn't yet become aware of the pattern and broken its cycle.

This is where people normally ask, "Michelle, I get what you are saying, but why doesn't my body just go back to its original way of being once I leave home or realize I'm not in harm's way anymore?" The problem is that these trauma adaptations and the programs they create are frozen in time, lost in the moment that they were created. They don't know you are older now and have greater freedom and choice available to you than you did when they were created. They don't know the empowerment journey you have been on. They don't have the luxury of feeling hope, nor are they willing to experiment with novel responses, such as new behaviors and thought patterns. They only operate on what they can predict, and they can only predict based on past experiences and the "world point of view" that matches the point in time they were developed.

Let's go back to Steve. The health challenges in his 30s were rooted in what happened when he was a younger child. His current thoughts and responses are actually coming from the world point of view of a young child's consciousness, and ONLY what was available to him at that time. See the problem?

Steve's system didn't shift the habit and couldn't undo the programing because his survival systems insisted he stay hypervigilant to possible threats during mealtimes. This was based on the trapped trauma in his system operating as if it were still happening. His system was stuck in time.

The trauma in Steve's system is trapped because he was never able to "complete" the circuit and tend to the needs that were repressed. Steve's young system didn't receive the support he needed to make sense of what was happening in a way that allowed him to step out of hypervigilance. This is what is needed to clear the debris of the past.

When Steve came to work with me, he didn't identify as a person with early childhood trauma. Instead, he viewed his childhood as typical. Like everyone, he surmised, he had stressed out parents that argued a lot and it was no big deal. Yet now, as an adult, he couldn't understand why he'd go to restaurants with his friends and feel so anxious and nauseous before eating. He didn't understand why he got moody and snappy at his loved ones when they started making meal plans. He didn't understand why his body was still struggling even after dietary changes, medication and supplemental support, and stress level management. What Steve's body was doing had nothing to do with current choices and everything to do with trapped, unresolved trauma.

Once Steve was able to witness what was actually happening in his system, understand the needs it was meeting and why, and begin to establish new programs and ways of being with his body and what was happening in it, his health and wellness issues rooted in trapped trauma were able to shift, change, unwind, release, and repattern themselves.

We will shed more light on how to heal and repattern the system in the next chapter; however, the first step is always to acknowledge that trapped trauma, unresolved wounds, and stuck emotions within the system impact it greatly. This is why it is so important to befriend the Body Being as a sacred messenger, because it will show you what you need to see and help you mend it. Then you gain the freedom to match your actions to who you truly are now and not what you had to become to survive.

TRAUMA-INFORMED SELF-COMPASSION AND CARE

You might have heard the terms *trauma-informed care* or *trauma-informed interventions* before. It means that one providing care is aware and informed of these types of unseen effects. Ideally, a trauma-informed care provider will bring compassion and an understanding that current behaviors, symptoms, and patterns have their roots in survival belief systems and needs.

Richard Schwartz, the founder of Internal Family Systems (IFS) or Parts Therapy (which we will explore more in the next chapter) titled one of his books *No Bad Parts*. This title captures the perspective of the Sacred Witness, who knows beyond a shadow of a doubt that not a single Part of us is bad, no matter how much we don't agree or dislike them. Our protective Parts are ultimately trying to help us survive, to protect us, and to help give us a sense of control in a situation that resembles one we previously couldn't control.

When we bring trauma-informed care to the Observer Self, we agree to acknowledge that two survival needs may be battling it out inside of us—one Part that says, *Hey, there is something wrong here and we need to look at this,* and another Part that says, *No matter what, DON'T look at that wound. If you do, we will not survive.* Thus, Parts of us will jump at the chance to finally be seen and supported, while others will freak out and try anything to block and sabotage our healing. The trauma-informed point of view, is that the seemingly sabotaging Parts and the cheerleading Parts ALL think they are protecting you in some way.

I hope the house metaphor and Steve's story help you begin to compassionately understand that you are not crazy or being overly dramatic if you've experienced trauma adaptations and responses that you didn't understand, or felt a sense of hopelessness around healing the effects of trapped trauma that you know about. When we access the Sacred Witness within, we can remember to be trauma informed with ourselves. We can bring kindness to these Parts of ourselves we are observing *while* tending to them *and* helping to bring the whole of ourselves into present time. When we understand the house metaphor, we can hold the power of the Sacred Witness just like Schedule A did for me, and I did for Steve. Then we can actually tend to the Parts of ourselves that need us, bringing the grace of understanding and curiosity to ourselves—instead of shame, judgment, and blame.

THE LINK BETWEEN
TRAPPED TRAUMA AND SELF-REJECTION

This brings me to one of the most devastating, unseen effects of trapped trauma in our system: the trauma adaptation of Self-Rejection. When we are coming from a survival Part with unresolved trauma running the show in the background, we don't have access to the main healing energies of the Sacred Witness: acceptance, love, and compassion. This is the Part of us that can create healthy self-dialogue and support internal points of view like self-love, acceptance, and compassion are offline. When the Sacred Witness is being drowned out by a survival Part, the healthy self-dialogue and support it would provide us are cut off from reaching us. Without these, we have harsh inner judgements, anger, resentment, disgust, and fear around the Parts of ourselves that are wounded or behave "badly." and we end up believing these adaptations are the true us. When this happens, we cut off our connection to our Body Being and reject and forget our True Self.

The path of the Sacred Witness allows us to navigate our way back to true connection with ourselves by helping us open back up to radical self-acceptance, which leads us to radical self-love. *Radical* comes from the word *radix* in Latin—meaning root. I'm using the word *radical* here because I'm inviting you to reconnect with the true, original vibration of *acceptance* and *love*. Because of the trapped trauma and painful experiences held in our bodies, most of us have completely broken off from the radical (root) essence of these two words—*acceptance* and *love*.

Given that generations have developed trapped trauma due to shadow tribalism and shadow power and control dynamics, we have collectively de-evolved our ability to connect to true versions of our Soul Being's common core values, such as love, acceptance, compassion, understanding, and grace. We have entangled and bound love and acceptance together with elements such as performance, externally determined worthiness, and outside approval-seeking. I use the word *radical* here to help our Mental and Body Beings break free from these entanglements, both personal and collective, and reclaim their birthright.

When we can embrace *radical* self-love and acceptance, we can clearly observe, identify, and understand the active trauma adaptations within ourselves at any given moment. Remember, these programs run automatically in the background. The ability to cleanly observe what is happening in our whole system via the Body Being's messages is the only way we can see them and regain real choice within our system.

Survival programs don't slow down to ask, *Hey Michelle, we have a people-pleasing, fawning Part whose program excels at making people think we agree with them when we feel threatened. Do you want to hit play on that program now?* Nope, our system just loads up the program and enacts the response on autopilot, below the level of our awareness and conscious choice. However, we can develop the habit of befriending the Body Being and asking ourselves that very question. The Sacred Witness is going to tap us on the shoulder and say, *Okay Michelle, feel that tightness in your chest and the increase in your heart rate? It feels like Parts of you are being threatened right now. Your survival adaptation of pleasing people is getting ready to get off the bench and agree to something that doesn't match what you really want to do. Take a breath and give yourself a moment. What other choice can you make instead? Let me remind you that you have other options. You have an aspect of you that understands how to hold healthy boundaries based on kindness to yourself and for the other. Let's pause and not respond to them until we can connect with that aspect of us.* When we have an inner dialogue like this, we can respond to a request from a grounded, centered, present-moment point of view and in alignment with our True Self, not the trapped-in-time, wounded Part of ourselves.

I invite you to explore the idea that every time you are willing to become present and open to the messages of the Body Being, you are actively unwinding the cycle of unconscious and conscious Self-Rejection. When we are on autopilot and running off the old stories, we are really rejecting who we truly are—an amazing Being worthy of love and acceptance, flaws and all.

CHAPTER PRACTICE

The practices for this chapter are designed to help cultivate and/or strengthen your willingness and ability to offer yourself trauma-informed care and compassion via radical self-acceptance. As we start to embody the concept that there are no bad Parts or trauma adaptations, we can unwind self-rejection and harsh inner judgments.

PRACTICE 1: SETTING A LOVING INTENTION FOR YOUR SELF-WORK

I like to ask my clients to set a Code of Conduct with themselves. This is a set of intentions for *how* they want to work with themselves once they understand the impact trapped trauma is having on their system. This Code of Conduct or Loving Intention for Self-Work lets your whole system, especially your Body Being, know that no matter what type of relationship and tone of communication and connection you had with it in the past, you are now going to come through the doorway of understanding and self-love versus shame and judgment.

Here are some key components you might want to add to your Loving Code of Conduct for Interacting with your Body Being:

- I am committed to developing a connection with my Body Being so that I am not shaming and shunning myself anymore.
- I am aware and accept that my Body Being likely has a bunch of trauma/survival adaptations and responses that I don't have a conscious relationship with. I want to change that.
- I recognize that many habits I don't personally like—and Parts of me want to label as bad, destructive, or undermining—are actually wanting to be updated and reprogrammed

just as much as I want them to so they can serve me now in a more positive and supportive way.

- I believe that the wounded Parts of me are wanting to be found and brought in from being exiled and banished.
- I understand that my Body Being had to prioritize survival, seeking cues of safety and strategies of safety *at all costs* because it didn't feel it had other options at the time (and it may have been right in those contexts).
- I am committed to continuing to open to the healing energies of the Sacred Witness: compassion, love, and understanding.

I invite you to sit in meditation and explore the Code you would like to set for yourself and your Body Being as we continue through this journey of Embodying the Sacred Witness. Write them down and place them in a spot you can reference when you find yourself lost in your old habits and need to remember your innate true nature and how to be with the messages of the Body Being.

PRACTICE 2: ANCHORING IN SELF-LOVE AND ACCEPTANCE WITH THE OBSERVER SELF

Now that you have set an intention for how to work with your Body Being via self-love and compassion, we need to help your system anchor these energies into your Observer Self.

This guided meditation is designed to help you develop a felt sense of inner safety within your whole system by releasing the habits of destructive self-judgments and self-betrayals and replacing them with the intentions of self-acceptance and self-love. Afterall, how can we expect our Body Being to share its messages if we are just going to destroy them with harsh critical judgments? It definitely is not going to feel safe to come forward if it feels like any information or insights shared are going to be attacked, judged, or abandoned all over again.

MEDITATION

Take a moment to become present and centered by going through your Check-In.

First, invite your system to pull forward an image of your Self-Rejection Protector, a survival program that kicks you out of connection to yourself and the present moment.

This protector, Self-Rejection, is just that—a protective Part and not who you truly are. See if you can really get a good image of what Self-Rejection looks like. What descriptive words, feelings, and physical sensations are coming forward with this image?

Next, ask your system, how do you feel toward this long-time protector, a companion of sorts, within your system?

Remember, this protector isn't really you. At our core, we are all beings that love and can open to all the Parts of ourselves via the Sacred Witness within. At our core, we are trying to help bring the lost aspects of ourselves, like Self-Rejection, home again, to help them heal, release their trauma programming, and remember their light.

If it feels true to you, let this Part, Self-Rejection, know that you understand it had a very real reason for forgetting that love is always present and available to you. Remind it that love and acceptance don't have to be earned. They don't have to be awarded or granted based on "goodness" and achievements.

This Part, Self-Rejection, has had to abandon these truths, for whatever reason. Yet, your Soul, your Heart, and Divine love and acceptance are always available no matter what. Nothing, not one thing, needs to change about you to be worthy of that love.

Befriending and Connecting with the Protector

Let it know that you totally understand that past aspects of you didn't have the luxury to remember these truths. But today, in this moment, you can offer this acceptance and radical love to all aspects of you, including the protector Self-Rejection, as reconciliation to whatever extent feels true to you in this moment.

See what is changing within the image and feeling tone of Self-Rejection as you are reading these words, which are coming from the energy of the Sacred Witness. Is it willing to soften, to listen? If so, thank it.

Let it know that you understand it was trying to protect you from the judgements and rejections of others. Ask it to remember that there is another way of serving you. To remember and open to the Body Being's wisdom, to help you step back into being with your Body, Heart, Mental, and Soul Beings all together as one unit; that *this* is an act of true protection.

Remind Self-Rejection that willingness to connect to the Body Being, as it is currently in this moment, *is* an act of self-love and True Self-acceptance. Feel into the response in and around your Body Being.

See if your system is willing to acknowledge that your Body Being, even with all its flaws and struggles, is still serving as a beautiful temple to house your Soul in this incarnation. Your body is your constant companion. It provides you with a way to interact with the world, with others, your whole system.

From this space, ask Self-Rejection to step back even more for a moment and allow you to find a deeper direct connection with your Body Being—open to a felt sense of it, whichever part of your body it feels safe connecting to.

We thank and honor this protector, Self-Rejection, for its willingness to allow you to partner directly with your body.

Connecting with Your Body Being

If you are having a harder time connecting to the body, you might connect through physical sensation by touching the body—a hand on the heart center, a hand on the top part of your thighs, or wiggling your fingers or toes. You can also connect by feeling the breath moving in the body, to whatever extent it feels comfortable and safe. Even if the breath isn't what you would like it to be, can you bring your conscious acceptance, love, and gratitude to what the breath is able to do for you in this moment? Can you acknowledge that to whatever extent your breath is currently working, it is trying to feed your body with your Soul's life-force energy, infusing your body with life and love?

Notice what might be shifting. With Self-Rejection willing to step back, you may experience more willingness to be here in the present moment, merging with your Body Being, befriending the body as your sacred companion, just as it is in this moment—*that* is True Self-acceptance and self-love. This creates the healing space to allow the old automatic stories you have about your body and your relationship with it to change to match the intentions you have for this connection now.

Not because you are forcing it to change, but because of your willingness to just BE with your body as it is right now without judging it, allowing the different aspects of you to have their opinions and old running stories, *and* not attaching to them as truth or absolutes. Acknowledging that they developed their point of view and programs for a reason, and we honor that, and are inviting them as well to step back and allow this current-time connection to be there too. Are they able to calm down and feel seen?

This is a healing presence. This is what grounding is. It is the willingness to be with What Is without trying to fix or judge it. When we can be open to accepting What Is, changes throughout our whole system become possible.

Is the Body beginning to feel less like a separate chunk of something you are stuck with, that you are dragging around like a foreign object that keeps betraying you? By gaining permission to return to connecting with the Body Being, its sensations can finally show us what created them and begin to make sense.

Now, the Body Being has a chance to talk to you, share with you, open to you, and invite you into helping and tending to its needs and the messages it holds for the rest of the system.

Notice where and how you can find this connection right now.

What shifts do you sense from being with your body?

Does it bring forward the Sacred Witness energy of curiosity?

What if your body can be a place where you feel more at home and safe with?

What if it could become your dearest friend?

Do any of your expectations of the Body Being and yourself need to shift?

Can you begin to hold the perspective of relating to the Body Being like you would a wonderful, beautiful soul friend? In friendship, we know that neither of us is perfect. We give each other grace, compassion, and understanding in the moments that we are not on the same page or feel like we are not supporting each other. Can that same grace be present in this relationship too?

Can you bring love and kindness to moments when you feel the physical body has stumbled, or when you have stumbled and hurt the body? Can you make a promise to yourself that you will do your best to repair and tend to each other in those moments, just like you were dearest friends?

Can you make the commitment to keep opening to the Sacred Witness energy to help you access curiosity and compassion toward your body and yourself?

Can you set the intention to create more ease and freedom in your connection with your Body Being?

Notice how just reading these questions might be allowing you and the Body Being to settle and open to each other. Perhaps there is a flow of welcoming, warmth, acceptance, and love.

The Body Being no longer needs to be at war with anything within you or you with it. You are learning how to welcome it all. This is radical self-acceptance and the energy of the Sacred Witness.

Right now, maybe you and your Body Being are willing to soften even more, welcoming each other as if you were long-lost companions finally coming together again. You are setting the sacred place for your True Self, your Heart, and your Soul to come forward and be present within your Body Being.

Inviting in the Mental Being

We don't want to leave the mind behind. If it feels good to you, invite the Mental Being to come forward as well and witness the shifts. We will work more with this aspect of us in the coming section. For now, we are welcoming it into the sacred space of the Heart, Soul, and Body Beings. Our mind has been faithfully acting as our main sentinel, guard, and constant protector, working SO hard to figure everything out and help us try to fix everything. We are inviting the mind to take a little break, soften, and open to the innate wisdom of our Body Being and Sacred Witness.

Perhaps the mind can also get curious about a new way of being. Can it be awake and working in collaboration with my Body and Soul Beings without stress? Can it open to the idea of recognizing what's happening in and around me from a present-time point of view and release its attachments to old stories and ways of being based in past experiences?

We honor and understand the value of always being alert and at the ready, staying with a low-level feeling of danger or threat lurking behind every action. We are so grateful to the Mental Body for all it does to keep us safe. However, right now, let it know you are okay. Just for this moment, ask if it is willing to release its hypervigilance, just like the protector Self-Rejection did. Invite the Mental Being to release its allegiance to stress and fear for just this moment and open to connect with this level of self-love and acceptance to move into action from a place of wonder, curiosity, play, and creation.

If it feels available, and to the extent it feels safe, ask your system to open to your True Whole Self. You might listen and receive, or offer a prayer such as:

I am open to re-engaging with grace, wonder, awe, and the radical concepts of self-love and kindness. I know that built within my True Self are the radical versions of love and compassion, ones that include healthy boundaries and actions that create a true sense of safety within myself, and that this includes experiencing as much health, wellness, and joy as I possibly can. All of this doesn't mean I'm naive. It doesn't mean I'm blind about the difficulties and suffering in this world or in my life. It doesn't mean ignoring the things I want to work toward and change.

Radical self-love means that as I come home to my Body Being as my portal to my whole self, I have so much more to offer to myself. I am willing to learn how to deal with whatever life brings me and to thrive, grow, evolve, and remember my wholeness through life's ups and downs. I know that I'm building these connections in this and every future moment when I am willing to come home to the Body Being, connect with What Is present, and empower my mind, heart, and soul to choose how I want to meet that moment.

And so it is—peace, peace, peace.

Now that you have an understanding of the multilayered and inter-woven effects of trauma on the Body Being and how it creates discon-nection, repression, and survival programming, we can step into the next part of Awakening and Befriending the Body Being: learning a few techniques to shift, unwind, release, and heal the trapped trauma so we can reprogram our system to match our True Self through the healing power of the Sacred Witness.

Chapter Six

Healing Trapped Trauma in the Body Being

Once we become willing to shift our system's default from being harshly judgmental and self-rejecting to offering self-acceptance and nonjudgment, we can keep developing our ability to clearly observe what our system is trying to share with us. Remember, we lose clarity and connection with our Body Being because we have survival mechanisms and trauma responses that skew and filter what we are observing to match belief systems and programs created to help us survive or make sense of our situation.

The last step of befriending the Body Being before we move into working with the Mental Being directly is to help our system realize that, because we have begun to connect with our Observer Self and become aware of the Body Being's messages, we have more freedom and choice points available to us now than we did in the past. The Sacred Witness perspective invites us into a dialogue to discover what the best response can be now, in the present moment. I like to call this reclaiming and reprogramming the "highest good and benefit for all" guidance system. When we can reclaim this state, we are now willing to have this mean, *I know I'm a part of the ALL. And I also know and accept that what is good for me is included in that guidance.* Self-rejection takes us—what is good and best for us—out of the "All" in that statement, and we get to put it back in now.

In this chapter, I'm going to share two more frameworks and practices I find incredibly helpful in:

- further understanding the hidden impact of trauma on our nervous system and our ability to access true choice.

- Learning how to witness and observe different Parts of ourselves and differentiating them from our True Self.
- Showing us how possible it can be to actually unwind, rewire, and unbridle our innate inner healing power—believing and knowing that we can recover what trauma takes away from us: the ability to act on our free will, guidance, and choice.

The Sacred Witness point of view opens us up to innate discernment—something that trauma, and the adaptations we had to make to survive, disconnect us from. When we can work with the Body Being as a sacred companion, we gain the ability to match our actions, thoughts, and attitudes to who we are now, in alignment with our True Self, not a self we developed to survive.

Throughout this chapter, we will explore various ways to cultivate non-dual thinking as a key component to our Observer Self. We are more than one thought, one idea, one perspective, one anything. We are full of competing points of views, needs, wants, and desires. We don't always match or make sense within the different aspects of ourselves. And that is normal. When we begin to receive the messages coming from the Body Being, it will feel as if we are constantly getting different stories and conflicting points of view—because we are.

The trick, or the *magic*, as I like to call it, in this stage of Embodying the Sacred Witness is to gain comfort with the idea of holding different perspectives without making one wrong or right. In this stage, we develop what I like to call the *yes, ands*. Yes, a Part of me feels tired right now and just wants to stay home tonight, *and* a Part of me is super excited about seeing my friends tonight. Both are true from their own point of view.

When we open to accepting ourselves just as we are in any moment—the good, the bad, and the ugly—we don't try to hide, run away, or agree to follow the old playbook from our trauma responses, which tell us we don't have options. Rather, we can be open to illuminating what actions to take that are optimal, true, and empowering to us and the other in that moment—for the highest good and benefit for all. That is true healing—remembering our wholeness—that creates evolutionary change throughout our system.

REAL-TIME PRACTICE OF CONNECTING WITH THE BODY BEING

As you read this chapter, I invite you to bring the skills you have been cultivating so far through your practices into motion. Jot down notes about the body sensations and/or Inner Narrator thoughts you notice as you work your way through this section. Writing them down helps us truly witness them and see just how dynamic our Body Being is as a messenger ALL the time.

Please remember, trauma and survival responses turn off our ability to connect to our Body Being and track our body as a messenger in REAL time. In the past, some part of our system believed it was a threat to us to stay connected to and aware of the body's needs. Therefore, it would not have been kind and helpful to stay in communication with our body as a sacred messenger. This is one of the hidden impacts of trapped unresolved trauma. Most of our systems have become incredibly adept at numbing out, giving false stories, and taking offline our conscious ability to tend our own needs fully. Unresolved trauma and survival responses literally diminish our ability to choose tending our own needs in the moment. Instead, we slip into deep survival responses like dissociation, fighting, fleeing, and freezing to survive.

I often share this image with people about trauma responses. Imagine you are locked in a room and watching yourself through a one-way mirror. You can see what you are doing, but you can't do anything to influence it. No matter how much you yell and scream at yourself to do something different, nothing happens. You are stuck watching a different you doing what it is doing. That version of you has no knowledge that you are on the other side of the mirror trying desperately to break through and support yourself. There is a version of you running a program completely autonomous to your personal choice. That is what trauma does to our ability to choose. Parts of us respond and act differently than we would want to. While others must watch and do nothing. Eventually the latter Parts stop trying to influence us and just shut down. However, every time we can witness and acknowledge a need in our Body Being, we are re-building connection. Every time we notice the body has a need and we "allow" or enable ourselves to answer as best as we can, we are healing the effects of trapped trauma. That is the healing power of the Sacred Witness.

Now, let's explore two modern theories as tools to bring more understanding and compassion to why our system is doing what it is doing, why it is hard to bring consistent connection to our Body Being, and why it is hard to have discernment around the conflicting messages we start to receive when we connect with the Body Being.

POLYVAGAL THEORY

Polyvagal theory, developed by Stephen Porges, totally shifted our collective understanding of the nervous system. Prior to Porges's work, the mainstream understanding of our autonomic nervous system was that it only had two parts:

- Sympathetic or flight-fight-freeze. This part's main job was to help us survive in the face of a real or perceived threat.
- Parasympathetic or rest-digest-restore. This part allows us to digest our food, have a sense of calm and peace, and heal and restore cellular function.

Stephen Porges's work illuminated a third part of our nervous system: our social engagement system. He identified that our social engagement system was a part of our central nervous system (CNS) that was utilizing the structures of mirror neurons and our interpersonal neurobiology networks to constantly scan for cues of safety in our environment. Remember, in the beginning of our lives we are dependent on others for survival and safety. Survival includes having acceptance and approval from those around us. Thus, it would make sense that these functions are hardwired into our nervous systems. In his work, Porges discovered that we offer and receive cues of safety with another mainly through our vagal nerve, a long branch-like nerve that goes from our head and face, down through our chest, into our abdomen, and all the way down to the pelvic floor.

Porges's pioneering work combined beautifully with the work of other pioneers like Peter Levine. When you combine these somatic theories, you gain a more complete picture of our basic biological drivers, including a survival desire to seek connection and be in connection with others at all costs. As a result of these drivers, we can develop unresolved or trapped trauma that impacts our whole Body Being, particularly when we develop Inner Narrators who say being in connection is not safe, or that we need to seek connection outside of ourselves all the time in order to be safe. Both extremes are problematic.

With the addition of the third component of the central nervous system, Polyvagal Theory recognizes three states of the nervous system:

One: Sympathetic—The Flight and Fight Responses

These are the impulses that mobilize us to take actions that help us survive. The inner sympathetic or flight and fight stories might sound like, *Wow Michelle, you know they [someone that just triggered you] are acting like that on purpose. They are disrespecting you and you have to stand up for yourself and fight back* . . .

Two: Dorsal or Shutdown Responses

Dorsal responses correspond to the back branch of the vagal nerve. These behaviors and stories are more extreme responses to our perception of danger, and can include the following survival strategies:

- depression
- fawning: momentarily releasing your own personal thoughts and actions to match another's for safety and protection
- folding: collapsing your own personal thoughts, wants, and desires to match those around you for an extended period of time
- dissociation
- numbing
- appeasing and submitting

Our shutdown stories take us even further into different trauma responses, and might sound like, *Wow Michelle, they are going to really take you out if you keep disagreeing with them, you better just agree and tell them you're sorry. Then they'll back off and you'll be safe.*

Three: Ventral Responses

Ventral responses correspond to the front branch of the vagal nerve and with the presence of the Sacred Witness. The responses and stories generated by this part of the system help us register that we are safe (internally or externally) and can move toward connection. The Ventral state opens us to accessing the parasympathetic responses we previously knew about via the older two-branch system—such as rest, digest, and recharge—so we can heal.

Additionally, we now understand this third ventral-vagal part of the nervous system lets us stay in motion and complete actions such as: working with requests on the system and making micro-adjustments to shift, change, create, and engage with our own thoughts and desires and the world around us. We can meet the needs of the moment without dropping into a full blown sympathetic or dorsal response that floods our body with toxic stress chemicals and chain reactions.

Ventral storylines provide us another option other than reactivity so we can respond in a way that matches our True Self. I call these the *whispers of our Sacred Witness*. These nudges and their guidance are trying to help us gain a greater perspective based on a clean read of what is really happening—beyond the influence and filters of our old tapes and trapped trauma responses. An example of this Sacred Witness voice and guide (which is there supporting us all the time in the background, by the way), is something like,

> *Okay Michelle, I know you are really triggered right now by that person's response to you and their opinions. It is causing you to feel threatened and I can see that a Part of you is taking it personally. This Part wants to scream at them and make them understand. I can also see that Part of you is wanting you to adapt your opinion to match theirs and apologize so that you can feel safe. Remember, their actions, tone, and ideals right now reflect what they are struggling with. It's not your job to shift it, change them, enlighten them, or take it personally. What do you need right now? Does your safety really depend on them, or can you keep yourself safe in a healthier way? How can you meet your needs right now in a way that works for you, staying true to your inner guidance and your True Self?*

These ventral story lines create more freedom for choice aligned with our True Self and help us connect to others in more supportive ways.

What's important to note about our system is that when we drop into a sympathetic or dorsal survival response, it takes our body at least ten to twenty minutes to switch over and access our ventral vagal responses. That is a LOT of time. When we attune and strengthen our body's willingness to stay in a ventral vagal-based response, we are able to make any micro-adjustments we need to remain in the flow state or in a state of openness and curiosity, instead of dropping into knee-jerk survival and trauma responses that kick us into flight, fight, shutdown, and freeze.

When the body feels safe to access a ventral vagal response (with its corresponding actions and thoughts) as its main way of operating, you develop a default pattern of play, curiosity, openness, healthy self-esteem, and seeking cues of safety within your own system, in addition to the people around you. Simply put, you can access an internal felt sense of safety and connection independent of the input you are receiving around you.

Polyvagal Theory and the Sacred Witness

Why is it helpful for us to know this theory if we want to develop the Observer Self and embody the healing presence of the Sacred Witness?

First, it can help reduce our shame and blame for being unable to get our body to "just calm down" at the snap of a finger when we are triggered into a sympathetic or shutdown response. This understanding further supports us because science now KNOWS that we can rewire our nervous system to increase our access to a felt sense of internal safety, thereby diminishing that default process of being continually dumped into a dorsal or sympathetic response in our nervous system (i.e., locked in that room with the one-way mirror). We can reclaim and develop the capacity to access more choice within our own system. The practices in this book help us do this a little bit at a time.

Let's look at an example of Polyvagal Theory in motion, to give you a clearer idea of how it works. Let's say you are a small child engrossed in your own little flow of doing something you love. It might be playing outside, dancing in the hall, or singing your favorite song. You are in the wonder, joy, and flow of your innate creative beingness. You naturally do what your little system cues you to do: look to those around you for subtle cues that you are safe and that everything is good.

As you look toward your caretaker in that moment, instead of seeing a smiling face that looks back at you with joy and approval, you see the flash of non-verbal signals (in facial expression or body posture) of their own disgust, inner shame, and guilt for abandoning what they used to love. You notice this one time, not that big of a deal. However, if you receive these cues repeatedly from those you look to for signs of safety, your system develops a belief system. Even if they don't verbally say "Stop, I don't like that," their body language and the non-verbal cues of their Body Being are communicating things like, *I could have been that happy, if only . . .* or, *Sure laugh and play now, the world will cut you down soon enough.* Some might experience verbally explicit cues of shaming, messages that they were not good enough, and so on. Some might even endure rapid jarring experiences that rip them out of the state of feeling good and into being afraid and needing to match what the caretakers want in order to gain safety and survive.

Can you see here how our nervous system, at the safety-seeking cues of our Body Being, slowly begins to abandon our ability to move into action, social engagement, play, and creation from a compassionate ventral vagal response? It is easy to see how we would switch out a kind Inner Coach for a harsh Inner Critic or Drill Sergeant. We swap out our loving approach to co-creating, and learning through play and exploration, to growing and learning through threats, bribes, fear, and submission. Creating and moving into action from this latter mode is crazy costly to our entire Being.

I used to mostly create from relentless sympathetic states, with rare moments of creating from a ventral vagal response. Here's an example of how I learned to meet stressful demands from a supportive ventral vagal response. When I was with Schedule, I wanted to work through the pain and gain more movement in my body. This desire to step into a new way of being was not coming from a place of fear and compliance. It was coming from a core desire for deeper and deeper connection and movement within myself through connection with Schedule. I wanted to experience connecting even deeper and doing more things together, like trotting, cantering, jumping, and being more and more in sync as a unit. I wasn't striving for survival-based acceptance from Schedule or an outside authority figure. I was being driven by my desire to explore more ways through which Schedule and I could experience deeper connection via movement, play, and fun.

Compare this to creating from the sympathetic power center. I have had labels of learning disabilities attached to me since age six. Attention Deficit with Hyperactivity Disorder (ADHD), severe dyslexia and dysgraphia, speech and hearing issues. Next, add the labels that came from my illness at thirteen years old—traumatic brain injury, post-traumatic stress (disorder), anxiety, and so on. I had the support of special education and IEPs (individual education planning) from the time I was in second grade. While I don't identify with the labels as any reflection of my intelligence, many teachers did. I had a teacher in twelfth grade who believed his AP (advanced placement) class was one in which a student with my labels could not be successful. I fought to get into the class and once there, I felt like he made it a point to prove that no special education student would succeed. My own inner anger and frustration at being told what I couldn't do spurred me on to produce an A in his course and a passing grade on the AP exam. Great! However, I "succeeded" not from a place of loving and being excited to learn and expand. I produced success from a driving force of shadow judgment, anger, hypervigilance, worry, and fear of failure. If I had been centered and grounded in my own authentic love of learning, I would have created a similar success without constant stress and fear of failure driving my actions.

Creating and acting from sympathetic responses can sound like:
- *I'll prove them wrong . . .*
- *I'm not going to let them beat me . . .*
- *Look at what they are doing, it is so much better than me, I need to step it up . . .*

Creating and acting from shutdown dorsal responses can sound like:
- *I'm never going to be as good as them, so why bother . . .*
- *Everyone has success but me . . .*
- *I can't do anything right . . .*

Creating and acting from ventral vagal responses can sound like
- *Wow, I'm not sure how this is going to work out, but wow, I'm excited to see what comes forward . . .*
- *I see a few speed bumps ahead right now, and I know that I'll have the ability to work through them in my own unique way . . .*
- *I love creating! I do it my own special way and that is all good because you do it your own special way and there is room for both . . .*

The ventral vagal responses open us to being in the flow, taking actions, AND working through the ups and downs of life without dropping into an unhealthy fear response and detrimental reaction to stress. The more we literally shift the relationship we have with stress, the more we can release our attachments to scarcity, fear, comparison, and shadow drivers. We step into new ways of being that open us up to our Body Being as a sacred messenger and help us step into play and expansion, while growing, shifting, and changing.

PARTS WORK

The second framework I want to bring in is Parts Work or Internal Family Systems (IFS), developed by Richard Schwartz, PhD. We all naturally do some version of Parts Work, but most people do not know they are doing it. In fact, I have already invited you into this approach by asking you to track the different sensations and trapped trauma programs in your system. Have you ever said, "A piece of me feels this way," or "A part of me always tells me that I should . . ."?

Dr. Schwartz's IFS theory brought our natural way of tracking these different aspects of us into a framework that honors the complexity of our neural pathways and that different Parts have very real impacts on our internal states and even how our physical body is operating and manifesting itself. Schwartz's system also illuminates that different Parts of us come with different belief systems, postures, and even body rhythms. There are even networks, or programs, of different Parts working together to protect us and help us survive. The job of Parts, so to speak, is to keep our body and mind functioning and safe at all costs.

What I love about Parts Work is that this model has truly brought a modern, easily accessible framework and approach to ancient healing practices. Master Healers and the Shamans of the past understood that true healing takes place when you access all the different subtle body beings together—body, mind, and soul. Parts Work helps people begin to understand that we need to look beyond just physically or mentally healing from trauma; we need to look deeper and recognize the hidden impacts of trauma in our system as a whole.

In the Internal Family Systems framework, we have three main types of parts:

- Protectors—managers and firefighters: the job of these Parts is to help us meet the requests of everyday life and keep us safe while in it. They don't have the luxury of trying out new skills or ideas because they were created from moments of adverse or painful experience and took on a "never again" approach to safety.

- Wounded Parts—exiles: these are the wounded Parts of us, like the young Steve his Protectors had to silence and push aside to keep safe. Exiles are disconnected from our system, or exiled, when our system believed we couldn't tend or protect them fully at the time. The system will continue to believe it can't tend to them in the present time until we can help it see that the circumstances are truly different, and we can now address the wounded, exiled Parts of us in a safe and supportive way.

- Core Self: The Self is not a Part of us per se. Rather it is our True Self which holds the core attributes of who we truly are. It is the Soul Being or Self that maintains our true nature, the Self that is not touched by the adaptations and reprogramming we had to make to survive.

PARTS WORK AND THE SACRED WITNESS

One of the core attributes of the Sacred Witness is an innate reverence for that which they are witnessing. The concept of reverence moves into motion through the active presence of the Observer Self by a willingness to not judge, shame, or blame what comes forward. Parts Work invites us to cultivate an inner stance of reverence for the different Parts of us when we are able to witness with our Observer Self. It does this by perceiving that every behavior or Part is working with a positive intent to protect us, even if it is very misguided and has forgotten its innate wholeness.

I love sharing Parts Work with my clients because it provides them with a more accessible intuitive system to seek understanding around all the different aspects of themselves, rather than taking an extremely harsh stance that the body or mind is trying to condemn and punish. When we can begin to realize that the protective mechanisms and aspects of us have their own sentience—their own autonomous survival responses that are designed to automatically try and help us survive no matter what—we can truly stand in awe of our multidimensional nature. We can begin to work with the different "Beings" within as parts of us that are very real.

Parts Work helps us to expand our Observer Self to look at our different behaviors, physical sensations, and symptoms from a place of honoring and reverence for what we are witnessing. It helps us support unburdening them, instead of villainizing, shaming, and blaming ourselves for why we can't seem to snap out of things and just make a different choice.

RESOLVING THE IMPACT OF TRAPPED TRAUMA

Let's take a look at how to integrate these two systems into the way we are connecting with our Body Being as a Sacred messenger to resolve the trapped trauma within. First, as we are observing our system, we need to develop the ability to sense and feel what point of view, Part, and internal state (i.e., flight, fight, shutdown, or freeze) we are coming from. Second, we must develop the ability to observe and connect with the Body Being from a place that is unblended from our trauma and survival adaptations' point of view in order to access the ventral vagal state. This is what allows us to see things from our True Self with the non judgmental point of view of the Sacred Witness. It is from the presence of the Sacred Witness within that we can tend to and heal our system and remember our wholeness again.

So what does the system need to complete its circuit so the body does not remain stuck in trapped trauma running the programs and protectors it created to survive?

To fully tend an unmet trauma wound, and complete the circuit, ALL the parts of the Being's needs must be addressed and answered—including offering whatever physical, emotional, mental, and spiritual care is needed. Healing is a whole Being process. This often requires that our protectors are willing to stand aside to allow the wounded and exiled Parts to finally express and get their needs met by our Body, Mental, Heart, and Soul Beings in a manner which feels complete and supported. And herein lies the main issue with healing work—what and who decides what is adequate support, care, and tending to?

To illustrate this further, let's go back to my illness and recovery at thirteen. Here, I will share how my physical body began to heal from trauma quickly at first, but how working with my Mental, Heart, and Soul Beings was far more complex.

MY BODY BEING

With the help of riding Schedule A three times a week, my physical body was able to heal. His body moved my body in the rhythmic motion of a walking gait. Since my body was in an open and receptive state when I was working with him—meaning that I welcomed and was consenting to connection and input from him physically, emotionally, mentally, and spiritually—I was able to access the healing power of the ventral vagal state within my nervous system. From this part of my nervous system, the repetitive motion allowed my physical body an opportunity to locate the damaged nervous system pathways and create new networks. My brain, spinal cord, and nervous system literally grew new pathways to provide the appropriate electrical impulses throughout my body, based on cues the muscles and tendons were being given. My body used what is called *neuroplasticity* to heal and make itself whole again. Within a year after my traumatic brain injury, my physical body fully recovered from the resulting paralysis to the point that I was walking, running, and trying out for the basketball team as a high school freshman.

The swelling in my brain had calmed down such that, while I still had light sensitivity and chronic migraines, the damaged pathways in my visual cortex had healed to the extent that I could physically see again. The swelling and trapped fluid in my ears causing deafness finally cleared after two years, and my hearing vastly improved. I was learning to speak again with the support of speech therapy. My cognitive skills, previously wiped out with memory loss, quickly caught up to my age range once my sight and hearing began to improve.

Notice I'm talking about healing at a purely physical level here. After just two years, the doctors deemed me cured and a HUGE success story, as I was one of the first survivors of this illness. Yet the true healing was far from complete.

EMOTIONAL, MENTAL, AND SOUL BEINGS

While my physical body healed well and essentially recovered within two years, the unseen and unresolved traumas were still present and compounding each day in my Emotional, Mental, and Soul Beings.

I was crazy hypervigilant; stuck in a body that had learned to appease and submit to survive. My body became attuned to always believing that I was either in, or about to be in, some form of pain—physical, emotional, and/or mental. I lacked any sense of self, ego structure, or personal consciousness, making me vulnerable to any structure I was given. My Mental Being believed the human world was not real and hostile. Earth school felt like a torture chamber. Outside of my three hours a week with the horses, interacting with people came with overwhelm, hypervigilance, and hiding within. I was becoming a hollow shell of a person and a puppet for anyone to move around as they pleased.

Spiritually, I raged at the concept of a God. I didn't want to believe that this God thing, to which my parents attributed my survival, was a good thing. To me this thing called *God* had sentenced me to hell, which did not seem very loving to me at the time.

My Internal State After Physical Recovery

Post-coma, all of the natural imprinting that comes from our bodies syncing to and being taught to comply with social norms, casts, religions, you name it, was gone. Because I didn't have the operating procedures most of us had installed in us by that age, I didn't understand why people did what they did and why I was supposed to conform to their madness.

I didn't understand why people subjected themselves to complying with different requests and actions when their bodies were screaming NO. I didn't understand why people hurt other people to make themselves feel better, because it didn't work. To me, almost nothing humans did or said matched what they were thinking, feeling, or what their Body Being was trying to tell them as a messenger of their True Self. I felt that almost no humans followed the guidance I heard coming from their Soul Being. I could hear, see, and sense their Team trying desperately to support and help them. Time after time, people blocked or ignored it. If I wanted to live and survive in the human world, I needed to find a way to deal with reactive, hurt, "mismatching" humans AND deal with what my system was showing and telling me, which was not often welcomed by the humans around me. Not an easy task!

This is where Schedule and the other horses taught me something about survival, counter to the way of the Sacred Witness. After twenty-five plus years of working with clients, I see that most people's systems have learned the same concepts the horses taught me, but through different experiences and teachings.

The horses taught me to comply, submit, and even dissociate from my consciousness, my needs, and my own Personal Heart's wants and desires as the main way to survive in the human world. I would watch them and their actions when other people were working with them. I watched the horse's consciousness leave their bodies and simply let their Body Being appease the human and go through the motions being asked of them. This was what I had learned to do in the hospital because I always lost anytime someone wanted me to do something. Every so often, I watched a horse snap back into their body and wake up, as I like to call it. They would come back into their body and ask a question of the human interacting with them.

Often, a horse snaps back into their body because something accidentally scared them and their survival needs kicked into gear, or their bodies were in pain and they were trying to tell the person, or they were confused by what was being asked of them. They would try to tell the person that was riding or working with them they were either hurt, scared, confused, or couldn't do what was being asked. I would watch the person's Heart try to tell them to listen and answer the horse's needs. Because I could see their energy bodies just as clearly as their physical bodies, I would then witness the person's Mental Being scream back at their Heart, almost whipping it back down through fears and judgmental expectations, until those voices overwhelmed the Heart's voice. Once their own inner judges and programs kicked into gear, the physical body would follow the directions of the Mental Being and they would often physically lash out at the horse, get louder, and/or keep asking the same question until one of two things happened. One, the horse appeased and did whatever the person was asking it to do to the best of their ability. Or two, the horse fought back, and the conversation would continue that way until one Being submitted to the other's will.

Once I saw this clearly in the horse-human relationship, I realized that this was happening over and over again in human-to-human relationships. I saw the same themes in my school groups, church youth groups, family, and even in my own body when I was connected to others. One day after riding lessons while, sitting in the pasture, I asked Schedule to help me understand what I was witnessing, I also asked why he didn't seem to check out and fall asleep with me. I was willing to listen to him and have a conversation in which we each supported each other, he explained. Because we allowed one another to share what we needed, neither of us had to protect ourselves. Because I was willing to tend to myself and open to the struggling Parts of me as he asked me to do, he had no reason to leave his body. However, he went on to explain, if I wanted to survive the human world with people who didn't know how to listen to their Hearts or the Hearts of others, I should check out and follow the horse's survival strategy. He said the best way to work with most people was to just leave your body and do what they ask (i.e., dorsal shutdown responses and Parts). If I didn't learn how to do this, I would need to be willing to fight until one of us submitted to the will of the other.

Then he gave me another caution I will never forget. He said, He showed me that if I choose to fight and to get louder, they will leave me or make my world worse. He cautioned me that I would never really win or get them to understand why I said no. He showed me images of horses that fought back, they either left the barn and often didn't return, or they were worked until there was no fight left in them. The horses that fought back were broken to the point that even when the humans left them alone, they still didn't come back into their bodies. He then showed me flashes of a few horses at our barn like that.

Later, I found a reason to visit those horses. They were truly not connected to their bodies. I searched for their light, the golden essence within their Heart, like I saw in Schedule and other horses: it was barely there. I asked them to meet me and connect from their Heart. *Nothing.*

They were a shell of a body with no spirit. Then, I started to watch people and saw the same thing: walking shells, bodies cut off from their Souls and Hearts. Nothing was left but compliance, numbness, and a Mental Being driven by and running off survival mode fears. These *ghosts*, as I came to call them, would consistently hurt themselves and others without awareness. These ghosts had lost connection to hope and their Soul's whispers of guidance and comfort.

The horses taught me how to dissociate, go into a shutdown response on command and become compliant and appeasing as the way to survive Earth school. They also taught me that if I dissociated too much, I would get lost, I would float too far out and become a hollow shell as well. That is when I started switching between floating out of my body, fighting, submitting, numbing, and overriding the messages of my Body Being and my Heart until, at twenty-three years old, my sacred companion Baron, saved me, woke me up, and launched me on the path of understanding and calling forward true healing and the lasting change I'm sharing in this book.

RESTORING CHOICE INTO OUR SYSTEM

These are the multi-layered and complex effects of trauma that require healing in addition to the physical body. Because Parts of me felt unsafe to tend, I didn't allow my Body Being to show me the pain held in my Heart Being. I didn't allow my Heart to guide me into my Soul Being. Because I didn't allow my system to connect to my Soul, my Mental Being didn't follow my Soul's guidance toward seeing, feeling, and listening to ALL Parts of me that needed attention.

The cycle of trapped trauma compounds on itself, growing deeper and deeper in the system. The deeper the unresolved trauma goes, the more our systems feel the need to disconnect to protect ourselves. The more we disconnect from our Body Being, the more we cut ourselves off from accessing the rest of ourselves and, ultimately, from choosing a different path. This means that we cannot access our greatest gift, the gift of choice, to empower ourselves with actions that support tending to the fullness of ourselves. It is a vicious feedback loop in our system that keeps us in a state of fear, suffering, comparison, and disconnection.

Another huge component to reestablishing choice in the system is to help the system feel safe in its parasympathetic and ventral response. A traumatized system often links being in a state of rest with being exposed to potential harm. In my healing journey, when I tried to support my body with things like mindfulness and meditation, it had the opposite effect on me. It became more stressed and kicked me into a fight/flight response versus the desired ventral response. In the next section, I will share more about how to help the system cultivate a deep-felt sense of safety. For right now, know that you are helping to create a new type of safety in your system through your work to befriend the Body Being.

Only in a true ventral response will our systems allow the body's innate self-healing capacity to do its job, unrestrained by protective mechanisms. When we are in a balanced ventral and parasympathetic state, the immune system can repair any ruptures to the muscles, tissues, cells, and organs that happened while in a sympathetic or shutdown response. From these parasympathetic and/or ventral states, we can tend to ourselves fully, release our attachment to what was, and open to What Is.

Let's go back to my client, Steve, and fast forward from how the experiences held in his younger body translated to his older self. Because of the unresolved trauma adaptations in his body, he had developed physical symptoms such as irritable bowel syndrome (IBS), food sensitivities, and other digestive issues. Through combining medical support with the inner Self-Work practices he was doing with me, he began to develop a new way to connect, hear, identify, and tend to the trapped trauma responses in his body. He experienced new inner dialogues around eating, helping him shift what it means to feel *safe* with eating while being in connection with his friends and family. Finally, his Body Being was able to pick a different choice within his system, come out of its hypervigilant state, and his digestion patterns began to shift. His symptoms went into remission. His body began to naturally heal the leaky gut, clear up the chronic infections, and address other trapped emotional and mental needs fully. Because he supported his mental/emotional states via befriending his Body Being, he was able to go from mere physical symptom management to whole system healing. This is the power of the Sacred Witness within.

The first step in rewiring and healing—for myself, Steve, and most people—is helping our system remember it can feel safe in a ventral response. We started working on this step with the titration practice of anchoring to an outside object or sensation in present time as a way to develop the sensory skills of interoception, or felt sense, without getting lost in the overwhelm. Titration and the ability to stay grounded in the present moment are key skills in developing the capacity to work with the Observer Self in a non judgmental and open Soul-Led point of view.

POWER OF THE PAUSE: EXIT RAMPS TO CHOICE

When we can work with the Observer Self via the Sacred Witness, we have the ability to watch and notice what ALL the different Parts of our system are doing via our Body Being:

- What is happening within it and our current nervous system state.
- Why our system might be doing what it is doing.
- Our arising fears, worries, expectations, desires, thoughts, and so on.

- What wounded Parts of us are wanting to come forward to be seen, felt, heard, and supported to complete their circuit.

Cultivating the ability to quickly notice and identify internal states, Parts associated with them, and the stories those Parts are operating from is a necessary step for befriending the Body Being as a Sacred Messenger. When our Observer Self is up and running in tandem with us throughout the day, we can actually sense, feel, see, and know when we are acting or responding from a point of view blended with a protective trauma or survival response. The ability to observe ourselves through the Body Being gives us access to our biggest superpower—choice.

Choice helps us activate the Sacred Witness within by allowing us to pause the automatic survival programs and intentionally pick a different path within our own system by turning toward our own Body Being with curiosity, sacred listening, and a willingness to tend our system to help it heal. I call this "taking an Exit Ramp" in our system.

Remember, the body is simply responding to programs and patterns that are already IN the system. The events, experiences, and belief systems that were born from them and the adaptations our system made to survive are what generate the stories and beliefs we interact with consciously and subconsciously all day long.

The first step of healing is to develop the ability to have AWARENESS of those different stories or Parts and identify the very real body responses that come with each of them so that when you are triggered you know their programs. We want to understand how these Parts and programs operate so we can begin to consciously decide if they are still working for us or not. If we notice the story or the way a Part is programmed that isn't working for us anymore, we can be open to asking ourselves, *What would be beneficial for me now?* From these new questions, we can begin healing and releasing those old trapped trauma tic tacs in our system.

Here is an example of this:

I'm in a fight story—this Inner Narrator starts up, *People are always against me. Nothing ever works out for me. I'm not going to take this anymore. I'm disgusted. It's that same old story of being left out or the world against me. Well, I'm done, no more, I'm not going to let them push me around . . .*

Once this train leaves the station, we feel the flush of hot fire pulsing through our bodies, taking us out of the lower freeze, folding, and fawning stages and up into fight. We need this burst of energy to help us break free of the old shutdown habits and stories. However, we don't want to get stuck here. If we stay in the protective fight mode, we may end up in resentment and victimization. Instead, we want to take an Exit Ramp—witnessing the flash of anger as a messenger showing us the old behavior and way of being is no longer serving us. Then we have the opportunity to find a better choice that truly honors ourselves and others.

By paying attention to the way our Parts are influencing and impacting our lives, interactions, and responses, we can take an Exit Ramp from automatic survival patterns and break free from the old cycles of reacting. Building out Exit Ramps in the system is the key to helping reclaim conscious choice in the system.

Building Exit Ramps

When you find yourself in the middle of an automatic trauma response, we want to help your system make a choice to create a new supportive healing program instead of the old protective one. We want it to hold up a stop sign inside, to give you space to check in and see if there is a better way to respond to a present stimulus.

Exit Ramps in the system help you create a wedge of awareness so you can recognize you are running from a protective Part, hit pause, and step out of a trauma response. Exit Ramps allow you to move toward curiosity to witness what is happening in your system. Exit Ramps step you into the present moment and invite you in to consciously tend the different aspects of you. When we take an Exit Ramp, we can remember that there is always another story that could be present—a healing one. By lovingly challenging the status quo of our Inner Narrators, we open to the healing guidance of the Sacred Witness's point of view.

The Sacred Witness energy allows us to stay connected and grounded to the present moment, anchored in a parasympathetic and/ or ventral state. Even while we are with a memory or witnessing the wound of another—which has the potential to stimulate and trigger a massive sympathetic and/or shutdown (or survival) response (such as harsh judging, defensiveness, denial, belittling, and so on)—we truly can remain unblended from that which we are witnessing. Being able to cultivate an "eye of the storm" refuge within ourselves via the Exit Ramps helps us gain a lifeline and stay non judgmental, curious, compassionate, and anchored in the Self's point of view.

Remember, the default patterns in our system are so often disconnected from our consciousness. We are lost in the inner web of thoughts of all the different Parts of us. Most of our energy and attention is in our Mental Being, caught up in the inner flow of thinking and narration. These thoughts might not even be ours but belong to the collective mind or those we are closely connected to. We may have accidentally absorbed these external thoughts via our empathic sensory systems.

Developing the skill of Exit Ramp building—pauses designed to shift us from protection to connection—we can choose the Sacred Witness's point of view. From there, we can open to true healing—turning toward and noticing the sensations present in the Body Being, exploring them, and letting them guide us to what they need. This approach replaces the default process of trying to automatically fix or dismiss the messages from the Body Being.

Let's consider this example to really understand the power of the Exit Ramp. I'm with a friend and I find myself feeling defensive and shut down when I'm trying to share my thoughts, which they disagree with, about a movie we just watched. I notice an Inner Narrator telling me to be quiet, make myself invisible, and simply nod in agreement instead of sharing my own thoughts. I notice another Part is shaming and judging me for being so weak and never sharing my own thoughts. Once I notice these different thoughts and impulses to shut down, based on an old program of fawning and people-pleasing, I have a choice to make. *Do I want to stay with these protective mechanisms or not?* If the answer is no, I can take an inner Exit Ramp, turn toward understanding, and cultivate new possible choices, instead of letting these old programs run their course. Once I decide to take an Exit Ramp, I:

- First, remember that the voices and desire to self-abandon aren't due to my lack of integrity or any other shame-and-blame story from which I have previously judged myself. Instead, it is a way of being that is trying to protect and help me.
- Next, I curiously observe what insights my Body Being is sharing with me about what is happening in or around my body. In the above example, I may feel a collapsing within my core, slumping of my shoulders, the dropping of my eyes, and overall fatigue and heaviness.
- Instead of projecting an old automatic story on what my body sensations are, I remind myself that my Body Being is acting as a messenger for Parts of me that need me to work with them, see them, and understand what created them, and how they are trying to protect me.
- Next, I remember I'm not powerless to my own inner systems. I can step into the practices I have cultivated to help myself find center, re-connect to my heart space, and open to the Sacred Witness within for support.

As we strengthen our capacity to hop off that disembodied state superhighway in our system and exit over into the ability to stay curious, open, and observing via non judgmental stances, we can regain the ability to remain in connection and open to the Sacred Witness energy within.

Know that it takes practice and repetition to gain comfort and confidence with these Exit Ramps and these new pathways of curiosity and non judgement, especially if we have reprogrammed our system to stay in more vigilant states. Practicing the skill of Exit Ramps is easiest to begin during personal reflections when you realize you previously made a choice or response that doesn't match your true choice. If you try to put this skill into practice right away when actively in the middle of a conversation or feeling the pull of different Parts of you, your protective programs may not be willing to step back and allow a new choice. The practices for this chapter will help you take the first steps toward developing this skill so that eventually you can use it both in your reflection practices and in real time.

CHAPTER PRACTICES

Accessing healing energy, and the ability to hear and follow the helpful whispers of the Sacred Witness within, lies in our ability to shift our awareness toward listening to the somatic sensations in the Body Being as a sacred messenger. Once we connect to the Body Being through this point of view, we can start identifying where we're dysregulated—and where the trauma responses are held in our body.

The two practices below, when combined, can help give you a basic format for how to work with somatic awareness to gain more comfort with interacting with the Body Being as a sacred messenger.

PRACTICE 1: CREATING AWARENESS AND CULTIVATING EXIT RAMPS

The first practice is a deeper version of the Body Scan in which you walk through a somatic awareness of the different sections of the Body Being to see what is present and what Parts might be associated with any sensations. The insights you gain from the scan begin to help you sort through the different sensations and create a "list" of what is currently most present and active in your Body Being. Next, to gain a greater depth of healing support for your system, you can take this list of somatic sensations into a reflective journaling process. This combined practice allows you to witness the different survival and trauma response patterns and programs that might be held within them. From here, you can begin to discover the power of Exit Ramps.

Part One: Creating Awareness—
Scanning the Body for Different Activated Parts

Practice Note: In the course of this practice, if you get lost or notice random thoughts unrelated to the part of the body you are scanning, it's okay. Simply acknowledge that some Part of you is potentially nervous about cultivating these ventral pathways. Ask your system to let you continue practicing and remind it that it is safe now, even if a Part doesn't think that is true. Then simply reorient yourself through reconnecting to your feet, the surface that is holding you, or your breath.

Check-In: Start with a short Check-In and centering.

Step One: Your Feet

Notice and bring your attention to your feet on the floor. If it helps, wiggle your toes, move your feet back and forth in a rocking motion, or push down with your legs to increase the pressure of your feet on the floor, which will cue your body to connect and focus on your feet further.

Take a moment to let your feet rest and notice what they are doing.

- Are they open to meeting the surface below them?
- Are they clenched up or tense?
- What does the arch of your foot feel like? Your heels? Your toes?
- Is there a difference between your left and right foot?

Take several moments to allow your consciousness to explore, feel, and sense your feet on the physical sensation level.

Next, check for the arising of any narrative, such as: *I don't like my feet, My feet are always hurting,* or *I need a foot massage.* Simply notice any running dialogue present.

Notice if the sensations you felt are tied to any old stories or memories. If that feels like too big of a leap, stay with just noticing the different "levels" of information you are receiving—physical sensations, narrative dialogue, and information via old stories.

If it feels supportive, ask your feet what they need right now to relax, soften, and open to the support of your attention. For example, maybe they want you to wiggle gently, flex, maybe even reach down to rub or massage your toes or feet.

Step Two: Your Seat

When you are ready, let go of your foot focus and now notice where your body meets the surface on which you're sitting or reclining, feeling the points of contact in your buttocks, back, arms, legs—wherever your body is connecting with another surface.

Follow the same check-in we did with your feet.

- Notice any sensations such as tension, relaxation, pulsing, numbness, clenching, and so on.
- Notice any differences between the left and right sides of the body.
- Open to the narrative arising: *My left hip always hurts because we were hit by a ball there too many times; My lower back is killing me, I never can seem to relax it*; or *Wow, I actually feel relaxed through my hips right now, that never happens . . .*
- Open to any old stories or memories being activated.
- Ask those areas of your body if they would like any support right now. Maybe you feel guided to help release any unnecessary tension, gripping, or holding you are noticing through movement. If so, allow your body to stretch, move, and answer that request. Alternatively, you can invite your life force energy to tend to the request of those areas by imagining they can breathe, exhale, and release some of that trapped energy now.

Step Three: Upper Body

Next, ask your attention to flow to your neck and head areas.

- Check in to any physical sensations held within these parts of your body—tight jaw, tension behind the eyes, a softening of the brow.
- Again, see if you feel any difference between the left and right sides of you.
- When you are ready, release the attention from the physical and move to see what narratives and stories are present. *I'm clenching my jaw again, I always do that when I'm concentrating; the back of my neck is so tight, I can't remember the last time I felt relaxed back there.*
- Ask this part of your body what it needs right now to support it. Maybe you slowly open the jaw and let a yawn or a sigh move through you. Maybe you answer the request by massaging your brow line or the back of the neck with your hands.

Step Four: Gratitude

When you are ready, thank your Body Being and all the Parts of you for being willing to share and connect with you today. Thank your Mental Being for stepping back and letting you practice observing both your physical body and the stories that might be present with it. And come back to center.

Deepening the Practice
Part Two: Cultivating and Taking Exit Ramps

Once you feel that you can gather different insights into what is happening in and around your Body Being with a basic Body Scan, you are ready to deepen this practice by taking what you found during the Body Scan into helping you both sort the different types of Parts the sensation is a messenger for and identify where you can build and take an Exit Ramp from your old protective or wounded stories. The second part of this practice is essential in a healing process because it takes us into committed actions that free us from unmet needs and helps us establish a new program in our Body Being. To help illustrate Part Two, we'll be bringing Steve back and use his process with this full practice as an example. After Steve learned the Body Scan you just practiced, I asked him to begin using it to track and sort the different Parts and their messages before, during, and after mealtimes. He began to see where he could take different Exit Ramps when he found himself falling into an automatic trauma response. Combining the Body Scans with this reflective journaling process allowed him to gain nuanced insights and information into the different shifts, patterns, and stories that were all hidden under the blanket feeling of overwhelm in his Body Being. You can use this practice to see beneath your own patterns, Parts, and protective strategies as well.

One: After this scan, make notes that help you sort through the different types of sensations and insights you gained from the scan.

For example, maybe you noticed the chronic tension in your shoulders or lower back. Maybe you heard the voice of an Inner Narrator that shames and blames you coming from the pit of your stomach. Maybe your jaw is clamped tight and you feel like you are holding back a scream of inner rage and resentment.

Two: Ask your Sacred Witness to help you pick one core issue or chronic "posture" you found during your scan that would be optimal to explore at this time.

For Steve, the first sensation he felt guided to work with was anxiety around mealtimes. He developed a practice to drop into a short Body Scan before mealtimes and track when "anxiety" started to show up, what it felt like in his body, and what circumstances it showed up with—was it there all the time or only in certain circumstances?

Three: Once you can see what the physical sensations are and what circumstances activate them, notice what inner narrator stories accompany these body sensations. Notice also what nervous system state you are in.

> *Journal about the messages, sensations, and patterns of the chronic inner "postures," and their accompanying nervous system states.*
>
> *For Steve, he noticed that behind the anxiety was a fearful young Part of him guiding him into thinking that he needed to just stay quiet and not share any of his thoughts or experiences with anyone during mealtimes because it might set them off. So therefore, he stayed withdrawn and disconnected during meals whether he wanted to or not. That would trigger another Shaming Part because he felt bad and sick to his stomach for not engaging the way he wanted with those he cared about.*

Four: Ask the question, "What else is there?"

I love this question because it invites our Body Being to share other subtle Parts that we might not notice because our focus is on our main sensation or "posture." This allows us to fill out the picture more to see all the survival programs present with that sensation.

> *Once Steve was able to break down general overwhelm into anxiety, he also noticed that after the anxiety he experienced a Part that desired to run away. This was a protective mechanism of withdrawal and shame. From there, he noticed another sensation of a hot flare in his chest and hands. The hot flare was from a Part he had never consciously noticed before. That Part was angry and hated mealtimes because he always felt sick no matter what he did. This Part didn't even want to allow food to enter his system (the reflux and indigestion symptom). He noticed that this Part got louder and stronger if he was eating with other people at a table compared to him eating alone in front of the TV or at a location other than a table. He also noticed that when he ate in a grazing and snacking pattern alone, the angry Part wasn't even there, and neither was the reflux and indigestion.*

Five: Bring the Sacred Witness to what you're noticing.

Let the Parts, sensations, thoughts, and feelings know that you see them and thank them for sharing. Ask for support from the healing power of the Sacred Witness to tend these hurt Parts of you. In Chapter Nine, I share a sample protocol for a deeper healing for this step, but for right now you can offer the healing prayer:

> *Even though I might know how to change these habits and tend to these wounded Parts of me fully, and a Part of me doesn't know if it's safe now to change them, I am open to the healing power of the Sacred Witness to help bring forward the grace of love, understanding, and new possibilities.*

Closing: Journal on what changes, shifts, awareness, and new choices come forward from your willingness to dialogue with the Body Being as a sacred messenger.

Healing Tip: Also, please note, the stories you find during these somatic reflections don't tell us about ourselves in terms of *who* we are. Instead, they give us insight into how our system is currently functioning. When we can begin to recognize that we are NOT our stories, our Parts, our emotions, or even our thoughts—that they are all simply outcomes of our experiences (both known and unknown)—then we can be open to true empowerment. When we can listen to our body in the moments we are being pulled into a survival or trauma response and say, *Wow, my body is really struggling with some old stories, patterns, and protective Parts right now. Okay, I'm not going to respond to the trigger right now. Let's lean in instead and see what is there. I think I need to pause for a moment, take an Exit Ramp, and ask my Body Being what is present for me and how I can tend to it.* Now, that is true empowerment and true choice!

PRACTICE 2: DEVELOP AN ONGOING RELATIONSHIP WITH THE BODY BEING

Practice keeping some of your sentient awareness—i.e., your awareness via your five senses—on the body, even while you're reading, meditating, sitting at the stop light, shopping at the grocery store, and so on. It's a challenge at first, for sure!

Set the intention and commitment to run a short Body Scan a couple of times a day in different environments. This helps you gain insight into the automatic ways in which your body changes and holds itself to match the different aspects of your life.

By creating (or strengthening) the ability to both be in a doing rhythm *and* sense and track your physical sensations, you are creating a transferable skill and neural pathways to take Exit Ramps into the ventral part of your nervous system. The more we build out these new pathways, the more your home base within the ventral part of your nervous system will become linked to your everyday life and interactions. These practices are one way of learning how to stay in connection with the Sacred Witness throughout your day. The more we are connected to our bodies, the much better chance we have of working with whatever activation arises in a grounded compassionate way, rather than defaulting to the survival networks of our nervous system.

Now that we have begun the process of befriending the Body Being as a beautiful soul companion and sacred messenger, we can step into the next phase of our journey.

Please remember to bring forward the skills we have cultivated in this section—the observer self, understanding the often unseen and complex impacts of trauma on our system, and our willingness to cultivate radical self-love and acceptance. These skills allow us to release harsh inner criticism and judgments as we bring curiosity to the messages coming from the Body Being. From here we can open to the next stage of developing the Sacred Witness, befriending the Mental Being, an aspect of ourselves also in need of support and connection.

Section Three
Awakening and Befriending the Mental Being

Overview

"Mind can be our greatest enemy or our best friend."
— GURUDEV SRI SRI REVA SHANKAR[1]

THE MENTAL BEING—
OUR FIERCE LONE WOLF PROTECTOR

The next stop on our journey of cultivating the Sacred Witness is to befriend the Mental Being. In trauma work, we say that the mind is a dangerous place to go without a Guide. Like the quote from Shankar shares, so often the mind feels like our enemy, not our friend.

I would like to give you an Exit Ramp right here by sharing that the mind is not our enemy, and neither is the ego. We need them both. They are here to help us make sense of the worlds in which we find ourselves. They provide us with a construct and a working ability to tend to all the functions and facets of our Being we experience at any given moment.

The Mental Being is way more than just our physical brain and its circuitry. While many of us simply equate the Mental Being with our thoughts, it is actually much more complex. The Mental Being includes both the implicit and explicit belief systems, thoughts, concepts of self and others, consciousness, and the unconscious. The Mental Being helps give our thoughts, feelings, inner impulses, and guidance structure through labeling (language), categorizing, sorting, and defining, as well as providing different frameworks that allow us to interpret and form personal opinions. All of these components are actually stored in our physical body and subtle energy systems, such as our chakras and aura. The Mental Being is like a super cloud storage system that allows us to access both our own individual mind, the collective conscious and unconscious, and ultimately even the Divine or Cosmic mind.

The Mental Being is how we store and work with memory at all levels—our own, ancestral, soul, and collective memories. This includes the collective mental field of your family unit, your local community, your nation, and then out into the global collective (both for humans and all Beings). The Mental Being not only *thinks*, it helps us tend to ourselves and others. It also holds the dial, determining the degree to which we access or restrict choice within our system.

The Mental Being interfaces with everything we sense, feel, touch, see, hear, taste, and understand. And we know from working with our Parts and inner storytellers, both aspects of the Mental Being, that they see the world through very different filters, based on various combinations of our past experiences, beliefs, and traumas. These points of view greatly affect how we process what our senses are picking up on and interacting with. Perception is really in the eye of the beholder and not necessarily a clean and clear read of the world with a capital T truth. A significant part of the Self-Work necessary to cultivate the Sacred Witness is to clear our Parts' various filters, those with distorted perceptions and points of view, so that we can open to What Is, instead of distorted projections based on trauma and survival needs of the past.

We have already begun to identify and tend the Mental Being through our Body Being practices. Let's have a quick look at our road map to see where we have been on our Embodying the Sacred Witness journey. You have begun to:

- Remember your original language of connection: Somatics. You have an awareness that you are experiencing different sensations within your body and those sensations are gateways through which your Body Being sends you important messages.

- Cultivate the ability to witness the Body Being through the Observer Self—getting curious about what the Body Being is experiencing and listening to its messages. You understand that those sensations are linked to different Parts that carry their own stories, beliefs, postures, and programs meant to help you survive and function to the best of your ability. You are practicing working with the point of view, which helps you shift from harsh judgmental or shutdown responses to access more insights into your behavior and underlying motivations.

- Embrace that, when you come from the Sacred Witness perspective, you have the ability to compassionately understand and heal the wounded Parts of you born from trauma and survival responses. You see that the wounded Parts, thoughts, and actions aren't *you*, and are limiting your full present-moment expression. This activates your biggest superpowers: Choice and Self-Agency.

- Develop a willingness to tend the wounded Parts appropriately so they no longer need to drive your responses to life. This frees you to respond to life by being with What Is while connected to your True Self.

In this section of the book, we'll expand our ability to identify different Parts of the Mental Being and how their survival- and protection-based filters are limiting our ability to access the True Self of our Sacred Witness. As we continue to explore, unwind, and heal our relationship with our Mental Being, we want to remember that we are not forgetting the Body Being. Instead, we are starting to strengthen or re-establish a Bridge of Connection between our Mental Being and the Body, Heart, and Soul Beings.

Over the next three chapters, we will explore how we can begin to:

- Cultivate working *with* the mind, not *against* it, through a unique process called the Bridge of Connection™.

- Build willingness in the Mental Being to be with our full range of emotions instead of trying to by-pass them.
- Understand why the Mental Being struggles with transformational change and healing work.
- Unlock an inner healing mindset by developing a willingness to walk with grief, which is one of the main keys that unlocks presence and our ability to meet life from our center.

Throughout this section, I share how to work with a simple, yet powerful Self-Work, or inner contemplation, frameworks needed to cultivate and embody the Sacred Witness. This whole section is dedicated to helping us develop the skills of the fifth stage of Embodying the Sacred Witness: Non-Dual Thinking.

The Mental Being loves absolutes, black and white choices, and rigid structures designed to ensure our safety, protection, and control. Awakening and befriending the Mental Being is going to ask the Mental Being to evolve its relationship with the unknown and gain more and more comfort with flexible thinking. This allows different levels of truth to be held in our system at one time, and ultimately invites the Mental Being to partner with the Body, Heart, and Soul Beings through the power of the Sacred Witness.

BIG PICTURE ROAD MAP CHECK-IN

Through befriending the Mental Being, we can establish a strong, trustworthy connection between our mind, body, emotions, and the Sacred Witness within. This re-connection is what creates the essential internal felt sense of safety that allows the Mental Body to switch from a fierce lone wolf protector to a faithful Sacred Companion. This faithful companion willingly shifts to help us tend and heal the trapped trauma held in our Personal Heart Being, which it has been loyally protecting.

Chapter Seven

The Bridge of Connection: Creating a Trusted Connection Back to Our True Self

To start us out on our journey of befriending the Mental Being, we first need to understand and accept that the Mental Being's foremost job is protection. For many of us, our mind has been the ultimate Lone Wolf Protector. Some of us develop well-defined "thinking" Parts that have sought to help us avoid feelings or being in the body as a means to protect us. Another protection method is a wall of thoughts and judgements that might keep us from connecting to our Mental Being as a partner. For many of us, our Mental Being's constant chatter has been our closest relationship in the absence of safe connections in the outer world.

Whether we like the mind or not, it doesn't really matter, the Mental Being is one of the biggest protectors we have. Therefore, there is a true hierarchy of needs we need to respect. Survival is the priority of the Mental Being, first and foremost. After survival needs are met, the Mental Being allows us to have access to creating our own Personal Heart's desires and needs. Lastly, once survival and personal needs are being tended adequately, our Mental Being can open to willingly partnering with the Soul Being or Sacred Witness within.

Let's look a bit deeper at the three levels of consciousness held by the Mental Being.

Default/Survival Level of Mental Being

Our mind starts out with a default program, or basic level of operation. It likes and learns best when things are predictable and have a repetitive rhythm to them. It is through repetitive actions and exposures that we can develop predictability. Predictability allows our nervous system to access a felt sense of "safety." When we can predict something, then we know what to expect. When we know what to expect, then we know how we are supposed to respond. When we know how to respond, we know what we need to do to keep ourselves safe.

This means that our system must meet our survival needs first. The survival level of us is necessary because we are in a physical body that needs to be fed, have shelter, and access connection. We want our Body Being to react and alert us to potential harm or danger. Our survival level also has amazing positive traits—it helps us adapt, change, and meet the needs of our changing surroundings. It can also support us in opening to and inviting the personal level of us to release what is no longer serving and open to new ways of being.

Personal Heart Level of Mental Being

Once we understand and know what to expect and how/what we need to do in a situation, we can shift from responding to the world from a survival-only point of view and open up to the level of our own personal heart. This helps us create experiences that are pleasurable and aligned with our heart's desires. However, the change from survival mode into taking actions that help us pursue our Personal Heart's desires only happens when we feel an internal sense of safety with ourselves and the world around us.

Our personal sense of self, what some call the *ego*, or the mental construct that allows us to know ourselves separate from the whole, is an absolutely necessary level of development required to embody true choice in connection. As a person that ran without an ego or personal self for years, I was in a constant state of self-abuse and outer abuse. Any Being I came in contact with could manipulate my own personal beliefs, wants, needs, and actions because I didn't have any access to "self" if they didn't honor it for me. I was an empty vessel for anyone to pour their own personal wants and needs into, a puppet for them to move and interact with. We need to have a strong sense of personal self, of who we are, and what our own Personal Heart feels, wants, and needs in order to access true consent, choice, and union.

Sacred Witness Level of Mental Being

The last level of needs the Mental Being allows us to access is the Soul preference, or Sacred Witness, level. Once our survival and personal needs are being tended, we can access aspects of ourselves that are beyond the sheer survival and ego/personal experiences of this lifetime. We are able to partner with our Soul Being and Wise One Team and discover how to approach our life with more and more choice, while honoring and valuing the form (body) we have, the experiences that form allows us to have in the physical world, and the person we are in this lifetime.

Ultimately, when we befriend the Mental Being, we are asking this whole system to function with trust in the Soul Being to help us meet all levels of our survival and personal needs from a place of connection to our True Self. This allows us the ability to return to center when we are triggered and a capacity to maintain connection to our True Self—and therefore, true choice—even in a storm. We'll work on developing these abilities and qualities in this whole section on the Mental Being. The first place we need to start is with building our Bridge of Connection™, the focus of this chapter.

THE BRIDGE OF CONNECTION™

To help clients cultivate an inner felt sense of safety and belief in their own amazing ability to meet life on life's terms without trying to wrestle the Mental Being into submission, I have developed a simple framework[1] over the past twenty years of working with both my own and clients' journeys of healing complex relational trauma—physically, emotionally, mentally, and spiritually. This way of working with your whole Being system can help you quickly identify where you are hemorrhaging your power of true choice to the different survival and trapped traumatized Parts held within the Mental Being.

As you now know, complex unresolved traumas and attachment/relational wounds are linked to chronic illnesses and disease. Just telling someone to release their attachments to the wounds of the past doesn't work. It shames them, and doesn't honor the fact that very real pathways and freedom of choice have been altered or restricted because of past experiences and the adaptations we make to survive. I developed the Bridge of Connection™ model to provide my clients with a very tangible, sequenced process of rebuilding a strong and secure connection back to their True Self. Working with the Bridge of Connection™ truly helps remove the blocks of shame, overwhelm, and hopelessness from the healing process.

Underpinning this model and practice are two key tenets. One is that our True Self, which includes the Sacred Witness, is always present and can never be damaged by our traumas and woundings. The second is that our traumas and woundings can create separation between our functioning-in-the-human-world self and our True Self. Sometimes this separation is the width of a small steam or a river, and sometimes this separation is oceans-wide.

While it might feel impossible to cross those bodies of separation to reconnect to our True Self, I believe that we can rebuild a strong secure connection to our True Self and invite our whole system to rewire itself so we can actually embody our true nature and way of being once again. The way you do this is by building the Bridge of Connection™. The Bridge of Connection has five basic pillars of connection based on the way we develop a felt sense of safety: Trust, Respect, Choice/Willingness, Connection, and Purpose/Values.

Ultimately, the Sacred Witness within creates a solid Inner Bridge of Connection that flips the hierarchy of needs from survival, personal, and then Sacred Witness, to one where the Sacred Witness leads and supports us in tending our survival and personal heart's needs. The Mental Body is pretty suspicious of this order at first; but that's okay, because that's its job. Again, we are working to help it remember that it is not a Lone Wolf Protector but rather a team member to our whole system.

Before we fully explore the Bridge of Connection™ together, let's talk about common strategies in personal growth and spiritual spaces that don't actually work.

THE PERVASIVE MENTAL BEING TACTIC OF SPIRITUAL BYPASS

Spiritual bypassing **is a term** that describes one of the main protective tactics the Mental Being employs when we start adding spiritual and/or mental health approaches and practices that help us override or change our basic hierarchy of needs. By-passing is when your Mental Being grabs hold of different high-level concepts or truths and uses them to do very fancy work-arounds to avoid the uncomfortable aspects of Self-Work.

The Mental Being believes the emotions and vulnerability we will encounter in our authentic Self-Work will somehow threaten our system; therefore, it wants to bypass the uncomfortable emotions held within the Heart Being and go straight into the esoteric impersonal teachings of spirituality. To do this, it tries to convince us that we are actually connected to our True Self and the Sacred Witness energy when we are really not.

To help illuminate a common bypass pitiful we all tend to fall into when working with mindfulness and other self-help practices, let's look at the three levels of the Mental Being from a slightly different perspective, using neurology as our lens now. We have three main parts of the brain: our brain stem, which is responsible for prioritizing our survival-level needs in our system; our mid-brain, which is responsible for helping us access and store memory and process emotions; and our pre-frontal cortex, responsible for our higher-level Mental Being functions.

What most of our Mental Beings seek to do with spiritual or self-mastering practices is to bypass the lower and middle part of our brains, which hold our survival fears and worries and our access to memory, emotions, connection, and relational thinking. Our Mental Being falsely believes that we can rid ourselves of survival-level or emotional responses or needs permanently. It thinks that if we can "heal" ourselves to the point where we are connected to our "Soul and Spirit," then we have reached the promised land within our own system and will no longer allow our "lower level" feelings and emotions to disconnect us from ourselves again. This is the Mental Being's attempt to bypass and take out the real Bridge of Connection. It skips the messy but necessary middle you will find when working with Parts that were exiled into the oceans of pain and trauma to survive.

This bypass causes our systems to not be fully integrated with all the different Parts in our Being. This is why we can be deeply engaged in some spiritual or mental health best practices, but not have that sense of calm and capacity translate to the rest of our lives. What the Bridge of Connection™ does is create true pathways that help us utilize the relational part of our system to help us tend our different needs from a place of true connection. We can't go around the emotional or survival aspects of our nature; we need to include them.

This is why just doing mindfulness practices without the Bridge of Connection doesn't work. In my working definition, mindfulness is about training the mind to focus on what we are asking it to focus on. But if we just exert our will over the Mental Being, in demanding its focus on something, without first pausing to check in on why it's doing what it's doing, it will likely get pissed.

For example, let's say I'm trying to ask the Mental Being to calm down and stay focused during a mindfulness-based breath work and mantra practice intended to cultivate inner calm. Every time I start my practice, all I feel is a blanket of general anxiety and a laundry list of what I need to do. I keep telling myself that I'm supposed to notice the felt sensation and my mind wandering and then command my mind to focus back on the mantra and breath. Over and over again, I redirect my focus back to the meditation. Yet I never allow my system a pause to lean into the messages coming from my Body, Heart, and Mental Beings and instead just keep overriding them to stay on target. Because I never addressed the Parts of my Mental Being that have real concerns with the idea of cultivating calm, I'm bullying the Mental Being. (And, quite frankly, this really dismisses and marginalizes the Body Being too.)

When we do "just" mindfulness, a whole bunch of our Parts come forward to sabotage our very well-meaning practices. Why? Because they believe we are creating a threat to the system. Think about it— how long are you going to stay willing to do something if you keep being told you are doing it wrong and that your needs don't matter? That is the very same harm we have been working to unwind in the Body Being. Just bullying the Mental Being into compliance won't work. No amount of willpower is going to make it work.

If you try to drop straight into a mindfulness, spiritual, or contemplative practice designed to shift your hierarchy of needs and how you show up in the present moment, without first inviting your system to partner with you in this new way of being, you'll just sling shot back and forth between the Parts that LOVE those practices and the Parts that view them as a threat and really dislike them. In the end, you will be in an inner battle. Avoiding that battle is totally possible through the Bridge of Connection work to follow. But first, one more common misconception that creates a lot of trouble as we work to befriend the Mental Being and cultivate our Sacred Witness presence.

THE MYTH OF SELF-REGULATION

In our spiritual and personal growth worlds, there is a pervasive, hyper-individualistic, and unfounded belief that humans are wired to self-regulate and self-soothe naturally. Remember back to Polyvagal Theory and Internal Family Systems from the last section? They helped us realize that self-regulation is a myth. Our neurobiology is hard wired for co-regulation. The Mental Body uses the co-regulation of our Body Beings from the very beginning to create a felt sense of safety and connection internally, relationally with others, AND collectively.

In the early years of our life, our Bridge of Connection is constructed between our little systems and the outside world via our main caregivers. We literally can only access an internal sense of safety and self-soothing when we feel "safe" in our environment. (Hold on to this word *safe* because we are going to revisit again shortly.) Therefore, in the beginning, we seek cues of safety from those around us first, in order to then express and tend to our own personal needs and wants, internally and externally.

We are way more interconnected than our individualistic ideologies would have us believe. We are inherently multisensory Beings utilizing our physical five senses and our empathic intuitive wiring to constantly scan the somatic messages and emotional energy fields of our caregivers. We are always registering the seen and unseen worlds around us, both consciously and unconsciously.

For example, we start to sync up to someone else's heart rate, breathing pattern, and gestures if they are in our field and we want to be in connection with them. We start to naturally mimic and match our verbal words and actions with another without consciously intending it. This lets the other person literally see, sense, and hear themselves in you, cueing them to bond to you and therefore include you in their protection. We are doing the same thing in reverse, witnessing ourselves reflected back to us, which increases our desire to connect and bond to them and bring them into our protection.

This social engagement system utilizes way more than our vagal nerve. It has a whole host of components, which include our subtle Body Being's electromagnetic field, the chakra system, the intuitive senses in our gut-brain and heart-brain (the gut and heart have their own neuronal networks), and these things called *mirror neurons.* Mirror neural networks are designed to quickly imitate the internal states and rhythms of the other. We create a carbon copy of their bio-rhythms and actions within our own system—down to the chemical make up of their own internal states: flight, fight, shutdown, or ventral vagal. Our own personal system of body rhythms and internal states are quite literally extremely porous and changeable based on the whole-body systems of those around of us.

You might have heard the word *entrainment* before if you have studied any somatic or sound healing work. *Entrainment* basically means that the more organized, or stronger, nervous system can help regulate a more disorganized or lost system.

So, what does this mean in relation to befriending the Mental Being and building a bridge that helps us integrate and align all aspects of ourselves? What we need to understand is that we all start out in early life with some semblance of an Outer Bridge of Connection to our caregivers, which provided us with a template for how to be in connection with and regulate ourselves. However, for most of us, this Bridge is missing pillars and is dicey if not downright dangerous. This is why so many of us struggle with trust, intimacy, and vulnerability in our present-day connections with others.

Let's bring this to our three levels of the Mental Being. At the survival level, we are co-regulating with the strongest outside nervous system to survival at all costs, which often leads to self-abandonment. At the personal level, we are co-regulating with our internal needs and wants, versus different shades of self-repression. At the Soul or Sacred Witness level, we can actually begin to co-regulate with the fullness of our True Self, helping the Body Being, Mental Being, and Personal Heart Being find connection with the help of our Sacred Witness within the fullness of our system. This helps us operate from self-acceptance and respect that stems from within, instead of having to seek regulation solely from outside of us.

Being able to cultivate an Inner Bridge of Connection allows us to co-regulate and source safety from within and not have to rely on others to provide it. This is a complete game-changer and liberator of our systems. Let's take a look at the Outer Bridge of Connection next.

OUTER BRIDGE OF CONNECTION

The first Bridge we build is to an external bridge, first to our caregivers and then to others. We then often replicate some version of this original Bridge through all other relationships in our lives as we grow, leaving us somewhat dependent on others to access our True Self until we consciously transcend how we connect with ourselves from an outer to an internal bridge. Because the external bridge is our first phase of development, we'll explore this Outer Bridge of Connection before we explore what it is like to build this bridge internally. Here is an overview of each pillar of our first Outer Bridge of Connection and their main questions and purpose.

Pillar One: Trust—*Can I predict you?*
Our system asks the questions:
- Can I predict the different ways you are going to show up around me?
- Can I predict the basic reactions and behaviors that you are going to make?
- Are you going to say what you mean and mean what you say?

If I can predict these things, good or bad, then I know what is expected of me within those predictions, and I can adjust to keep myself safe. Remember I mentioned the word *safe* above; let's revisit it now. We have done a very interesting thing with the concepts of trust and safety that feels good to our heart, but isn't actually true from a nervous system point of view. Trust is created from predictability. A felt sense of safety is created when we know what to expect and feel confident that we can produce, or show up, in a way that will meet the needs of that experience. From a sheer nuts-and-bolts perspective, how we *feel* or what we desire in a connection is a second tier priority above the survival need for predictability. The question of how I feel about what I can predict is asked in the next pillar of connection.

Pillar Two: Respect—*Does the way you interact with me feel fair and just?*
Once I can predict you, and therefore know what I need to do to survive and what is expected of me, then my system can ask:
- How do I feel about that interaction? Is this something I want for myself?
- Does it feel fair and just? Meaning, can I make sense of how you show up with me?

- Do I feel like you have regard for me in what you are doing and how you are interacting with me? Meaning, does it feel like our interactions honor me as a sentient Being who has their own thoughts, feelings, wants, and needs?

First, notice that like trust, I didn't say it feels good and "I" (meaning my personal system) like it. Rather, I said "honors my sentience," meaning the interaction offers me true choice. This might seem like the same thing, but they are very different. For example, Schedule didn't do everything I wanted; however, I was able to understand that when he said no, it was for a reason—such as I was off balance or asking him to do something he was confused about.

I am willing to give and receive a sense of respect and esteem to you if I feel you have regard for me as a Being as well. When I can understand why you are interacting with me in a certain way and it feels like you are trying to consider me and my feelings in that interaction, I am willing to move into consent within our connection, which is our next pillar.

However, if I do not feel that you have basic regard for me, I begin to respond to you not from a place of connection to my True Self, but rather my Mental Being takes over and begins to seek safety by utilizing survival tactics such as appeasement, compliance, resistance, shutdown, and even submission. Thus, the rest of the Bridge goes dark. I don't use it and instead stay solidly in survival reactivity mode instead of personal connection mode.

Pillar Three: Choice and Willingness—*Can I be in this connection from a place of true choice? If so, am I willing to be vulnerable?*
Once I can predict (i.e., trust) you and feel that you respect me, I must consider whether I feel free to come to the connection from a place of true choice. The third pillar is a huge choice point in the system in which the Mental Being either grants us access to continue along our Bridge of Connection or not. It makes this evaluation by asking a single question: Can I be my true authentic self in the connection?

I teach my clients and students that requests in a connection come through one of three basic doorways:

- **The Doorway of Fear and Intimidation**—This is the "big stick" doorway. If I have to connect through this doorway, I am coming from the point of view of compliance AND resistance. I feel like I have to relate *or else*, and parts of me are defending myself. Because I don't feel a true sense of choice and the ability to be myself in the connection, not all of me is willing. Therefore, I'm only there to survive.

- **The Doorway of Bribery**—This is the "carrot" doorway. Coming through this doorway, I really don't want to do something for whatever reason, but I am willing to do it for a "price." Depending on the "price" and the reason behind it, I may or may not be able to maintain connection with my True Self. This lure of some benefit takes away my ability to make an authentic choice free of coercion or manipulation and may keep my survival systems activated. We will dive into this option more in Section Four, where I introduce you to the four protectors of your Heart Being.

- **The Doorway of Choice and Consent**—This is the "just right" doorway. This doorway is one based on compassion, the freedom of choice, and a mutual agreement to be in the dance of connection. When a connection is offered through this doorway, I feel I have the ability to say yes, no, or maybe without fear of retaliation or withdrawal of your connection as a way to manipulate and control me. It has room for healthy compromise.

In order to access genuine willingness in our systems, we have to feel we can come to a connection with the ability to say yes, no, and maybe without jeopardizing the connection. The Mental Being will want to ensure we don't have to trade our authenticity for belonging.

This pillar does SO much of the heavy lifting in the Bridge

of Connection. If you don't have the willingness to step into true consent (choice without a survival fear driving that choice) within a connection, then you are really not present to open further in that connection. The Mental Being will shut down access to true connection and drop you into by-passing and protective mechanisms instead.

However, once we can establish that true choice and consent are present, we can make a choice to be willing and enter into vulnerability. Making this choice is a necessary piece of building our Bridge of Connection and reaching the next pillar.

Pillar Four: Connection—*Working with the true version of "safety"*,
When I'm willing to be vulnerable with you, I can step deeper into the movements asked of me during the dance of connection:

- I feel free to make requests of others.
- I'm willing to be in the dance of healthy compromise.
- I'm willing to tend to the other and ask them to help tend to my needs as well.
- I'm open to allow myself and the other to make repairs after any rupture, therefore maintaining the presence of true choice for myself and the other.

At this point I'm able to open to connections that are not based on perfection. I am willing to give Clean Compassion (more on this in Chapter Fourteen) to both myself and the other and allow for a sense of safety that doesn't just come through predictability. Once I have this pillar of my Bridge online, I am able to hold connection to my True Self and lean into growth opportunities during mis-attunements that might otherwise activate a full-blown threat/survival response. I honor that what actually creates a felt sense of safety is the intention of doing no harm AND when/if harm happens, we are both committed to offering each other any repair work needed. At this pillar, when I find myself feeling shaky with trust, respect, or willingness, I feel both of us are committed to addressing those issues and tending each other to make our Bridge steady and strong again.

**Pillar Five: Purpose—*What does my Heart Being and
Soul Being want to create?***
If I can trust you, our relationship feels respectful, we honor one another's choice, and I am willing to open to our connection, only then can I allow my "purpose" to be present. I am free to ask questions like:

- What do I want to create and experience through this connection?
- What does my Soul Being, Sacred Witness, and inner guidance want to co-create through this connection?

Purpose means that we can go past basic survival needs and that I feel that my own personal heart's needs are also being tended. Thus, I'm willing to open to my Soul Being and to my True Self to guide us beyond that which our Mental Being and base survival programs might limit us to. Therefore, I'm unlocking the highest potential of any moment, connection, and co-creation that wants to come forward for myself and the other. I am willing to take leaps of faith and be in the unknown. As a result, I start to believe in myself, my inner guidance, and my True Self, to be able to create a felt sense of safety within me, even if I can't predict the other or the outside world.

When we can activate the last pillar of the Outer Bridge of Connection, we are willing to allow our True Self to guide us and work with our various aspects of Self. The ocean that separated you from your True Self starts to drain and dwindle.

However, there is one small issue with this path to ourselves. This path is dependent on an outside source that shows up to get us started. In order to release the need to gain an internal sense of safety only by predicting the movements of the world around us, we have to pick this WHOLE bridge up and move it inward to befriend the different aspects of us—Body Being, Mental Being, Heart Being, and Soul Being. This is our Inner Bridge of Connection.

Before we explore the details of the Inner Bridge, let's look at an example of what this movement from the Outer to the Inner looks like.

EXAMPLE OF MOVING FROM OUTER BRIDGE TO INNER BRIDGE

Think back to the story of Schedule and me. My nervous system and internal felt states were a crazy hot mess. There was no coherence anywhere in my own personal body rhythms. After the coma, I wasn't able to gain any sense of "self-regulation" prior to beginning to work with Schedule again. If someone was upset around me, I was upset. If someone was scared, I was scared. It went beyond biorhythms and emotions. Because I had zero connection to the concept of Michelle and her own personal heart and mind, I would morph and adapt to the Parts of the people around me. I was a walking reflection of ANY system around me except my own. The different beliefs, protective mechanisms, and survival programs I was exposed to in others instantaneously became mine.

However, because I was willing to connect to Schedule through an openness of my heart and I felt safe with him, I allowed his heart, his breath, and his presence to start to repattern me back to my OWN system. Most importantly, Schedule helped me co-regulate back to me, because he was running the energy of the Sacred Witness. That is, he was not trying to override or fix my system with his stronger, more organized system. He was holding space, providing a safe, steady, nurturing rhythm for me to begin to claw my way out of my deeply entrenched flight, fight, and freeze patterns.

I was finally able to answer the first hierarchy of needs, survival, and begin to access the second tier of needs, the personal heart, via the ventral vagal part of my nervous system. This allowed my system to step out of sheer reactivity mode and start to heal on levels I wasn't able to access before. Around Schedule, I felt safe for the first time I could remember post-coma. Because even though my conscious mind had no memory of my time with Schedule to pull from, the whole of my Being remembered. I innately knew I could trust him. I knew that I was always going to be accepted by him and I felt unconditional love with him. Therefore, I was willing to step out of survival protection and into connection, being vulnerable with him and allowing his field to guide me into coherence. We built an Outer Bridge of Connection.

However, in the beginning of working with Schedule, I only felt a sense of safety and calm in my system around him. The regulation I gained and the connection to my True Self didn't transfer anywhere else.

The reason I couldn't hold the same quality of self-regulation and self-connection anywhere else was because my Mental Being still felt under constant attack by entrainment with other people's flight, flight, or shutdown-based patterns. Therefore, outside of co-regulating with Schedule, I was dysregulating into hypervigilance, overwhelm, and disconnection with everyone else. I was continuously creating a bigger and deeper ocean between my conscious self and who I truly am. I was at the whim of my survival-based outer Bridge of Connection that sought safety however it could find it, matching the internal states of those around me to get them to bond, connect, and protect me. I didn't have a steady enough Inner Bridge of Connection to hold the "self-regulation" Schedule was helping me find through co-regulation.

The Inner Bridge of Connection is our own conscious ability to co-regulate, tend to the aspects within our own system, and hear and match our True Self. Think of it as internal co-regulation. We take the survival-based Outer Bridge we are wired to build and create the Inner Bridge inside ourselves. We substitute other people for our own Sacred Witness within to build the foundations of our inwardly-sourced safety, intimacy, and connection. In this way "self-regulation" is actually letting core parts of our Soul Being help us self-soothe, co-regulate, and become a great Healer in our nervous system to all the Parts of us that need regulation.

Now, let's dive into the five core pillars of the Inner Bridge of Connection and the essential tasks, skills, and inquiry required to develop each.

INNER BRIDGE OF CONNECTION

As we've explored, the amount of access we have to our own Inner Bridge of Connection in our natural progression of life is initially determined by the level of felt sense of safety we had growing up with our first caregivers. For example, if a person felt a good sense of external security overall, they naturally feel safe to try out new things, be vulnerable in connections, ask for help, and have their needs tended internally or externally. Because they had the opportunity to practice their full Outer Bridge of Connection on a regular basis, the second Inner Bridge of Connection, begins to naturally come online. This is because the body of water separating them from their True Self is naturally more like a creek or small river with a strong bridge to go back and forth on. They can quickly identify where they are losing power to a survival or trauma adaptation when they feel shaky and are empowered to tend their needs either internally or by seeking support, resources, and help outside their system.

However, most of us are a mixed bag of secure and insecure connections to ourselves and others. Unfortunately, too many of us are lucky to have any version of the five pillars of connection up and running at all. Therefore, we are VERY hesitant to construct an Inner Bridge of Connection and feel locked into seeking ways to give ourselves a sense of control and protection, mostly through the outside world.

However, that is exactly what befriending the Mental Body is all about. Consciously developing and shifting from the authority to gain a felt sense of security from the world around us to sourcing a felt sense of security from our own inner guidance and support from our True Self.

Ultimately, these pillars don't belong to anyone else BUT you.

- **Inner Trust:** Can I predict *myself*? Will I stay true to my own inner compass? Will I match my actions with my inner guidance and follow the lead of my Wise One Self?

- **Self-Respect:** Can I trust myself to remain fair and just with how I hold myself accountable while doing any repair work or Self-Work? When I catch myself shredding myself with inner shame, blame, judgment, and loathing, will I hold up a stop sign and say, *No, no we don't talk to parts of ourselves that way.* Am I willing to seek the Support of the Sacred Witness within to help me understand the Parts and aspects of me in need of healing, instead of condemning?

- **Choice/Willingness:** Will I faithfully step into my Self-Work with compassionate understanding and committed action? Do I allow myself to hold the stance of "all parts welcome," letting my whole system know that I am working from a place of wholeness instead of dualism, shame, and blame? Do I give myself the ability to say yes, no, or maybe and refrain from forcing myself through manipulation, coercion, shaming, should-ing, and so on?

- **Inner Connection to My True Self and Wise One Team:** Do I have a consistent, fair, and just practice that allows me to co-regulate to my Wise One Self and Team, thus helping me access self-accountability and reflections to make supportive course corrections when I realize I am out of alignment with my True Self or inner guidance because of a past wound, trauma, belief system, or habit that is no longer serving?

- **Purpose / Values:** Am I willing to liberate my true choice and actions from the fears of humiliation and trauma adaptations to unlock my clear inner guidance and discernment? Am I willing to hear my guidance and put my trust into knowing that this guidance always includes what is for the highest good and benefit of all (including me), even if Parts of me can't see it or understand it fully? Am I willing to be led by my Soul's values, instead of the survival values within my system?

THE BENEFITS OF THE BRIDGE OF CONNECTION

The Inner Bridge of Connection helps us develop incredibly strong self-esteem. With it, we are able to open to our inherent worth, knowing that it is present with us at all times, even in the moments where Parts of us forget and we show up in a way that doesn't match who we truly are. It helps us begin to keep our word to ourselves and do repair work with self-kindness and self-love. This automatically opens us to connect to the truth that our Soul and Wise One Team are available to us at all times. With this truth embodied in our system, we are able to hold our Mental Being when it gets nervous and wants to self-abandon, thus bypassing the Bridge of Connection by exchanging Parts of us for safety and protection. We can help it soften into the sacred space of our True Self, therefore softening to the willingness to take the leap of faith necessary to open to the Sacred Witness within and hear our inner voice and guidance and ours alone.

When we can walk through our lives from the point of view of our True Self, we have amazing natural self-esteem and healthy boundary systems. We hold the belief that everyone, including ourselves, have innate abilities to heal and support themselves. We also believe in our own and other Beings' innate wisdom, worth, and power. When our Mental Being is allied with the True Self, we know that the validations we are seeking outside of ourselves already exist within us and the same is true for others. When we are in connection with the Mental Being from the point of view of our True Self, we are willing to be in a state of curiosity, exploration, have more comfort with the unknown, and seek awareness and understanding versus harsh judgements and absolutes. Our mind goes from closed, rigid, black-and-white thinking to having access to flexible, growth-oriented thinking.

THE INNER BRIDGE OF CONNECTION AND THE SACRED WITNESS

With our Inner Bridge of Connection solidly connecting us to the Sacred Witness within, we can avoid the unfortunate bypass that sounds like, "It's all good, no worries" (which we often do as a defense and shutdown method of protection) and open to what I believe Rohr is referring to in his fifth stage: opening and working with non-dual thinking and non-attachment as a point of view that we can hold within ourselves.

A really amazing thing happens when we develop and strengthen our Mental Being's belief in our own Inner Bridge of Connection. We truly shift from needing the world to be perfect for us to feel safe, into sourcing safety within ourselves via accessing our True Self. Our Mental Body releases its unachievable goal of needing complete prediction to feel safe (first pillar of the Outer Bridge of Connection) and begins to have more trust and faith in our ability to walk with life on life's terms. When we build the Bridge of Connection within ourselves, our Mental Being naturally remembers that the Heart and Soul Beings are the actual co-captains of our ship. The Mental Being can release the Lone Wolf Protector position that says, "It is my job and my job alone to protect you!"

and realize a whole support system exists within us, which it didn't remember was there when it had to adapt to survive.

The Inner Bridge of Connection gives us the ability to think and act from the point of view of Non-Attachment and Non-Dual thinking. Non-dual thinking opens us to be willing to not know, to be curious, and to open to the grace of wonder. At this point, the Sacred Witness helps us be guided and informed by what we are observing—letting it shift, change, and transform us. When our Mental Being is certain what is needed, we are most likely blocking any other insights, different possibilities, and capital-T truths from coming into our awareness.

The Inner Bridge of Connection opens us to working with and allowing the "yes-ands," the point of view through which you can allow and even welcome opposing truths to be present at the same time. Cultivating the Inner Bridge of Connection grants us access to walk with paradoxes and become comfortable with the uncomfortable. Without inviting in the stage of non-dual thinking, we remain locked in dualist absolutes, over identifying and trying to protect and justify old beliefs and systems, thereby skewing what we are observing or what is trying to work its way through to co-create a new way of being.

Once the Mental Being awakens the full Bridge of Connection, it remembers its wholeness and willingly yields and opens to the Heart Being. The Heart Being then can lead us to our Soul Being, which has the ability to center us as one whole unit, supporting our body, mind, and heart. The Soul Being has a completely different protection approach, as I mentioned earlier. It knows it is not possible to prevent pain or harm at all costs. Instead, the Soul Being has the wisdom to know that it can be open to support and guidance on how to meet the ever-changing rhythm of life. It meets life directly with LOVE and compassion and a willingness to tend the Parts of us our Mental Being believes are too dangerous to address and therefore has held in exile, trapping the past traumas within us.

CHAPTER PRACTICES

The first step to building our Inner Bridge is developing a willingness to bring awareness to what really is happening with the Mental Being before we dive into retraining the mind to be present, curious, and willing to release its attachments to the known.

To help with awareness, I love to help clients get a baseline read on their current relationship with their Mental Being and an overall feel for the current state of their Bridge of Connection. So often, people jump straight into neurofeedback, mindfulness training, meditation training, or some form of trying to "quiet" the mind and open to the heart center. Remember when I mentioned that I don't ask people to ground right away because *whole* inner systems come online with the stance that connecting with the body and/or another energy (like the earth) is not safe and should be avoided at all costs? Similarly, you may have protectors against befriending the Mental Being. For this reason, I typically don't recommend dropping straight into well-meaning mindfulness, meditation, or other mind management practices.

We have already been peppering in mindfulness and contemplation skills, or what I call Self-Work, by checking in with the Mental Being to notice the stories and Parts held within the Body Being. Therefore, we have been reestablishing basic trust and respect in the system already, hopefully leading to Mental Being's willingness to explore and connect with your True Self.

Additionally, as you walk through these practices, remember that our system doesn't do anything for giggles. It has amazing reasons for constructing itself as it has. Through awakening to and befriending the Body Being, you have already started to develop the skills of Self-Trust and Self-Respect: *Can I predict that I will show up consistently for my Self-Work in a way that is rooted in curiosity, seeking understanding, and witnessing what is happening, versus trying to strong arm or shame the system?* We want to use the same skills with the Mental Being, seeking awareness first before inviting it to change and grow into a new way of being. This allows the programming change to be guided by our inner wisdom instead of our Mental Being, which might still be running as a fierce Lone Wolf Protector outside of being connected to the wisdom of the Body, Heart, and Soul Beings.

The upcoming practices help us see the Mental Being and its purpose from a different point of view, gain basic awareness into how our Mental Being is currently working with the rest of the system, and discover what our current Inner Bridge of Connection to the Sacred Witness looks and feels like overall.

PRACTICE 1: PULSE CHECK ON YOUR RELATIONSHIP TO THE MENTAL BEING

In this practice, you have an opportunity to explore three different perspectives on your current relationship with your Mental Being: how you feel toward your Mental Being, what is your current working relationship with your Mental Being, and how your Mental Being views you. This might sound weird, but each of our four core Beings have their own systems and consciousness. In any relationship, you need to work with both points of view—you to the Mental Being and your Mental Being to you—to support willingness from the whole system rather than just one part.

Do your best to directly access the responses from each point of view, allowing the answers to come to you from either your personal perspective or the Mental Being's perspective as its own Being. You can work on developing this skill of "channeling" through a process called automatic writing. In this practice, see if you can release the filter of the narrator's mind and open to what the Mental Being is sharing. Automatic writing is pretty simple instruction-wise, but can take some practice to trust. Whether you write it, speak it out loud, or simply think it, give yourself a few moments to listen, sense, feel, hear, and know the answers that come forward versus having your constant inner narrator Parts answer.

Part One—How Do You Feel about Your Mental Being?

Write down as many of your thoughts, feelings, and stories about your Mental Being as you can right now.
>   *For example a Part of me:*
- LOVES my mind, it is smart, witty, intelligent, it has been my protector.
- Likes that I can escape into it and find refuge in my imagination.
- Loves that it has gotten me out of trouble; I can count on it.
- Believes my mind betrays me with dropping me into memories I don't like.
- Hates my mind and feels like it is a nasty inner critic more often than not.
- Disagrees with my mind, it thinks thoughts I don't agree with, but I can't seem to change or influence,
- Feels like my mind is foreign to me and something that "has a mind of its own" and doesn't follow my lead.
- Is annoyed with my mind because it always feels that it is foggy, lost, disconnected, not listening.

Part Two—How Do You Work with Your Mental Being?

Next, take a baseline reading of your CURRENT working relationship with your mind:
>   Please answer these questions from what is present:

- How much influence do you believe you have in partnering with your Mental Being?
- How much influence do you believe your mind has over your own inner will?
- How much do you believe your mind is protecting the past pains and trauma stories in to any given moment?
- How much do you believe you can notice when the mind is protecting an old story line in a current interaction?
- What level of influence do you feel you have to redirect the mind when you notice that a trauma or survival story line is guiding you versus coming from a present moment response from your core self?

Part Three—How Does Your Mind Feel toward You?

Next, we are going to switch to the point of view of the Mental Being toward you. Again, your Mental Being can run outside of your direct consciousness; therefore, engaging with it as a separate Being will help you gain awareness into why and where many of your hidden conflicts and disconnections are between how you are consciously viewing yourself and how your Mental Being and its protectors are viewing you.

- How old does the Mental Being believe you are in general?
- To what extent does the Mental Being believe you are willing to partner with it?
- To what extent is the Mental Being willing to work with the consciousness of the Body Being?
- To what extent is the Mental Being willing to work with the consciousness of your True Self?
- Is there anything the Mental Being would like to share with you?

Be aware, you might have more than one answer or point of view coming back. See if you can allow yourself to receive the different answers.

For example, it might say:

> *When you are scared, I feel like I'm the one that has to take charge because the body shuts down. Then, when you are not scared anymore, you judge me and blame me for the choices I had to make when other Parts of you froze.*

Or it might say:

> *When you ask me to follow your lead and trust you, I get nervous because I don't think you can protect yourself—you're just a little kid and you don't understand all that can happen and go wrong.*

Again, there are no right or wrong answers here. We are simply getting the lay of the land and mapping out some of the common threads and stories present behind the scenes so we can tend to them and discover what is supportive.

PRACTICE 2: EXPLORING YOUR
BRIDGE OF CONNECTION TO YOUR TRUE SELF

Now that you have an idea of how you and your Mental Being are relating, let's explore a bit more of the components of that inner connection by checking in with your Bridge of Connection—including the pillars of Inner Trust, Self-Respect, Choice/Willingness, Connection, and Purpose/Value. Remember, your Inner Bridge is dependent on your Outer Bridge. If you find one of your pillars of connection feels like it was blown apart or is entirely absent, you will want to practice the same activity again but from the point of view of the Outer Bridge of Connection. (To do that, you can pull from the descriptions of the Outer Bridge on page 390). In this exercise, we will also be looking at the nature of the Body of Water separating your Mental Being from your True Self.

Check-In: Complete your Five Senses Check-In to see what is present in the Body Being around the topic of exploring your Inner Bridge of Connection.

Body of Water: Extent of Separation: Ask your system to help you sense, feel, see, hear, or know what the current level of separation looks or feels like between your Mental Being (running as a fierce survival protector) and your True Self (the Sacred Witness energy within).

- Is it a small stream or shallow creek?
- Is it a larger river with deep banks and cliffs between your Mental Being and your True Self?
- Is there a large lake or ocean surrounding a little island of Self in the middle?

Inner Bridge of Connection: Now ask for an image(s), a felt sense, or a knowing of what the Inner Bridge of Connection is like overall.

- You might see an image of a strong and sturdy bridge with five pillars underneath holding it up.
- You might get a sense of a sturdy bridge; however, it is a draw bridge that can easily shift from connection to cutting off connection depending on who is in the guard house.
- Maybe you saw a spindly little bridge with suspension cables that seems to have no support but is trying to hold itself up.
- Maybe you see the remnants of a bridge with pillars that are tattered but standing and chunks of the top missing, making it hard to trust you can walk across with confidence.

However the images are coming forward to you, know that they are all able to be healed and reconstructed in a way that serves you now. However, we need to understand What Is before we can help ourselves heal.

Five Pillars of Connection: Next, we are going to gain insight into what each pillar of connection feels and looks like. You might make note of any memories or Parts that influence how a pillar is currently operating within your system.

- **Inner Trust:** What does your Trust Pillar look and feel like? Are you able to consistently match your action with your intentions—i.e., say what you mean and mean what you say? Write down anything you notice about this pillar's current makeup. Does this pillar struggle with particular aspects of your experience? If so, jot those down.

- **Self-Respect:** What does your Respect Pillar look and feel like? How do you feel you treat yourself when you realize that you have shown up in an unpredictable way with yourself? In what areas do you feel it is easy to remember and allow yourself positive regard for your own personal thoughts, feelings, and needs; and in what areas is it more difficult?

- **Willingness:** What does your Willingness Pillar look and feel like? Do you allow your system the choice to say yes, no, or maybe without bullying, coercing, harshly judging, or shaming it? Are you willing to be a work in progress, releasing the expectation of perfection? Are you willing to release the "survival-at-all-costs" point of view and be open to insights and choices that come from your Heart and Soul Beings?

- **Connection:** What does your Connection Pillar look and feel like? The dance of connection makes room for moments of effortless movements and creation as well as moments of misattunement, and even breaks in connection. AND the dance of connection knows that healthy compromise and repair work creates a strong bond to yourself and to others. How does your connection pillar work with this full range of relating? Does it feel exposed and need control to feel safe? If so, what does that look like for you?

- **Purpose/Values:** What does your Purpose and Values Pillar look and feel like? What might some of your different core values be? How do those values create a Code of Conduct, which seeks to help you align with those values? How willing is the Mental Being to partner with the Code of Conduct coming from your Heart and Soul Beings? What values do you find easy to match your actions with and which ones are harder?

Overall Impression: Finally, ask your system to give you any additional insights or guidance that it feels would help aid in your understanding and awareness.

When you are ready, offer your Mental Being and Bridge of Connection a blessing such as:

I offer to you, my fierce protector, my love and my gratitude. I know that you have been my constant companion my whole life and I am grateful to you and all Parts of you. I know that you have been trying to keep me safe, and sometimes that means acting in ways that other Parts of me don't like or appreciate.

As I witness the Bridge of Connection today, I know that a path is forming to bring us into wholeness, to heal. You are not alone—you have the wisdom of our Heart and Wise One Self and team to help protect us. It is time to come home, to remember you are not alone.

I ask for healing strands of Grace to tend any Parts of me willing to accept support at this time. I call in my Sacred Witness within to help support and tend any and all Parts of me seeking healing— physically, emotionally, mentally, and spiritually.

I ask for their support to hold us in their healing presence as we continue on the journey of healing and embodying the Sacred Witnesses within.

And so it is—peace, peace, peace."

Take a moment to let the healing presence of the Sacred Witness within offer your whole Body Being support. Write down any insights or awareness that come forward to support your continued Sacred Witness embodiment journey.

In conclusion, the pillars of your Bridges of Connection to the Mental Being directly impact how much access you have at any given moment to your True Self and your ability to be in the driver seat of your system. Being able to stay in your system's driver seat is one of the core skills for embodying the Sacred Witness energy.

In the next chapter, we will address one of the main concerns our Mental Being has about permitting us full access to our Inner Bridge of Connection and therefore the Sacred Witness: its comfort and permission to allow the full range of emotional experiences held within our Heart Being.

Chapter Eight

*Building Mental Being Capacity
for Our Full Range of Emotions*

Now that we have begun strengthening the Inner Bridge of Connection, we are going to support the Mental Being and its main protectors further by their building capacity and comfort with the full expression of the Heart Being and the wounded exiled Parts—so they can be seen, felt, heard, and tended. In this chapter, we will look at how the Mental Being tries to by-pass our Personal Heart Being to avoid feelings and the risk of becoming lost in the ocean of pain, emotions, loss, trauma, and past pain. In the next chapter, we'll focus more specifically on building allyship within the Mental Being for the inevitable grief that comes with change and growth.

The Mental Being often believes that the emotions we sense through our Heart Being have to be micromanaged and controlled, otherwise they will overload the system. The next step in befriending the Mental Being with the Bridge of Connection is establishing a willingness in the Mental Being to trust that you, in this present time, have more capacity to work with the sensations, emotions, and experiences held in your Heart Being than when you were younger and it had to run autonomously, as the fierce Lone Wolf Protector of your system.

You might be thinking right now, *Michelle, what is the connection between the Mental Being and our emotions? Don't emotions belong only to the Heart Being?* Well, yes and no. I see emotions like Hermes, the Greek messenger of the gods. The Heart Being uses emotions to deliver messages from our Heart and Soul Beings to the whole universe of us. The Body Being easily connects and works with the messenger of emotions. However, the Mental Being would rather bypass the ever-moving, often chaotic-feeling and unpredictable tapestry of emotions that the Heart Being uses to communicate, looking to swap out feeling tones for static logic and predictability, like we discovered in the last chapter.

Here is an Exit Ramp for any Parts of your Mental Being that still might be leery of allowing access to the messenger of emotions. Emotions themselves are neither inherently good nor bad and do not personally belonging to you or me. Instead, they are neutral and impersonal. Emotions are simply signals that our Heart Being uses to help us know what we want to move toward, create, and experience more of. They also can be used by the Body and Heart Being to alert us to an issue or need in the system that is calling for our attention and support. Emotions can also deliver messages about what we no longer want to engage with or expose ourselves to. All aspects of us use the messenger of emotions to share their thoughts, needs, wants, and desires with each other. What makes things tricky with emotions is the way our Mental Being holds, interprets, and gives different "value judgments" to what we sense and connect with through an emotion.

The good news is that you are already well on this journey of helping the Mental Being befriend the waves of emotions that come with the trapped trauma messages we encounter while witnessing. For the past seven chapters, we have been systematically sitting with, opening to, and inviting in both the emotions and stories trapped within your system so they can be seen and witnessed. Little by little, you have helped Parts of your Mental Being cultivate more and more Trust, Respect, and confidence in the Sacred Witness within to be able to hold space for its sacred messages. The practices have helped your Mental Being realize that we can work with the Heart and Body Beings' messages without being flooded and overwhelmed, lost in the emotional waters that come with the exiled Parts of you. You are cultivating a new way to befriend the Mental Being so you can stay in present time, return to center, and be grounded—while inviting yourself to listen to the wounded Parts of you, instead of arm wrestling them into submission.

In this chapter, we will continue this important cultivation, by supporting another aspect of the healing power of the Sacred Witness—the ability to be present, centered, and in a Soul-Led state—even when we are witnessing the throes and intensity of ours and others' emotional waters.

Let's first look at how our Mental Being tries valiantly to shield us from our Heart Being's full experience.

MENTAL BEING PROTECTIVE PARTS

The Mental Being's protectors mostly stand their ground on the projections of fear, doubt, and comparison. Their main job is to try to protect and disconnect us from the guidance of the Sacred Witness, which seeks to lean in and open to the wound versus shutting it down. Our Protectors are not trying to make our life difficult, but rather they truly believe they are the shields that make us safe.

Here is an example of how the Mental Being's Protective system uses storylines, thoughts, and feelings for getting us back into what it believes is safety from the Mental Being:

You have been trying to change a habit of always agreeing with what your friends say. You find yourself even folding on silly little things like what movies you like or what your day was like to match theirs. You know you are safe to share your own thoughts and that your friends do not need you to match them for them to like you. However, no matter what self-talk you do to prepare yourself to show up authentically, you find yourself backing off your own inner guidance to share your thoughts when asked. You felt the guidance of the

Sacred Witness within asking you to turn toward and explore the inner Part(s) causing you to show up differently than your Heart is intending. When you drop into your Self-Work, you feel a deep sense of emptiness or isolation in your heart center. You feel guided to call forward your metaphor of the Bridge of Connection to see what pillar of connection needs support and you get an instant hit—Choice/Willingness followed by Respect. As you start to follow your system's guidance, you are met with a wall of deep dread and fear. You feel a strong inner sense that might say something like, *If you keep trying to find that Part, you will end up totally overrun . . . or . . . This is silly you're fine, this really isn't a big deal, who cares if you share how your day was, they probably don't really want to know anyway.*

These types of statements come from Protectors that are trying to override the choice to tend to the hidden wounds in your system. A Protector shows up in our Self-Work because it is afraid that if you keep looking, you will not be able to maintain base-level functioning within the system.

We don't want to just bypass our Protector fears, because they are normally housed in a somewhat-truth. Most likely at some period in your life what their fears are based on were an overall true statement. From our example above, there probably was a time when you were overwhelmed after you allowed your system to share the fears and pain they brought to you. Most likely, their back-then reasons to pump the brakes were because you were younger and didn't have an outer support system to help you navigate and tend the full range of emotions and fears that came forward with a wounded Part of you.

A key component of befriending the Mental Being is acknowledging that these protectors have a real reason for being there. They were not created from thin air; there is a story held within them. Sometimes we need to know that story and witness it consciously for it to be tended and release its trapped pain, sensations, or emotions. Sometimes we don't need to consciously know the stories they hold.

In such cases, they are ready to simply be given permission to release and dissolve. However, it is not our Mental Being that makes that call from a protective stance. The wisdom of what needs to be witnessed and how that witnessing needs to come forward comes naturally from the Sacred Witness and the inner guidance of our full system.

We are asking the Mental Being to release control and its self-appointed role as the "healer" within our system—to pass that baton to the Sacred Witness and True Self within. Let's turn now to how we might begin to build comfort in the Mental Being with the full range of our deepest, most vulnerable emotions.

CULTIVATING COMFORT WITH EMOTIONS

It can be super difficult for the Mental Being and its protectors to trust and give permission to work with the Sacred Witness, because it brings a different kind of healing container and "protection" than the Mental Being is familiar with. Ultimately, we are asking the Mental Being and its protectors to step back and trust the wisdom of our Sacred Witness to hold a strong healing presence for the Parts of ourselves and others that are lashing out and entangled with past fears, harsh judgements, shadow beliefs, and protective mechanisms.

I love what Pema Chodron, American Tibetan Buddhist nun and teacher, shares in the very beginning of her book, *How to Meditate*:

Meditation [Self-Work] is a transformative process ... the more we practice, the more we open, and the more we develop courage in our life ... Because when we're developing this courage, in which we allow the range of our emotions to occur, we can be struck with moments of insight, insights that could never have come from trying to figure out conceptually what's wrong with us, or what's wrong with the world. These moments of insight come from the act of sitting in meditation which takes courage, and courage that grows with time."

As you practice cultivating the Sacred Witness, you develop this greater courage Chodron speaks of. This courage creates the willingness and capacity to interact with our full range of emotions. This then opens powerful insights we'd never reach by relying on the Mental Being's conceptual problem-solving and protection efforts alone. As we cultivate the ability to "sit" with all aspects of ourselves and no longer shun them, taking guidance from our Sacred Witness, we can allow the wound itself to lead us into the medicine and the healing inherently held within it.

Cultivating comfort with emotions allows us the ability to open to presence. In true presence, our fears, prejudices, judgements, beliefs, dogmas, habitual patterns, ways of bracing, and constant inner struggles fall away and become silent. From that silence, emerges a willingness to enter unbiased awareness. From this awareness grows acceptance of being with What Is. Accepting What Is allows us to stop bypassing, projecting, or trying to deny something so that we can open to understanding. Once we have understanding, then our true inner guidance, versus a protective Part's fears and beliefs, can give us insight into what is needed to help heal, shift, and grow. This understanding and presence always empower us and others with the Grace of Freedom. Freedom to break free from the weight and repetitive karmic nature of the past and the worries of the future, and to step into the Now Moment with willingness to not know and to make a new choice that matches our guidance and truth, not the well-worn protective choices.

Let's turn now to another case study, where we witness Jill shift from her Mental Being's fierce protection and Heart Being suppression ruling her inner world to an opening that took all of us by surprise and enabled her to make connections—both with herself and those around her—that her Wise One Self most longed for.

JILL TRUSTS HER SYSTEM'S
ABILITY TO RIDE EMOTIONAL WAVES

Jill is an amazing woman. She not only had a past career in the military, she was a wonderful advocate of veterans, helping them to reintegrate back into civilian life. She came to Unbridled Change because she was hitting a wall in her own trauma work. She was struggling to reconnect to her emotions without triggering a *ton* of protectors—some of which were totally committed to keeping her safe by keeping her detached from her emotions. They did this by evoking dissociation and no-will-to-live energy every time she started to feel anything—happiness, joy, excitement, hope. Anything other than neutral and on purpose was considered a threat to her Mental Being. Her Mental Being believed it was better to feel absolutely nothing than risk allowing the Heart Being to relay any felt sensations or emotions. It was afraid to let her feel the pain, suffering, and rage held in her wounded Parts. Jill had realized that this blanket of numbness allowed her to function and do her job, which she loved; however, it was not supportive to her marriage, her overall health, or her life. She wanted to change that protective mechanism.

She already had an amazing holistic team, office-based therapist, and medical team. Someone suggested she add in working with us to help bring all the work she was doing together. She joined our six-month Equine Partnered Coaching program we offer, that includes helping clients cultivate the Bridges of Connection. I started to work with her through the very same method I have shared in this book. Specifically, we were working on the first three Pillars of Connection: Trust, Respect, and Choice/Willingness. She quickly disclosed her background in a very robotic, facts-only manner. She was a survivor of childhood sexual abuse, and joined the military as way to get out and to help others. Once in the military, she survived more sexual abuse, emotional abuse, and moral injuries. Being an advocate was a huge part of her healing work. However, she would say she felt hollow inside and didn't know how to "fix" that.

Jill's Mental Being had a strong belief that she was a past, younger version of herself that didn't have the skills to work with the trapped trauma held in her Heart Being. Because of this belief, it only felt safe to allow Jill to work with her Heart and Body Beings from a very disconnected and numb place that said something like: *Yeah, stuff happened to me, but it's in the past. No use going there or crying about it because it doesn't change anything. I just have to keep pushing through.*

I could see from her energy bodies that she was one of the "ghosts" that Schedule taught me to see so early on. Her Body Being was present, standing in front of me. Her Soul was behind her. Her Heart Being was beside her, sending constant messages via her emotions that were totally being blocked. Her Mental Being was trying to keep the messages of the Body and Heart Beings offline and under control. Her emotions were pulsing at such a loud vibration energetically that it was like constant massive explosions within and around her. However, the Heart Being was totally and completely blocked from doing its job of relaying messages back and forth between all the different Beings to the Mental Being. All that Jill had access to was her Mental Being. It was front and center and in command. Nothing, and I mean nothing, else was allowed to be felt by Jill. After a few sessions, the main horse that came forward to partner with Jill was our little tri colored pony, Cocoa Puff.

Cocoa Puff wanted to help Jill find the hurt that was trapped, screaming out in pain, but was landing on the deaf ears of the Mental Being. Cocoa Puff is a survivor of abuse as well. When she first came to Unbridled Change as a young rescue at just three years old, she was so full of trapped trauma and hypervigilance that she was totally afraid to leave a small area or interact with any Being, including other horses. If you put her in a paddock or field, she would run so fast, and without any connection to Self. She would run herself into objects or run until she collapsed in exhaustion. To prevent that, I created a smaller space for her to be in that she felt more comfortable with. She would stand in the back corner of the space with her butt against the corner and her head facing the gate—ready to run, strike out, and do whatever she needed to do to keep herself safe. Slowly, I helped her rebuild her own outer Bridge of Connection to me and eventually her own inner Bridge of Connection with her True Self.

Cocoa's road to connection started with being able to predict my movements. She also could predict that I was not going to harm her or force her to do anything that she didn't understand or want to do. She could choose when to say yes to me and when to say no. She would always have her basic needs met—clean bedding, fresh water, good hay and grain and she didn't have to interact with me to gain access to those things. Little by little, Cocoa realized she had a choice, she had the right to tell me no, and I would respect that. After a while, she would follow me around while picking her stall area, and we could move her to a small paddock. She was eventually willing to partner with a beautiful older horse she felt safe with, and was eventually willing to go out in the paddock with him when I wasn't there. She worked her way back from total disconnection and began to remember who she was and that she had a voice, a Body, a Heart, and a Soul.

Cocoa tends to pick clients that are on a similar journey, offering them the healing presence that she found on her own healing journey as a guide for them. Jill, too, was drawn to Cocoa over all the other horses and wanted desperately to love on Cocoa Puff, to scratch her and groom her and just be with her. However, Cocoa wasn't allowing her to get within ten feet of her. Despite the distance, Cocoa was completely attentive to her. She would walk next to her freely, completely in sync with anywhere Jill asked her to go—but insisted on keeping a ten-foot gap.

One day, Jill felt totally defeated by the distance Cocoa kept creating. A Part of her was taking Cocoa's distance as a sign of complete disrespect and mistrust. She turned and screamed at me, "Why! Why after all this time doesn't she trust me! I haven't done anything wrong! Does she think I'm going to abuse her too! I'm not them! Why do I have to pay the price for them?"

Without waiting for a response from me, Jill threw down the brush she had been trying to get Cocoa to sniff in hopes to groom her, began to pace, and continued to yell and scream. Tears burst through the wall and began to flow.

"I haven't done anything wrong. I didn't do anything wrong. All I wanted was to love her. All I wanted ... all I want is love ..." Jill collapsed onto the ground shaking and crying.

Cocoa stood ten feet away, looking at Jill and lowered her head to match Jill's collapsed body on the ground. Jill looked up at me—every Part of this amazing, strong warrior was pleading. Pleading with the broken open heart of the wounds of her past. All she wanted was what she had wanted all along—someone to love her, a place to belong, a Being that she could love in return. I smiled back at her with tears in my own eyes and followed Cocoa's lead and squatted down next to Jill about ten feet away. I took a deep breath, let it out slowly, and then said, "Tell me more, it's okay, we are here and want to know."

Jill shook her head no, but she said weakly, "Sure, but I don't know what to say."

I followed her body's message. "It's okay, you don't have to say anything. You don't have to go into anything that you don't want to. Just know that we are here, however you need us to be here."

Her body softened. Cocoa moved a few feet closer and stopped. We sat in silence as Jill's body rocked back and forth. It would tense up, she would form fists and hit the ground repeatedly. Then she relaxed and cried. Round after round this pattern ran, Cocoa and I stayed with her.

Then Jill jumped up and started screaming, "NO!!!!" over and over. She started to back up, then lurched forward screaming, "NO!!!" Cocoa and I remained right where we were, holding space for the waves of trapped impulses, needs, and emotions that were rolling through Jill.

When Jill came to rest several minutes later, she looked at me and looked at Cocoa in utter shock and disbelief.

She said, "Why? Why did you stay? Didn't that scare you? Why didn't that scare Cocoa? I'm so sorry. I didn't mean to get too emotional. . ."

With that Cocoa answered her. Cocoa closed the gap and moved closer to Jill. Jill didn't know what to do or what to think. From her point of view, she had just uncontrollably raged, screamed, cried, threw things, and hit the ground. And yet, after weeks of distance, Cocoa chose to close the gap.

She asked, "Can I touch her?"

I reminded her that she can offer a "horsey handshake" and see what she does. We have a rule at Unbridled Change that you can't touch a horse before they touch you, to ensure consent is present in all our conversations. The handshake is simple, we offer our hand for the horse to sniff and touch as a way to access consent to connect via touch and not just our attention. Every time Jill had previously offered a "horsey handshake" to Cocoa, it had been met with a *No-thanks* snort, followed by a *What's up, I'm cool with just this level of connection with you* head nod in return. I could see the hesitance in Jill to offer this again.

I shared, "You might be surprised. Give it a try."

Jill slowly pulled her arm up and halfway stretched it out toward Cocoa, anticipating rejection once again. But that didn't happen. Cocoa reached out her nose and sniffed Jill's hand. Cocoa then moved in closer, running Jill's hand down her neck and under her mane. I stepped back and let Jill and Cocoa be together. Jill was smiling, crying off and on, and talking to Cocoa in hushed words that were meant just for them.

We closed out that session without much processing. I encouraged her to explore the experience in the journal she started with us, share it with her therapist if she wanted to, and that next session we could dive into any questions she had. Jill liked that plan. When she came back the following week, she said she wanted to see if Cocoa would say "hello" first before we checked in and processed the last session. She walked up to Cocoa and offered her hand. I could tell she was holding her breath. Cocoa reached out, said *hello* with her nose, and moved in to her for a little scratch on the side of her neck. As Jill turned to walk back over to where I was, Cocoa walked with her, this time only a small distance between the two bodies.

Pause and Reflect

I bet your Mental Being might be asking the same questions Jill's did.

If it feels good to you, bring a hand to your heart center to guide your attention into your own inner sanctum and connect with your Sacred Witness.

From this place, open to the state of willingness and curiosity. Ask for support to help guide you in reflecting on some of the questions Jill had as we processed her session.

Note: If a Part or protector starts to bleed in with fear or worry, acknowledge them and then ask them to step back into the support of your Sacred Witness where they can witness what it feels like to be held in this presence too.

Do you have any thoughts or ideas as to:

- Why it didn't scare Cocoa when Jill was hitting the ground and yelling?
- Why I didn't try to stop her process and reground her when her Heart Being came online with the large waves of emotional messages and actions?
- Why Cocoa trusted her after she had shown up differently and was unpredictable?
- Why that session changed Cocoa's willingness to allow herself to be in physical connection with Jill?
- Why that session changed Jill's Mental Being's willingness to connect physically with Cocoa?

Next, consider what made this session possible for Jill:

- What aspects of the Sacred Witness were present in Jill, myself, and Cocoa Puff?
- What Parts and Protector stories of yours popped up as you were reading and experiencing her session?

The short answer to what was happening for Jill during that session is that her Mental Being allowed her system to be Witnessed. The whole system was allowed to be seen, felt, and heard—not just the "facts" of the Mental Being. Here is what I saw her subtle energy Beings do during that session: Her Soul Being was holding her as it was being held by my field and Cocoa's. Her Body Being's messages were honored and therefore given permission to speak in their own way without having to edit themselves. Her emotions were able to lead her to connect with her Heart Being. Once she reconnected, even in that brief moment, to her Heart Being, she became present with herself as she was—the messy

Parts, the scared Parts, the confused Parts, the fearful Parts, the angry Parts—all Parts were welcome.

This healing session was possible because of the comfort Cocoa and I had created within our own systems for *big* emotional waves and our ability to allow the Sacred Witness within to guide us on how to show up to most support Jill in that moment. Technically, everything Jill did should have activated every survival and trauma adaptation in my own Body Being and in Cocoa's, given our trauma history. However, it didn't, because that history is no longer trapped in our system. Because our Mental Beings were comfortable and trusted the guidance from our Sacred Witnesses, it showed Jill's Mental Being that there was another way too.

After that session, Jill's Mental Being started to allow her to work with her inner Bridge of Connection to listen to and hear her Body, Emotional, and Heart Beings in totally different ways. It still got scared and had protective Parts jump up, ready to disconnect her. However, now it believed in Jill's own ability to manage the waves—because she had done it. When she would ask her Mental Being to step back, her Mental Being trusted her. It released its main belief that Jill had no way to open the trapped traumas in her system besides running the narrative fact-based Mental Being report (a bypass). Rather, her Mental Being had a real-time experience trusting another way.

When Cocoa said *hello* again a week later, and offered to stay close by Jill's side, that was the repeat predictability her protective Parts needed to further step into willingness to try this new way.

HEALING PRESENCE

You have heard me use the term *healing presence* many times already on our journey. The teachings, practices, and reflections for this chapter are designed to help you cultivate even more Trust within yourself and your Mental Being that you can hold center and stay connected to the healing presence of the Sacred Witness.

Take a moment to feel into the healing presence Cocoa and I held with Jill. You might sense:

- Warmth, openness, non judgment, and willingness
- A quiet felt sense of safety to say anything and be in a state of vulnerability with Parts of you that you might normally shun, shame, or judge
- A deep feeling or knowing that you are being supported
- This support may have felt soft and opening; it may have also felt like a strong solid field that you could feel "holding" you

Here are a few other qualities of that healing presence we offered, which can often be hard to articulate and even consciously know are there:

- **A willingness to walk with Truth.** When we are in a true healing presence, we innately have an inner knowing that we are going to be met with Truth. While parts of us might want to run from Truth, when we are in a healing presence, we can feel that challenge *and* unconditional support, compassion, and a deep understanding for this inherent difficulty. Because we can hold this paradox, a deep sense of kindness and love are present and available to us as we unpack any truths, as well as *all* the Parts that might struggle with what is illuminated in exposing that truth.
- **There is an innate feeling of strong boundaries.** When I feel a true healing presence within myself or in another, I also feel held by healthy boundaries with integrity and

strength. I know I'm being led from a place that will remain true and guided by my Soul's core values, rather than a container that can be swayed and pulled into the weeds by unhealed Parts of me driven by scarcity, comparison, fears, self-pity, and shadow control games. I know I'm not being held by the Parts of me that have forgotten the innate strength and presence of what is being witnessed. Yes, I feel compassion, and I also feel a deep sense that I can wiggle and push all I want, but this inner boundary of caring accountability will be there holding a loving expectation and boundary for me to step into empowered, committed action and accountability with myself in a way that matches the guidance I receive.

- **Surrender versus Submission.** Surrender and Submission are not the same thing. Submission is a state of shutdown, appeasement, and inner resistance. When I submit to something, I am doing so without connection or willingness from my Heart and Soul—it is a sheer survival action. Whereas, the state of true surrender is a combination of boundaries and the willingness to walk with truth, even the truth that Parts of me really don't want to look at or admit are true. Surrender invites me to follow the promptings of what needs to be seen, felt, heard, and witnessed so that I can move into healing—the process of reclaiming the awareness of my innate wholeness and choosing to align my thoughts, actions, and behaviors with my Soul.

- **Willingness to let go of the illusion of Safety.** An inner knowing that the Soul doesn't desire us to play only with what is safe and easy. Our Soul wants us to live fully beyond the limits of tribal safety and be with our own true wild, beautiful, and incredible life! To walk with the Soul as a healing presence, I need the Grace of Courage.

An Important Note about the Mental Being

Before we enter into our practices for cultivating this *healing presence* for ourselves, it's important to note something about this process. When we cultivate the ability to befriend our Mental Being and access our different states, emotions, and wisdom from the Heart Being, we are NOT going to erase the original survival responses and personal needs, fears, or worries from our system. The protective belief system that somehow we magically no longer have moments of survival-level thoughts, flares of emotions, and protective fears or actions is completely false dualist thinking and leads to *tons* of internal shame, guilt, and feelings that you are never going to gain the enlightenment and peace you are seeking.

Instead, we want to help the Mental Being remember, ALL the different "levels" of us are true and have their own inherent wisdom held within them. This helps us access the fifth stage of our Sacred Witness road map, which is cultivating comfort to walk with paradoxes and what can feel like two or more conflicting points of view. The healing presence of the Sacred Witness works from the point of view of holism, accepting and honoring all aspects of ourselves—the light and shadow, the faith and doubt, the fear and trust, the worry and optimism, the struggle and surrender. We have all the different shades of these within us. Ignoring any aspect, or letting a protector trick us into believing these aspects no longer influence us, is a risky move.

For example, Jill held within her a belief that she needed to stay composed and not emotional to be a safe Being. Parts of her were stuck and trapped at different ages and consciousness—little ones that could barely talk, young adult ones that wanted to break free, soldier ones that told her to stay on the mission and ignore anything else. Other Part and Protectors shunned emotions and any physical sensations, because they didn't know how to connect without opening to the pain of the abuse trapped in her body. She had thinking Parts that believed, *life happens but you can keep moving,* which while not wrong also didn't hold the capacity to simultaneously care for the hurt Parts of her while also moving forward with daily life. She was missing the ability to hold different levels of her at the same time. She had Parts that thought it was all or nothing—this is dualist thinking. Either she was past her trauma and healed or she was stuck disconnected, and, in her words, "damaged." In the beginning, she felt so defeated if she had a wounded need pop up within her. She worried it was a sign that she wasn't "doing this healing thing right" or that a piece of work she did wasn't holding. She would beat herself up and judge herself if she had a moment of sadness or mistrust within her.

What was happening to Jill was a very unfortunate, massive Mental Being bypass, which creates an immense amount of suffering and anguish for so many of my clients. When we can acknowledge that different states are held within us all the time, we can accept that even in a moment of responding from a different state of our system, we can always consciously choose *who* and *how* we want to embody and walk with ourselves. When we shift our Mental Being into functioning from a level of holism held within empowered consciousness and stop shaming ourselves for our inner struggles and impulses, we can hold sacred space for *all* the parts of us and help them remember their wholeness too. When we can make this fundamental shift, the Mental Being goes from the Lone Wolf to an amazing Guardian in the light that honors our struggles and invites us to remember something else is there too.

CHAPTER PRACTICES

Remember, one of the Mental Being's main jobs is to get us out of discomfort by any means necessary. Being a healing presence means that we are going to be asked to sit with, lean into, and open to Parts of ourselves that are potentially submerged in toxic guilt, shame, rage, fear, and other big emotions. It is through a healing presence that they can finally be seen, felt, and heard so the trapped trauma begins to unwind and unburden, and fractured parts can be reclaimed and healed. This means that we are going to have to be with Parts of ourselves and others that aren't all gumdrops and roses. IF we are going to get the Mental Being on board with allowing the Heart to share its deepest pains, humiliations, and wounds, we need to cultivate a willingness to sit with the uncomfortable, and even at times downright scary, Parts of ourselves with courage, strength, and love.

I want to share two practices to help you create a healing container, what I call *Healing Rooms*, and a process for how to work with parts of you, via *Healing Interviews*. These are the main tools you can use to help your Mental Being open to your full emotional range and better align to working with the Sacred Witness within.

PRACTICE 1: CREATING YOUR HEALING ROOMS

You might be thinking, *Okay Michelle, this all sounds amazing. But Jill had you, she had Cocoa. She didn't have to maintain the center. She was able to let you and Cocoa hold that space and presence for her. She didn't get lost because she had you two helping to co-regulate her. How am I supposed to do that for myself and also let the wounded parts of me share their messages and unwind?*

That is a great question.

First, please know that every time you pick up this book or work with any of the practices, you have my own Sacred Witness *and* your own Sacred Witness and Wise One Team to help co-regulate and hold you too. They are with you, right now as you read. You are also consciously cultivating the ability to hold a healing presence to help the Mental Being develop trust in you too! And, please remember, healing occurs in connection—both connection internally and externally. It is okay to seek outside support just like Jill did, to create an outer team as well.

Next, it is helpful to construct a "space" for the different Parts of you to be held in. I call it the *Healing Rooms* or *your Sacred Space*. The Healing Room is a metaphoric place within your Mental Being that can invite the different Parts of your Mental Being to rest in, step back, and allow your Parts to access the essence of a Healing Presence. While these feel like only mental constructs, they are also very real energic structures and spaces that bring forward the healing energies of the Sacred Witness to provide the presence of love, compassion, honoring, courage, curiosity, healing, *as well as* boundaries, protection, and deep respect for the whole system.

The Healing Rooms are a safe space that allow Parts of you to share their stories, ask for help, and get their fears, worries, and concerns tended. The space helps the system realize that there is now a container that can hold the waves of emotions in a way that allows other aspects of us to witness from a distance surrounded by a field of grace that holds everyone involved. Just like Jill was held by her own field, my field and physical presence, Cocoa's field and physical presence. In actuality, the holding field was even greater—the Beings of the Earth, the Herd, the Trees, the Creek, the Stones, the WHOLE of Unbridled Change and all its parts were there to hold her.

I use this technique to help support your Mental Being in realizing that it isn't being overridden or shunned when we ask Parts to step back and give us permission to witness a wounded Part of us or connect with a sensation held in or around our body. The technique of the Healing Rooms gives the system the structure it needs to witness the different conflicting Parts, stories, and levels of consciousness held within, without Parts bullying each other because they view them as a possible threat. As you cultivate the ability to witness the dualistic perspectives held within your own system, you will also begin to see the different "levels" of consciousness held within your system too—survival, personal, and soul or cosmic levels.

During this practice, you will set up your initial Healing Rooms; and you can always continue to evolve these spaces as you feel guided. We want to use these tools to help us titrate into these waters a little at a time, beginning to gain understanding and awareness of what the Protectors' fears are first so that the Mental Being realizes that there is always an incredibly strong lifeline of support present with us. Because the truth is our Soul and Wise One Team don't leave us, it is our Mental Being and its protectors that cut off the connection to those amazing parts of ourselves via an ocean of past pains, traumas, and fears.

To create your Healing Room, we want to create a space that contains the resources needed to provide a strong and capable holding field. Some Beings we want to consider calling in include:

- The Elements: Fire, Water, Earth, Air, Light, Sound, Color
- Wise One Team members: these can be the avatar of the Sacred Witness you created at the beginning of this journey, avatars of your Wise One Self and team, angels, animal or nature guides, past loved ones
- Comfort items: a place to rest, witness, and be soothed

This is your sacred healing space that can hold, contain, and be a refuge within your own system. As you develop a comfort working with your Parts in the Healing Rooms, the Mental Being will begin to establish deeper inner trust in this structure to provide the safety and co-regulation it has been seeking, granting more willingness to allow you access to the Heart Being to help bring forward the wounded Parts that need support.

When you are ready, let's begin:

Check-In: Take a moment and run through your Check-In.

Creating Your Healing Room: Call forward your Sacred Witness within to help you create a Healing Space or Room for the different Parts of you to come, soften, and open so that they can access the Sacred Witness.

Sense, feel, see, hear, and know that the Healing Room is being created within a crystalline orb waiting for you. This orb contains the healing presence of your Sacred Witness, Wise One Team, and any other appropriate healing Beings. Within this orb is a sacred space that can meet the needs of any Part of you that needs help and support.

Creating Your Entrance: Next, imagine the gateway or doorway to enter this space. This gateway is special and only allows you and your Wise One Self and Team to access it. When you call on it, your Wise One Team can help escort Parts of you or trapped energies within your system to enter the Healing Room so you can safely connect with and support them.

Placing Your Orb: Now, we need to establish where you would like this orb to be kept—within or around your Body Being or Field? For example, you might find that you want it to sit about three feet out from you and slightly to your left side. You might want it to be further out and to the right. Or maybe you feel guided to hold it in your mind's eye or heart space. There is no right or wrong, only that which serves you in this Now Moment.

Now that you have the room created, see if you can imagine walking into the space.

Calling Forward the Healing Elements: Call forward the healing elements you would like to have present in this space. Perhaps a sacred fire or water element. A soft place to sit and reflect. Or an intention that whatever you or a Part of you needs to help support it will be available when it is needed, trusting in the wisdom of your system to shift, morph, and adapt to customize the healing room as needed.

Practice Inviting in the Parts of You That Need Support: Now that you have created a Healing Room, let's try it out. Sometimes it helps to say out loud to your full system something like,

> *I call forward my Wise One Team and guides to support me today. To all the Parts of me that are nervous, worried, or have fears that I will become overwhelmed, lost, or disappointed by what I might find during my meditation or Self-Work check-in, I ask those Parts and Protectors to move with my Wise One Team into a Healing Room so that we can hear the guidance and wisdom of my Heart and you can have a safe place to witness what is happening as well. I know you are trying to protect me from harm. I need you to trust me and honor me as I trust and honor you. I am willing to be open to guidance and support. Thank you.*

PRACTICE 2: HEALING INTERVIEWS: UNDERSTANDING YOUR PROTECTORS AROUND EMOTIONS[1]

This practice is designed to provide you with an overall template for working with Protectors and Parts.

When you are doing this on your own, I highly suggest starting with topics and/or emotions that you have a *low* charge around. Don't go for the biggest struggle or emotion that you would normally deem off-limits. Remember, these dialogues and healing sessions are about building trust, respect, and willingness within our system, not taking on the toughest topic right off the bat.

For the purposes of teaching how to invite a Protector to share its fears, worries, or concerns with the Heart Being, I have selected one of the main emotions we all tend to have protective Parts and programs around: Anger. When you are doing this practice on your own, you can invite your system to bring forward any topic, sensation, or Part that you would like to gain more connection and dialogue with.

As we explore an example of a Healing Interview using Anger as our focus, please let your system know you can stop the process below at any point if it feels like too much. Let your system know that you can work with this process as many times as needed to gain more permission to explore the different layers and aspects of this topic and its related feelings, sensations and emotions. For example, on the first pass through, it might only want to share from a global or general conceptual perspective on anger, then move into a more personal level, and finally from a survival level. Trust your system to guide you in the who, what, where, and when, versus the Mental Being having to figure out the best path.

Healing Interview with Anger

Check-In: Start with your Check-In and Body Scan.

Call Forward Your Healing Room: Invite your Wise One Team to bring forward your beautiful Healing Room to help support you and your system. Let your system know that you are wanting to connect with one of your Protectors related to the emotion of anger. You are seeking to better understand and maybe even tend to some of its fears or worries.

If your system gives you permission, ask one Protector for Anger to meet you in the Healing Room so that you can gain a better understanding of what its job is and how it believes it is helping to protect you.

Healing Interview: When you feel ready, walk through the following check in with the emotion anger:

Up first, ask the Protector what level of comfort they have with anger, on a scale of one through ten—ten being that it is totally freaking out and dysregulated with any anger in or around you, one being it is pretty okay to witness inside or outside anger, in general.

Now invite it to share more insights into any of the following:

- What judgments or belief systems are present with just the word *anger*? Be real here—the good, the bad, and the ugly. For example, were you taught that anger is a sign of weakness or something you will get into trouble for if you express it?
- What is its comfort level with your own personal anger?
- What is its comfort level with witnessing anger in someone else?
- What is its comfort level with feeling like anger is being directed at you?
- What hidden or known boundaries do you have within your system around the emotion of anger?
- What are the benefits of anger?
- How can you hold the presence of anger differently within your system?

Locating Any Parts That Would Like Healing Support: Are there any wounded Parts or Protectors that are ready to shift how they historically respond to anger? Ask it/them to come forward at this time.

- Where can you feel this Part, in or around your body?
- Sense into what it feels, looks, and sounds like.
- Ask it to share with you what it feels, thinks, and believes would happen with anger.
- What is its fear about anger?

- What is its main belief system about allowing anger to present?
- What else might it want you to know about anger?

Healing Support: Is it willing to release some or all of its limiting beliefs and attachments to the emotion of anger? If so, what does it need to help it release?

- Ask if it would like the support of an element (water, air, earth, fire), energy (Yin or Yang, for example), guide or color to help cleanse, clear, and release the limiting thoughts, pains, fears, and trapped emotions from the system.
- How would the system release the burden of these limited beliefs or trapped emotions and traumas from your whole body being?

Take a few moments to work with how the Part would like this support.

Repatterning: Now that you have made room in the system, what would your system like to reclaim and rewire so that it can witness and work with anger in a healthier way? What adjustments are needed? What new boundaries and ways of being would you like to upgrade within your protective parts so that they are now guardians in the light for you?

Ending the Practice: Thank your system for its willingness and thank the Parts that stepped aside for you to work with this emotion—anger—in whatever fashion you were able to interact with it today.

Make note of any follow-up parts or wounded parts that might still want your attention and tending—either with this emotion or another—now that this healing practice has taken place. Set a time in which your system can trust you to continue to work and explore those items.

When you are ready, take three beautiful cleansing breaths. Ask Air to help cleanse and clear your system. On the inhale, gather up all thoughts, feelings, emotions, habits, and postures that are no longer serving and release them on the exhale. On the next inhale, call forward healing strands of grace to help soothe and balance the system.

Wiggle your fingers and toes, gently stretch, and call yourself fully back to the present moment and time. Honor yourself for your willingness to explore often uncomfortable and avoided emotions and thoughts.

And so it is. Peace, peace, peace.

Continue to work with this practice, at your own pace, with many different topics. Use it as a format for Self-Work to explore an emotion or topic your system normally tries to avoid, distract you from, or has skewed projections around. Ask your system to share insights around the fears, worries, and stories behind its normal response. Ask your system to see if there is a wounded part behind these protective stances that needs tending. As you continue to work with this type of practice, your system can release its avoidance and step into a willingness to be with different emotions or topics with greater and greater access to your core self—a true healing presence.

In the next chapter, we are going deeper into allying the Mental Being with our Heart Being through the Bridge of Connection by exploring the grief and loss that inevitably comes with being human. We'll discover how to navigate this grief and loss in a way that supports cultivating the Sacred Witness within and greater harmonious functioning within our entire being.

Chapter Nine

*Helping the Mental Being Cope
with Change and Loss*

As we explored in the last chapter, the Mental Being struggles to allow the full range of our emotional expression. It often seeks safety by trying to bypass the emotions held in the Heart Being all together. Additionally, by its default nature, the Mental Being also struggles profoundly with change and its inevitable companion—the emotion of grief. In this chapter, we are going to work with the Mental Being's ability to navigate change by increasing its capacity for tending and befriending grief.

You might be thinking that grief belongs to the Heart Being; however, Grief Work is key to helping the Mental Being and its protectors build out our Bridge of Connection to our True Self and the Sacred Witness within. Without allowing the Sacred Witness within to help our Mental Being hold and work with grief, it will be hard for the Mental Being to allow us to befriend the next aspect of us—our Personal Heart Being—as a means of self-protection.

Please stay with me during this chapter and resist the urge to skip it. Developing a willingness to welcome and walk with grief is a key part of the Sacred Witness. Without it, our Mental Being can hobble the Sacred Witnesses' ability to support us fully in our healing and growth.

I know that the subjects of grief and loss are hard ones. Many of us are not taught how to walk with grief as a healing partner and companion. The subject is almost taboo. People often run from it or try to dress it up in pretty, neat little packages. This subject is definitely not gumdrops and roses. However, the practices I share in this chapter will provide you with the real deal, boots-on-the-ground practices for working the very real, messy parts of transformational change—namely that something has to die to bring in something new.

Over the years of supporting clients on their healing journeys, I have come into awe of the truth that our Body, Heart, and Soul Beings actually carry their own healing wisdoms when it comes to meeting grief and loss. It is the Mental Being that struggles and blocks the inherent wisdom and acceptance held within these other aspects of us.

Transformational Change and Grief

We are in a transformational age. The systems we created that have seemingly served us all so well are no longer serving. There have been and will continue to be massive changes in our personal and collective lives. Many of us are not only feeling the discomfort in these shifts, we are grieving. Parts of us are clinging desperately to the known, comfortable rhythms of earlier times in our lives. Other Parts of us might feel trapped in our old creations like a tomb—wanting to change a habit, a relationship, a job, but paralyzed with fear over what else we'll lose before it is all said and done. Parts of us that worry that the changes we're facing won't yield the future we want, or may make things worse.

I'm not just talking about big picture domains, such as governments, education, food and energy sources, climate and resources, and/or global economies. I'm talking about how these transformational energies are playing out on the personal level too.

What does transformation, change, death, and rebirth feel and look like?

- It looks like a person who has spent a better part of their adult life building their mastery in a body of work, who is now being asked to change, to walk away from their current work, and to reinvent and allow themselves to go in what feels like a totally different direction. This may lead to the loss of identity, fear of being able to provide for themselves and their commitments, fear of failure after success, and so on.

- It looks like the couple that has grown and built a family together, starting to feel the rumblings of growth and separation churning in their guts. They can feel their values shifting, crashing together, and separating like tectonic plates in the earth. They desire to hold their relationship together at all costs because they do love and value each other. However, they know deep inside that they are pulling apart from each other and that eventually, it will create a void that can no longer be overcome.

- It looks like a young adult realizing that their life experiences have put them in a box in which they don't belong. Their heart is calling them to break free and make their own future versus following the well-laid path of generational trauma beliefs, which are strangling them and cutting off the whispers of their soul and potential. They experience a war between their innermost desire to change and the weight of past belief systems and learned helplessness.

- It looks like the parent struggling to connect to a child that is growing up and coming into their own voice. They find their growing child pushing back on the pathways laid out for them to follow and realize that they have blurred the line between seeing their child's life as a reflection on them and allowing the child's life to belong to the child instead.

- It is in the look a young mom sees flash over her doctor's face when they share the news that she has an illness that puts the odds against her, or will impact her and those around her in a significant way. The dread that washes through her mixing with a sense of calm, a sense of determination, and also a desire to run away and hide instead of meeting this new world head-on.

- It is when a person realizes the business and life that they so carefully and thoughtfully built is being torn down by outside forces beyond their influence. They hear the whispers of their Soul telling them that they must pick up their bed and walk, even if not everyone will walk with them.

If you can relate to one or more of these scenarios, you are not alone. If it is bringing up feelings, stories, protectors, and other sensations, know that is normal, and you're in the right place. The first practice at the end of this chapter will help you work with scenarios like this. The Sacred Witness invites us to notice that these opportunities for great change are calling us to embody our lives, empower ourselves with choice, and be willing to meet each moment with a full Bridge of Connection.

But before we go to our Sacred Witnesses' gifts in the face of change, let's explore why change is so very hard for our Mental Beings.

Why Change is Hard on the Mental Being

From the Sacred Witness's perspective, accepting and welcoming grief means you are welcoming alignment with the Soul's desired changes, evolution, and transformation. The cycles of death and rebirth, old ways dying and new ways being birthed, are always present as we move forward into an unknown "new" way of being that becomes available during an act of witnessing ourselves or another.

The Mental Being says a resounding NO to all of it—the grief, loss, death, rebirth, unknown, and evolutionary change.

Why? Because the Mental Being can't predict what will come with any of this. It doesn't really know what is on the other side of the canyon after we leap. The Mental Being loves the comfort of knowing how to show up, how to act, and what the rhythms of daily life are now and will be in the next moment. It really doesn't even care if those rhythms don't match your true nature. Our mind would rather cling to the devil it knows then the devil it doesn't. It would rather hold tightly to a connection it understands, even if that is a past wound and protective program, than risk constructing a new way to meet life. Change means loss. Loss means pain. Pain can equal suffering. But we do have some ability to influence the degree to which we suffer.

Grief Work is courageous, messy, illogical, and unreasonable. Our mind naturally wants to run away from it, and cram it into a short and sweet condensed sentence of condolence. Our mind feels the stigmas and fears of people around us too. People often try to hold up pro-verbial crosses and Xs at anyone they witness walking with grief, in a futile desire to ward off the reach of death and its impact on their lives. It is very natural for our Mental Being to be uncomfortable with holding space for loss, grief, pain, and sorrow. People fear grief and view it as an endless pit of pain and suffering.

THE TRAP OF BY-PASSING GRIEF WORK WITH NON-ATTACHMENT

One of the Mental Being's favorite ways to avoid true Grief Work is to convince us we are connected to an esoteric version of non-attachment. Again, spiritual teachings often sound beautiful and great on paper. However, they can look and feel totally different when we are first asked to embody, live with, and welcome them into our everyday lives.

I believe that the great mystical teachings are all meant to support us in reconnecting to our everyday lives with tremendous love and honor for them. I do not believe that most spiritual teachings are asking us to step out of our lives into a life without connections and attachments.

Here are some of the common spiritual statements our Mental Being loves to use to dress up our feelings about grief and trick us into spiritual by-passing, insisting we are okay with Grief Work and have no problems with the cycles of death and rebirth:

- *there is a season for everything*
- *the world keeps turning*
- *to love is to lose*
- *everything is connected so there is no true loss*

And so on.

Here is what it might sound like when we brace against and skip the grief process:

- *it's time to release and move on*
- *there are greener pastures*
- *I decide when it is time to leave or let go*
- *I'm the master of my reality*
- *I will just freeze a room in time, not change one thing and that will prevent the wheel from turning*
- all the ways in which we DO freeze our responses based on the wills and beliefs of the past—(Such as, *This is the way we have always done it, so this is the way it will always be,* or, *This was their wish so I'm bound by it,* or even forbidding people to mention a loss as a way to avoid processing the loss.)

So how do we navigate healing and transformation consciously, without slipping into the Mental Being's traps, which desperately attempt protection by disconnecting us from our personal Heart and hopping straight into the shadow version of non-attachment via Spiritual By-passing? How do we stay present when it feels like the universe is trampling over our carefully constructed lives? How do we break free of the different habits and protective ways of being that we have created but no longer serve so that our innermost heart's passions and joy can come forward?

I could stay esoteric here and talk about the law of non-attachment, with fancy words and teachings. Honestly for me, true non-attachment isn't about stepping out of being attached to our lives, like so many people believe it means. As a person who has walked hand in hand with death multiple times, who walks with one foot in the spiritual plane and one in the physical, the esoteric versions of Grief Work and the boots-on-the-ground daily practices of Grief Work are not synonymous. It took me a few dances with loss and death to finally be willing to work with grief as a companion, releasing my attachments to what a spiritual practice is and is not.

Here is a massive insight I finally came to understand in my healing dance with cancer. Staying in the ethers with spiritual teachings by-passes the gritty parts of being in physical form. Spiritual by-passing can gloss over life's messy parts, painful parts, amazing yet mundane "ordinary" parts, and disconnect us from the everyday breathing in and out with our lives. When I realized I was using my spiritual practices to protect myself from physical, emotional, and mental pain instead of actually *being with* them and tending them deeply, I had to go back and totally dismantle the myths and hidden agendas I used to build a spiritual practice in the first place. I realized that in a desire to escape the pain I felt in my Personal Heart Being, I allowed my Mental Being to adopt the spiritual by-passing myth of, *I am spirit and my earthly body is nothing more than an illusion. My life and its choices are simply an experience I am creating just to have an experience.*

I had a very pretty barrier in my Mental Being cutting off connection and communication with my Body Being, Heart Being, and Soul Being. My Mental Being, in its tremendous cleverness, found a way to protect me by using spiritual non-attachment teachings to keep me from their true embodiment! I created this barrier from living and being connected to my life because Parts of me thought that actually being connected would render me deeply vulnerable and open to even more loss and painful moments. This by-pass of denying my human-ness and the physical world as a valid world was dualist thinking and kept me from growing, expanding, and truly connecting to the sup-port and wisdom of my Soul.

However, the alternative to the by-passing version of non-at-tachment was truly feeling life. Ugh, that didn't seem like a very fun idea. However, it is what true non-attachment is about—being able to release my bracing and avoidant beliefs so I can be with what is and meet that moment in its entirety.

Remember, the Sacred Witness can open us to the state of being which is true non-attachment. I can have Parts of me that are sad, upset, grieving the loss of some part of my life or connection that I wish was still present *and* I can find joy in the little moments, allow myself to laugh in a present connection, and feel deep love for that which is leaving. With the help of the Sacred Witness, we can walk with paradoxes held in our Heart Being and the different perspectives of the Body Being and Soul Being.

True non-attachment allows us to shift from being stuck in con-stant defensive and reactive positions to opening to the pause, calling forward the Sacred Witness within, and seeing what choices serve the *whole* of us best now. When we are in true non-attachment, we are willing to release the rigid dual thinking or polarizations that can happen in our Mental Being and allow ourselves to step into the point of view of the Sacred Witness, seeing beyond our trauma and survival responses and beliefs.

Examples of Dualistic and Non-Dual/ Non-Attachment Thinking

Dualistic point of view:
- "I must have this to survive."
- "I can only calm down when _____ is present."

Non-attachment points of view:
- "I like _____ in my life and it makes things easier. However, I would figure it out if I didn't have this."
- "I prefer to be surrounded by people that share my point of view, however it isn't necessary for me to have an internal sense of belonging to my own ideas. Therefore, they can have their opinions and I am still able to remain safe in my own beliefs."
- "This morning, I held this core belief. However, this afternoon I discovered a new piece of information. Do I desperately cling to my old belief system and try to undermine or resist what is present in my awareness now? OR, can I shift my belief systems and also be willing to let it shift again if a new perspective comes in?"

When we can become comfortable with the uncomfortableness of not knowing what is going to come next, we can also release the need to know "why." *Why is this happening? Why is something I love being removed from my life?* These questions will never have an answer that feels good to all Parts of us and that's okay because not all of us has to agree with the changes. However, if we can accept these Parts as they are and open to what is present within, then we can open to the next question of, *What else is also here?* too.

This truer version of non-attachment became my lifeline through the muck, pain, and grief of my cancer journey. Life became a "yes and." *Yes, we are spirit and live on beyond this form so therefore there is no true loss. AND yes, we are also humans and life here on Earth is constantly changing and finite. We have human Parts of us that grieve and feel pain;*

things do transition from one form to another and we are allowed to deeply be touched and saddened by this. To walk hand in hand with our mind, body, and soul takes an immense amount of prayer, courage, contemplation, and true non-attachment work.

Our Mental Being is trying so hard to hold onto and block us from feeling the brunt of the pain we experience in grief and loss. It really doesn't want us to be with or interact with the world as it is. Developing a Grief Practice helps us be with What Is and be willing to allow the process of death and rebirth to guide us in what to create from the ashes. A Grief Practice steps us into connection with our beautiful, crazy, insane, joyful, and sometimes painful life, full of twists and turns, working edges, and expansion beyond what our Mental Being can imagine.

My own Mental Being Struggle with Grief

I'd like to share with you an example of how easily we start to lose our Bridge of Connection to our Heart and Soul Being's nudges when the Mental Being is trying to protect us from grief. This story highlights my own avoidance and by-passing true connection in a tender encounter with one of my longest Soul companions, Diesel.

Over the past twenty-three years, Diesel has been a teacher, guide, friend, rock, and Sacred Witness for me and countless other Beings through Unbridled Change. He is another amazing horse Being that I was lucky enough to bring into my life when he was just two and I was twenty-four years old. Diesel and I crossed paths just after Baron had launched me on my journey of remembering my True Self. Now, twenty-two years later, he is getting older and nearing the end of his physical life. My Soul Being knows the truth, that he will always be present with me, just in another form. And it will still be an immense loss when that moment comes. There are Parts of me that do not even know how to be in this world without him because they found their way back from exile through my connection with him.

After a scare with his health, without my conscious choice, I started to shorten my time around him. I was still caring for him, grooming him, and everything that I needed to do to care for him. However, I wasn't lingering. I wasn't sitting with him during my morning or evening meditations like I normally did. I found myself coming up with excuses and distractions instead of spending quality time with him like I used to. I would give him a pat after feeding time and return to the house.

One morning, my Wise One Self was able to break through my Mental Being barrier and into my consciousness. It pulled at me to stop while I was walking back down the hill from our barn to our house. I heard a Part of me say, *Go back and meditate with Diesel.* Even though it was summer time, I felt a cold sweat rip through my body. Almost every Part of me was screaming at me to keep walking. A part of me thought, *Diesel is fine, he is hanging by his fan, it's hot, just keep walking and you can meditate with him tomorrow.*

Another part of me said, *What if there isn't a tomorrow? You heard your Soul. Are you willing to listen? It's okay . . . it will be okay. I know it hurts. Which would you rather do? Stay separate from him for the rest of his life and lose those moments or love him?* This second voice was the voice of my Sacred Witness within. Thankfully, I know that voice so well that I knew it was trying to help reconnect my Inner Bridge back to my Heart and Soul, showing me that I had lost willingness and, therefore, connection to my true Heart's values and choices.

However, despite knowing the truth of the Sacred Witness within, I couldn't get myself to turn around and walk back up the hill. I didn't want to ignore it either, so I sat down in the pasture and began to sob. Deep waves of grief rolled through me. *What would my life be like without him? I was lost and struggling to find purpose before he came into my life. He helped reground me and tether me to my life. I* felt a wave of compassion and love move through me, holding me and inviting me to lean into that fear, that pain, that sorrow. All of a sudden, I saw and felt Schedule A again standing next to me. He leaned down and nuzzled my cheek. I could feel the warmth of his essence once again holding me.

I asked him for help, to guide me as he once did. I told him I didn't want the pain of losing such a close Heart companion again. Then I saw a flash of that afternoon, the summer before my senior year of high school, when I came to the barn for one of my riding lessons. Even though Schedule had been retired at that point and I was no longer riding him, I always went straight to his stall or paddock to greet him first before I went to work with another horse. That day, my instructor met me at my car. She was looking down and said that the owner of the barn wanted to see me in her house.

I knew instantly that Schedule was gone. I refused to move. Instead, I looked around. I saw the other riders and employees going about their business. There was a riding lesson happening in the ring. Horses were grazing in the paddocks. Everybody was moving in their normal rhythms. I screamed, "Why are you all moving? Don't you know that Schedule is dead!" I never made it into the house to see the owner of the barn or let her share the news. I collapsed down in the parking lot and sobbed and sobbed.

As I sat there in my pasture, I watched the memory of that past summer day come forward. I watched the young seventeen-year-old girl feeling that she had no one to comfort her. No one understood how she knew that Schedule was gone without being told. She felt totally and completely alone once again in a world that she didn't want to be in without Schedule.

The Sacred Witness within asked me at that moment to hold her. She was a wounded fractured Part of me that was still so lost, scared, and overwhelmed. The only way she had found to connect to her True Self was no longer in physical form. She was angry and mad that no one seemed to care. She felt betrayed by Schedule that he would leave her so suddenly. She was angry that no one understood that he was not just a *horse*, he was her friend, mentor, and protector. To her, the only Being she trusted, felt respected her, and didn't see her as damaged was *gone*. She had just lost the only Being with whom she was willing to let down her protectors and expose her True Self. Losing Schedule was losing the one and only lifeline she had in the storm she perceived life to be.

I realized in that moment of witnessing the younger version of me that Parts of me were totally terrified that I would lose myself again like I did after Schedule died. It took me years to find some type of tether again after Schedule's transition. I had a whole host of Protectors that remembered how lost I became. My system was afraid that would happen again. However, this time the price I would pay if I lost connection, my tether, again felt too great to Parts of me. They thought I might walk away from my life with my girls, my partner in life, my business, my friends, and family. From their point of view, I had reconnected to my life and created a willingness to embody my life at this point to such a greater degree than I was willing to connect at age seventeen. My Mental Being was sure I was going to be swallowed up into the same hole that this fractured Part of me was lost in once Diesel died. So, to protect me, it was distancing me already and starting to sever the connection between Diesel and me. I had Protective Parts that were giving me other focuses, things to do, and letting my willingness to be in connection with Diesel go.

As I witnessed all these different parts, I reached out to the younger me in my heart and sat next to her in the gravel parking lot. I whispered to her, *I know. I know what pain you are feeling right now. I know that you feel like you are going to be lost, and you will be for a bit, but I'll be with you. Schedule will be with you. You are not alone.* As she was crying, I asked her to tell me everything. I wanted her to share her fears, anger, worries, and pain. She leaned into me and I held her.

Together we cried. Together we welcomed the waves of grief and emotions that were crashing through us.

When she finally looked up, I felt Schedule come forward to her. She was hesitant to reach out to him. He asked for her forgiveness. He knew Parts of her were not ready for him to leave. He understood it ripped through her like a knife, cutting her off from herself. He was sorry he couldn't have stayed with her longer. He was here now and would never leave her alone again if she wanted to stay with him. My heart witnessed her standing up and walking to him. However, she paused and looked back at me. She asked me, *What about you? What will you do with Diesel?*

I didn't know. I didn't know what I would do when Diesel passed. I had helped so many amazing Horse Beings transition over the years, but *this one*. I didn't know. I realized in that moment that because Parts of me felt lost and trapped in a reactive Being that didn't respect herself or her life at all after Schedule A died, that other Parts didn't trust me now. Therefore, they didn't believe I would have respect for myself or my life now, so they were trying to shield me from that pain again. I let those Parts of me know that while it would be incredibly hard and I couldn't predict when it would happen or how I was going to react, I knew that I would be held and that I wasn't alone anymore like I felt back then.

I felt the prompting to turn around again and walk back to Diesel. This time I was finally able to turn my body and look up the hill toward the barn. I saw Diesel walking down the hill. He was closing the gap in real time, coming to me. When he reached me, he gently placed his massive head up and over my shoulder drawing me close to him, just as Schedule A did the first time I re-met him after the coma. In that moment, I felt Diesel, Schedule A, and my seventeen-year-old Self holding me. We all breathed together. We all witnessed each other. My Mental Being softened and my Heart was able to open once again. I thanked the Sacred Witness within and Schedule A for helping me find this wounded Part of me and the fears my system had about what might happen when Diesel passes. As I pulled back from Diesel, I watched my younger self and Schedule A walk away together into my Heart. I turned back to Diesel and asked for his forgiveness. I felt him reply, *No forgiveness is needed, I love you. This is hard and will be hard. I am here and want you here too.*

The Sacred Witness supported me in becoming aware that my Mental Being was scared and trying to protect me behind the scenes from the shadows. From that unconscious fear, I had inadvertently avoided stepping into true connection with someone I deeply love. The promptings of the Sacred Witness invited me to stop avoiding and courageously lean into a willingness to connect with my inner guidance, thus allowing me to discover and ultimately heal what was driving the avoidance.

How the Sacred Witness Walks with Grief

During the act of Sacred Witnessing, we allow all the levels and Parts of us to be honored, valued, and heard. We witness their stories, their fears, and the ways in which they feel lost in the sea of separation or stuck in their survival and trauma adaptations and programs. Every healing that is born through an act of Sacred Witnessing includes a willingness to connect to and engage with grief, just like I did with finding the younger exiled Part of me. Without knowing it, the protective Parts of me had disconnected me from my own Inner Bridge of Connection. However, once the Sacred Witness was able to break through the separation and invite me to stop and go back up the hill, I finally saw what was happening and my Body Being helped start the conversation—the cold sweat in my body and the screaming from Parts of me to urging me to run, run back to the house and not lean in. From there, I followed the Inner Bridge to help me co-regulate back to my True Self. I let myself see behind the curtain of my Mental Being and its protective stories to understand the drivers of my actions and thoughts.

Once I had awareness and understanding of what I was doing and what was driving my actions of disconnection, I was able to tend to the stuck and wounded Parts of me. From that awareness, I regained my power of Choice. It didn't have to start out perfect, just a willingness to pause and not run away from the message of the Sacred Witness. From the pause, I was able to step into a reflective Self-Work practice and illuminate where I was losing my power to past pains, limiting beliefs, habits, fears, and coping skills that were no longer serving me. From this place of true connection, I was finally able to turn my physical body around and match my actions to the guidance that came from my Heart and Soul Beings, opening to Diesel, thereby healing the rupture that was forming within and opening to the paradox of love and grief.

THE SIXTH STAGE OF GRIEF

Elizabeth Kübler-Ross[1] **was** groundbreaking in helping us track the stages of grief: denial, anger, bargaining, depression, and acceptance. Yet, most people mistakenly get the idea that grief is a linear, ordered process. To me, it looks and feels more like overlapping spirals and circles where these stages bleed and mix with one another—dancing within each other and shifting back and forth. The process eventually creates a larger and larger area in the center that opens us up to more acceptance. Acceptance drops us into what I call the sixth stage of grief, it's natural companion—creation.

Creation walks with grief because when something dies—a habit, a job, a career, a loved one, a friendship/a romantic partner, a partnership, a home, our own life—something else rises from that ending and opens us up to a new creation cycle.

The big question is, are you able to co-create with death and rebirth cycles as a willing partner or does your Mental Being act like an anchor in the ever-changing waters of life, trying to hold you in one moment, stalling it out, prolonging it, or sabotaging the next moment at all costs, even after the "death" has come?

Our Heart Being knows the truth that, one way or another, the creation cycle will keep going. What does your Mental Being do with this truth? Whether we like it or not, we all actually do have a Grief Practice sorts. The question is what *type* of Grief Practice do you have? Is it helpful to you, your life, and what is wanting to flow through you into creation? OR are you holding onto what's dead, cutting yourself off early from a connection, or laying down in a preferable coffin-of-what-was, just waiting out your life cycle?

Sacred Witnessing is not a passive act, it is an active agent for healing, change, and living. The Sacred Witness supports us in deeply connecting with the organic movement of our lives—our messy, insane, glorious, painful, joyful, overwhelming lives. Additionally, when we are tending to the grief of what we lost, we are also tending to the loss and releasing our attachments to the life that we thought we should have, could have, or wanted.

The Sacred Witness is constantly inviting our Mental Being to open to the movement of creation. It is asking our Mental Being to accept the mystical laws of Death and Rebirth to help us honor, release, and move from one aspect of our lives into the next one. When we allow ourselves to truly embody the Sacred Witness as a constant companion, we are inviting ourselves into change and creating new life beyond our wounds, beyond the loss of something that parts of us would rather remain in connection with—a Being, a job, a home, a time period of our life.

Here is what I have come to deeply understand about grief: it is a part of our daily lives. Either we are willingly walking with it or we are avoiding it—therefore shutting down, blocking, and by-passing our full Bridge of Connection to our lives and relationships. Grief means I love something, I cherish it, and I wish it would be and remain with me forever. Grief means I honor something and the moments we have together and I honor and hold space for the moments I wanted to have together but was not able to. When I open to grief, I open to connection. When I fear, avoid, try to block, or by-pass the fullness of grief; I block love, I block connection, I block actually being present to what I have right now in this present moment—my family, my job, my hobbies, my companionship with other Beings.

CHAPTER PRACTICES

The practices for this chapter are designed to help you cultivate greater comfort with holding space and witnessing Grief. The first practice is designed to support you in developing willingness in the Mental Being to meet the deeper layers of Grief in a specific situation of unfolding change in your life. The second practice will offer you a supportive tool you can use on an ongoing basis to work with the grief that emerges in the course of your ever-changing life. It uses the easy-to-remember Mantra of LOVE to help you work with Grief on a daily basis.

PRACTICE 1: BEGINNING TO EXPLORE THE GRIEF BENEATH CHANGE

Let's go back to the examples of transformational change at work in many people's lives today (found on page 190). Which of these did you resonate with? Perhaps you could relate to one or more of them. For this practice, please choose one to work with through the process below. If you didn't find that one of these examples quite fit, I invite you to consider a situation of change present in your own life right now and explore it using the following inquiry practice.

Step One: Check-In
Start with your Check-In and Body Scan. This process can be found on page X.

Step Two: Ask for Willingness in the Mental Being
Next, consciously ask the Mental Being to offer some space and a willingness to explore the good, bad, and ugly perspectives of all your Parts as it relates to this experience of change. Remind the

Mental Being that it has trust, respect, and the capacity for choice here. Remind your Mental Being that we are going for awareness and acceptance of What Is so in our whole system, but that no specific action will be required without its buy-in.

Step Three: Enter the Healing Room with Parts That Arise

Once you have gained the Mental Being's willingness to explore, enter the same or a new Healing Room (using the practice from the last chapter). Present your system with the situation of change you are working with, and notice what Parts, stories, and emotions arise in you. Give them space and work with them as you have been practicing working with Parts.

Write down the stories, Parts, wounds, and emotional experiences your system is bringing forward. Remember to meet them with presence and compassion, as we learned in the last chapter.

Step Four: A Healing Interview with Grief

Take some time to ask the following questions to the brave Parts of you that have stepped forward. Write their answers in your journal.

1. What has been so in this situation since it began? This could be a review of the relationship, the career path, the educational choices you've made, whatever you are working with.
2. What motivated you to engage in this situation or experience in the beginning?
3. What have you contributed to this situation in terms of your energy and resources?
4. How has this situation served you? In what ways has it been aligned with certain values you have held? What needs has this situation met for you?
5. How has this situation contributed to your sense of identity?
6. What is true, here and now, about this situation or experience?

7. What needs to be grieved as a result of this unfolding change?
8. What feels like the hardest part of allowing this situation to change?
9. What is this change really about for you?
10. Let grief speak: What does it need you to know or do to honor it and your whole being?

Step Five: Check In with the Sacred Witness

Lastly, invite in your Sacred Witness to hold all of what you have found here. Take your time to be with what has emerged. Remember that you don't need to fix or change anything you are noticing, just simply allow it to be here and accept what has arisen.

Now that your system has had some space to explore what is beneath an unfolding change in your life, invite your Sacred Witness to step forward and share with you the following. What wants to be created now? What wants to emerge in this ever-changing, unfolding moment? Allow yourself to fully feel and hear your inner Sacred Witness and take time to be with what arises.

PRACTICE 2: DAILY LOVE AND GRIEF PRACTICE

Every client I work with is walking with grief in their journey of healing and growth—either consciously or unconsciously. The following daily practice will help your Mental Being learn how to meet Grief as a way to unlock the Love it has been keeping at bay in its protection efforts. It is a practice of non-attachment, can serve as a Grief Practice, and also works in tandem with the Bridge of Connection.

To help my clients open to the mantra of LOVE practice, I share with them a poem by David Whyte called "Start Close In" (see Appendix A). In this poem, Whyte offers a call into courage, movement, and love by giving advice to the reader to stay in present time and not get lost in getting too far ahead of this present moment. He suggests that we, "start with the first thing close in, the step you don't want to take."[2] Inviting our Mental Being to meet what is right here helps it cultivate a willingness to open to the LOVE and support that flows from the Heart and Soul Beings.

The Mental Being needs to be reminded it isn't alone within our system protecting us at all costs from potential loss and grief. It can lean in and start with the first step it is afraid to take—to trust you, trust the Sacred Witness, trust the wisdom of your system as a whole Being—body, mind, heart, and soul. This practice helps you start to close in.

THE LOVE MANTRA[3]

Get comfortable and complete our foundational practice, found on page 389. Once you are centered, I invite you to repeat the following mantra to yourself.

Today I open to and call forward LOVE:

L—Letting go of trying to control, so that I can let things be

O—Opening to what is, in this moment, without filtering, resisting, or blocking it

V—choosing to be Vulnerable with others and with myself

E—Experiencing All! All emotions are welcome without getting grippy with or bracing against them. I'm willing to witness and feel: joy, happiness, excitement, pain, hurt, desire, fear, anxiety, worry, laughter, peace, ease, safe . . . every emotion in my current experience.

From here, invite in greater support with the following healing prayer.

Thank you for the breath I'm taking. Help guide me today so that I am able to be in my life, open to LOVE—to the connections that are offered today and to the connections you would like me to offer myself and others today.

I open now to the healing strands of grace to support my whole Body Being so that I can have the courage to stay close in. Please get my attention when I am drifting too far into the past pains or into the future with worry, fears, unproductive questions, and unfounded predictions.

Help me stay in my life today and open to the wonders and beauty surrounding me.

For the parts that I am struggling with and desiring to control, help me access the grace of patience and understanding. Help me see that which I do not want to see and hear that which Parts of me are blocking. Help me have compassion to open to What Is, so that I can make empowered choices in alignment with my Heart and Soul and what is wanting to come through to support myself and those I will interact with today.

Infuse my heart with love, compassion, and understanding.

Infuse my body with light and courage.

Infuse my aura with comfort and support.

I ask for any guidance now to support me and release my attachments and beliefs to the troubles held within my heart, body, and mind.

Take a moment of silence to listen within.

Listen for the messages of your Body, Mental, Heart, and Soul Beings.

What insights are wanting to come forward?

Track for any emergent felt senses in your body that draw your attention.

Listen to your thoughts. Allow yourself to release the reins of what you want to hear, sense, feel, see or know, and instead wait for the Sacred Witness to guide and answer you.

Please know that sometimes there are no words, no pictures, no felt sense in your body. There is only silence. Sometimes a whirlwind of images and words may emerge, showing you what you might be holding onto so tight from the past, or revealing fears and gripping sensations about the future. Sometimes an emotion like grief knocks on our door and asks to be witnessed. Sometimes there are words of encouragement—*keep going, you got this, you are doing okay.* Sometimes we hear our Soul whispering insights and invitations such as, *You have been avoiding this person and that discussion for three days now. What might be up with that? What else do you need to explore so you can move into action with the guidance you received three days ago?*

Allow yourself to explore this mantra and healing practice on a regular basis in your practice.

Now that we have explored the Bridge of Connection, the Mental Being's capacity to meet our full range of emotions, and our Mental Being's ability to meet change and its accompanying grief, we are ready to enter deeper into the Heart Being with the Mental Being as our friend and ally.

I invite you to continue to work compassionately with your Mental Being, giving yourself the gift of time and practice. Invite the Mental Being to willingly illuminate its different main protective Parts so you can gain a greater understanding of the working edges and default survival drivers keeping you from full presence with yourself, your life, and your guidance system.

In the next section, we'll move deeper into the layers of our Heart Beings, working with these aspects of our Being to continue cultivating the Sacred Witness within.

Section Four
Awakening and Befriending the Heart Being

Overview

*"The entire Universe is condensed in the body,
and the entire body is the Heart. Thus, the Heart
is the nucleus of the whole Universe."*

—SRI RAMANA MAHARSHI[1]

We are now halfway through our journey of embodying the Sacred Witness as a healing presence for yourself and others. Congratulations on coming this far.

We have begun befriending the Mental Being, helping to establish its willingness to release its Lone Wolf status and remember that safety and healing support come from the wisdom held in our Body, Heart, and Soul Beings too. You also learned how to use the Inner Bridge of Connection to reestablish pathways through which you can help the protective Parts of the Mental Being release their dualist black-and-white points of view and remember their wholeness. We also helped the Mental Being develop willingness to connect with and allow you to experience the different emotional waters you will hold in the act of Sacred Witnessing, from which the Heart Being doesn't shy away. The Heart Being easily allows us to flow with the messengers of emotions and feeling tones as one of its key languages.

In this section, we are continuing our journey by connecting into the nucleus of us—our personal Heart Being.

What is the Heart Being? In the quote above, Maharshi invites us to see the Heart Being as the nucleus of the whole universe that is

Us. A nucleus is the central organizing structure around which other parts are gathered and grouped. Therefore, our Heart Being is our central organizing point that allows us to connect and sense into the multi-dimensions of the worlds within and around us—the Seen and the Unseen, our Soul Being, other Beings, Earth, and even out into the Cosmos. It is the portal that allows us to sense and connect with the sacred wisdom and knowledge from our own Soul's, the Collective's, and the Divine's Hearts. Our Heart Being can lead us into a felt sense of deep union. It can invoke a felt sense of belonging. It also serves as our personal gateway into embodying our Soul Being. Through our Heart Being, we can have the felt sense of embodiment and BEING in our lives, versus simply feeling like we are skimming the surface of our lives—disembodied and separate from our lives, our Soul, and our purposes.

When our Mental Being allows us to connect to our personal Heart Being, we establish a direct connection to the Sacred Witness within, a constant companion that tends our core fears and wounds (which arise from how our system constellates itself around different trauma and survival adaptations). The Heart Being helps us continue to unlock our inner willingness to take leaps of faith into fully believing in ourselves. In the role of the Sacred Witness, connection with our Heart Being is a key component to helping us hold a healing presence of love and willingness to connect with all the aspects of us, providing the palpable experiences of being truly seen, felt, heard, and tended to.

In this section, we are going to learn how to work with the main language of the Heart Being—the language of symbolic metaphor in the realm of archetypal patterns.

Learning how to work with the symbolic nature of the archetypal realm within us (instead of viewing them as something to master and control from a Mental Being perspective), we gain access to the Sacred Witness stages six and seven—having the ability to stand with the point of view of the True Self. Our true Heart Being has the capacity to remain centered and connected to the Sacred Witness, even in the midst of strong emotions and experiences around which the Mental Being's protective mechanisms typically throw us off center.

Befriending the Heart Being allows us to shift from being emotionally manipulated and blended with wounded and protective Parts of ourselves and others, which are scared, fearful, resentful, or looking to derail us from true healing or growing. Befriending the Heart Being allows us to re-constellate the nucleus of us, shifting center from the Mental Being to the Heart Being, allowing us to hold ourselves in alignment with the Sacred Witness and access the skills of acceptance, curiosity, and non-attachment.

Over the next three chapters, as we Awaken and Befriend the Heart Being, we will explore:

- How to identify and work with archetypal symbolism as a main tool for perceiving through the lens of the Sacred Witness.
- The four main Survival Archetypal Patterns we all have in common and how these four patterns act and serve as the Four Guardians of the Heart, bringing forward Healing Invitations and Messages from our Heart Being.
- And how to befriend the Four Guardians of the Heart Being and understand how they help craft the nucleus we constellate our WHOLE system around.

Big Picture Road map Check-In

Through this section, we will gain more comfort working from the realm of the Heart Being as our nucleus of "us," instead of the Mental Being. The shift, from the Mental Being to the Heart and Soul Beings as our nucleus, grants us greater access to the Sacred Witness as a constant daily companion and healing support to ourselves and others.

As you engage this section, a friendly reminder—please don't leave behind the Body and Mental Beings. This is a journey of embodiment, creating a felt sense of connection through bridging together ALL aspects of us. As we bring our attention to one aspect of us, like the Heart Being, it is simultaneously healing and reestablishing lines of communication with our Mental Being expanding our willingness to sense more in the Body Being and opening us up to new choices and ways of being to come forward from the Soul Being, which is the final stop on our journey after exploring our Heart Being. Through befriending the personal Heart level of ourselves, we are one step closer to creating a new level of inner leadership in our whole Being, shifting from our default automatic survival level functioning, to letting the Sacred Witness guide us from our Heart Being.

Chapter Ten

Introduction to Archetypal Patterns

In the last two sections, we have been exploring the idea that trapped trauma and unmet needs held within our system have altered and limited our thought patterns and how our body runs. You have engaged practices to work with protective Parts that helped you survive environmental challenges and relational wounds in the past. Over the next three chapters, we are going to focus on developing a key skill of the Sacred Witness—the ability to see what is driving our behaviors and actions *archetypally.* Learning how to identify and see the different archetypal patterns at play, within ourselves and others, gives us the ability to understand how our Heart Being is trying to guide us.

You might be thinking, *Michelle, you already taught us about Parts. Why do we need to look at archetypal patterns, aren't they the same? What do archetypal patterns have to do with the Heart Being?*

Great questions! Short answer: no, Parts and archetypal patterns are not the same thing, which we'll explore more here. By adding in how to work directly with archetypal patterns, we access a deeper level of unburdening our system—which will increase our access to the Sacred Witness's profound support. We'll discover that if we only work with Parts or only archetypes, we can't fully unlock the potential of the Sacred Witness. We have to meet ourselves at both levels. Similarly, if you are befriending and working with just one aspect of you, such as your Body Being or Mental Being, you will only get so far.

I have watched so many people chase their tails when they are solely working with Parts and not connecting back to the Archetypal realm within them. Similarly, I have witnessed people become detached from, undermine, and by-pass the wounded Parts of them when they only work on the impersonal archetypal level. When we bypass either, we cannot fully tend to the aspects of us that need our support, nor integrate and evolve our system into greater wholeness. Learning how to distinguish Parts from archetypal patterns allows us to honor each of their roles within our system so that we can fully befriend, connect, and integrate them, avoiding the pitfalls that happen when we only work on one level of us.

Let's explore the difference between a Part and an archetype, or archetypal pattern, now.

WHAT ARE ARCHETYPAL PATTERNS?

An archetype, or archetypal pattern, is a set of universal symbols, images, constructs, and innate potentials held in the collective unconscious (and thus shared by all) that can be expressed in human behavior and experiences. By their nature, they are impersonal and universal, even though we can assign a level of personal attachment to them.

Whether we realize it or not, our whole way of operating and working with the world is through the lens of archetypal patterns. Swiss psychoanalyst and mystical teacher Carl Jung pioneered our modern use of working with archetypes for personal growth and understanding, helping us gain insight into our own inner world and our unconscious workings, both individually and collectively. Contemporary spiritual teacher and pioneer in energy work and healing, Caroline Myss,[1] added her visionary gifts to our understanding of how to use archetypal patterns for personal and collective healing. Her methods of teaching people how to identify and work with their core archetypal patterns revolutionized the fields of personal development, mystical healing, and the spiritual arts. Her model gives people a foundational practice for working directly with these patterns, which has the potential to unlock their own self-empowerment and self-healing. We'll be using her framework to explore archetypes and how working with them will help us unlock the full potential of our Sacred Witness.

Just as the Heart Being works with us through metaphor and symbolism, so do the archetypes. The trick to speaking the language of archetypes is to not only interpret them literally, but instead realize they carry with them a full range of different emotions, programs, thoughts and ideas, traits, belief systems, and behavioral patterns that transcend any one point of view. For example, let's look at the archetypal pattern of the Artist. You most likely got an image right away of the Artist archetype in your mind's eye. Artists have a talent for creation and can bring ideas into form. While they might certainly create art via a medium of painting or music, they could also be oriented around their desire to create beauty and unleash creative expressions. Someone who embodies this specific archetypal pattern may see the world through the lens of the Heart, be open to the emotional realms, and love to explore the full spectrum of experiences. They are typically not concerned about being conventional; instead, they are driven to create and express themselves in their own medium.

A core trait of any psychological archetype is that they can be expressed at varying levels of us: survival, personal, and the collective and "universal" realms. They also have a range of expression in the Light, meaning in ways that are in alignment with our True Self; and in the Shadow, ways that are heavily burdened by our survival and trauma adaptations. For example, the Artist expressing themselves at the survival level might seek to exchange their creative talents to meet their daily needs. This can be in the Light, such as a commercial artist who enjoys their work and receives compensation for it. This exchange could also be in the Shadow, where the artist compromises their own integrity and style to conform to what will bring them acceptance from the tribe or meet other survival needs. Another way the Artist can express itself in the Shadow survival range is the Starving Artist, which may include those who refuse to deal with or value material matters for the sake of their art, or refuse to get a paying job because it is not aligned with their creative spirit.

The Artist can be expressed on the personal level as well. The personal level in the Light might be someone that creates art to bring themselves joy in their daily life or as a hobby and personal passion. The shadow side of the Artist on the personal level might look like a person using their eccentric traits or artistic ideas to judge, shame, or control another. Another shadow expression of the Artist can be the repression or even abandonment of the Artist within due to protective mechanisms. This repression would then turn their creative traits into self-harm and depression. The Artist can also transcend the survival and personal levels of us and express through us at the collective or universal level. At this level, the Artist feels a calling beyond their own personal preferences or survival needs and becomes a vessel for artistic expression that serves the collective in some broader way.

As you can see from this example, archetypal patterns run with a full range of expressions across the different levels of our consciousness and have both supportive ways they operate in the Light, and Shadow ways they operate through destructive behaviors and thought patterns.

WHAT IS THE DIFFERENCE BETWEEN ARCHETYPES AND PARTS?

Now that you have a basic idea of what a general psychological archetypal pattern is, let's explore the difference between a Part and an archetype so we can discover how to work with each.

As we've explored, Parts, both protective and wounded Parts, are fractured off aspects of us resulting from trapped trauma and survival adaptations. They are frozen "pieces" of us that are stuck in the time, consciousness, and beliefs from the moment in which they were created. Parts are locked into one rigid point of view based on the specific event or experiences that generated them. This means they cannot "see" or operate in any way other than what was available to them at the moment they solidified in our system. Parts exist at the survival and personal levels of us, and cannot reach beyond the personal into a more expansive range, like the archetypes can.

Parts cannot go beyond their original roles and mindsets. Therefore, they, by themselves, cannot bring us into true connection with our Heart Being because they were born and created from their personal survival and protection stories in a moment when our Heart Being and Soul's wisdom was offline. Therefore, protective Parts tend to compound on themselves, spinning off constant warring new protective and wounded Parts. For example, to combat the protective program of *Never Again*, we can develop an opposite survival program of seeking connections that are *totally* void of Heart Level relating. These risky connections leave us further exposed and in extremely unhealthy relationships. This new protective program spins off more wounded Parts and the cycle continues—creating, once again, more and more aspects of us that are holding unmet needs and emotions cut off from and drowning out the guidance of our Heart Being, which is trying to help us find a healthier way to work with what we're experiencing in the present moment.

Archetypal patterns are NOT bound and burdened by these restraints. Remember, a key trait of an archetypal pattern is that they can function at different levels of our Being—survival, personal, and transpersonal (i.e., collective, universal, and even cosmic)—in a range from Light to Shadow. Even though we interact with the themes held within an archetypal pattern personally (and they feel very personal when activated in us), they are actually completely impersonal in nature, which gives us access to a *full* bandwidth of different traits, guidance, and resources. Parts, on the other hand, whether they are helpful manager Parts or shadow protective Parts, are completely bound to only operating and seeing the world from their fixed point of view.

When it comes to distinguishing between an archetypal pattern and a wounded or protective Part operating at the survival level, people can understandably get confused. This is because all of our Parts are actually held within our different archetypal patterns. To understand the difference, it helps to work with the metaphor that Parts are like individual people and archetypes are the bigger containers, such as houses or communities, that hold all the different Parts. Therefore, learning how to recognize an archetypal pattern's full range allows us to distinguish between a Part that is stuck and locked into its point of view and the archetypal pattern it is associated with, which can move beyond the base survival levels to the highest expression of our Soul-level responses. Parts cannot evolve and grow; however, our archetypal pattern can develop, grow, and evolve.

Another misconception is that archetypal patterns cause us to disconnect from our Heart Being. Instead, it is the protective programs held within the theme of that pattern that create the disconnection and drown out the full range of how that pattern can support us. Because the archetypal pattern includes the ability to go beyond the survival level, learning how to work with them directly *is* our ticket to unlocking different states of being.

FOUR COMMON SURVIVAL PATTERNS: THE FOUR GUARDIANS OF THE HEART

In Myss's model, we all have four common archetypal patterns inherent to our survival system. I like to think of these core patterns as the four core leaders, or co-captains of our ship. They represent the main themes we all have to work with in some form or fashion to meet our daily needs of being alive, in a body, and having to care for and tend ourselves and our lives.

Our four basic survival archetypal patterns, which are the Guardians of the Heart, are:

· The Child—Guardian of Innocence
· The Victim—Guardian of Truth and Choice
· The Prostitute—Guardian of Worth and Integrity
· The Saboteur—Guardian of our Power

Together, these four survival archetypal patterns serve to protect us, keep us safe, and help us function in our daily lives. They are literally our own built-in survival system. Like I mentioned earlier, they are the main "houses" that hold and organize all our protective Parts within them. Without their innate drives and instincts functioning to meet our needs, we would not be alive.

I also refer to these four patterns as the Four Guardians of the Heart because it helps us remember that these archetypal patterns can express themselves beyond their survival level and shadow range. Working with the term *Guardian* reminds us that they innately hold full range archetypal potential, like all archetypal patterns. Ultimately, these patterns within us have the role of supporting us to meet the realities of life on this planet. As such, they are Guardians because they will literally not allow us to access our True Self if they believe we need to run a protective thought, action, or way of being to keep us safe. As the main Guardians of our Heart, they are the true gatekeepers that determine our access to the full Inner Bridge of Connection, as well as all the amazing gifts and other archetypal patterns held within our Heart and Soul Beings—such as the Artist, Visionary, Lover, Networker, Healer, and yes, the Sacred Witness within.

If we want to befriend our Heart Being and open to the amazing gifts and talents of our Soul Being, including the Sacred Witness, we need to learn how to work directly with these core survival patterns and unlock their full range.

When we can co-create with these patterns in their higher-functioning range, they enable us to thrive, stay in alignment with our True Self, and make everyday choices aligned with our true nature and power. When we learn how to work with their questions and concerns as healing invitations, they provide constant guidance on how to break free from survival-based functioning and remember our true nature. These four patterns are truly wonderful, beautiful, and *amazing* guardians for our True Self, which is why I refer to them as the Four Guardians of the Heart.

UNLOCKING GUARDIANSHIP
THROUGH HEALING INVITATIONS

When people hear the names of these four survival patterns, or Four Guardians of our Heart—the Child, Victim, Prostitute, and Saboteur—they often have a negative association and even a visceral sense of disdain. They see them as the Four Horsemen of the Apocalypse in our system, trying to keep our Heart offline and safe from danger by any and all means necessary. This is a common misconception because when these core archetypal patterns are driven by an unconscious wounded Part of us, our Inner Bridge of Connection is cut off. We find ourselves being kicked into the limited safety of the Mental Being's adaptive programs instead of being able to hear the real guidance coming from our Heart Being. If these patterns within us are heavily burdened and running in their shadow survival forms, then the Mental Being's Protective Parts are running the show—cutting us off from access to our true Heart's guidance and driving us into shutdown, flight, fight, fawn, fold, and/or freeze programs.

I could spend a whole book exploring these core archetypal patterns and still have more to share and explore. For the purpose of this book, I want to offer a basic overview of these four and share this simple truth: the health and conscious awakened relationship you have with these four patterns within you—at *any* given moment—will determine how much access and *accuracy* you have in hearing and interpreting your true Heart's guidance and the guidance of the Sacred Witness energy.

The more these four are running autonomously behind the scenes from base survival and trauma adaptations, the more skewed and filtered our inner guidance and access to our True Self will be. Therefore, to unlock their true Guardianship level, we need to understand how they function at each of their levels.

It is sometimes hard for people to believe these survival patterns are actually the biggest Guardians of our Heart. When worked with, as we'll explore in this section, these archetypes are our biggest allies in adapting to the changing needs of each moment and staying in connection and alignment with our True Self.

I invite you to an Exit Ramp to help your Mental Being release any preconceived judgments that might be associated with the names of these guardians. In the next two chapters, I will introduce you to the WHOLE pattern of each Guardian. This includes their survival and guardianship levels in the Light, the supportive traits and themes that open us to empowerment; and the Shadow sides, those traits and themes that are running from fear and protective point of views cut off from our Heart Being.

Knowing how to identify and talk with these four Guardians will personalize them for you so you can work with them more effectively. When we know how these patterns typically work within us and how they function in their different ranges, we can stay connected to the support of our Heart Being, engaging our system in a way that honors their worries and concerns *and* brings us into balance and harmony with our True Self—win, win!

LEARNING TO RECOGNIZE
ARCHETYPAL HEALING INVITATIONS

Because every archetypal pattern has a range of expression, they hold within them the ability to alchemize their survival pattern into Heart guardianship. To find and unlock this alchemy, I teach my clients to recognize what I call the Healing Invitations of each archetype. Healing Invitations are moments where we feel the nudges and guidance of the Light held within them coming forward to help us transcend the sheer survival level shadow functioning.

When we can answer the Healing Invitations, we help these patterns shift so they are free to function from their upper levels of Guardianship. Healing Invitations guide us to lean in and be curious as to what hidden needs are present within us, potentially trying to be met through the shadows. Knowing how to identify and work with the Healing Invitations of the Four Guardians of the Heart allows us to enter through the wounded Parts held within that pattern and transform them with the help of the full range of archetypal potential that goes beyond survival. From there, we access the true choice on how we can meet the needs a Part was trying to meet from the Shadow now and discover a way to meet it in the Light, in alignment with our True Self.

Remember, our Heart Being's guidance and Healing Invitations are often hijacked, skewed, or cut off by the Parts held within them that are intensely fearful and often resentful of the guidance these Four are trying to bring forward. The Guardians of our Heart are often heavily burdened and drowned out by the wounded Parts held within them. Unfortunately, when they are overburdened by the voices of our Parts, we can't access their true voice and form. Instead, we only know these Guardians through their false versions—the Inner Narrators of protective Parts that were forced to make certain choices to survive.

Learning how to identify and recognize the differences between the promptings of the Four Guardians of the Heart and protective

Parts is a key component in befriending the Heart Being. Learning how to identify the different themes of each Guardian will help you sift through and identify what Guardian, and thus Healing Invitation, is present. Being able to identify their key themes and drivers gives you instant access to their true guidance as messengers of the Heart Being. You can then consciously witness yourself and tend to the fears and pain held within the wounded Parts that are causing your whole system to run out of alignment and balance.

Another way to help identify a Guardian's Healing Invitation is the presence of an inner war or collision within. These collisions are a result of our survival needs, personal desires, and the guidance coming from our Heart and Soul Beings crashing into each other *and* the Mental Being cutting off access to our Heart Being by collapsing our Inner Bridge of Connection. I witness these collisions manifest in so many ways, both in my own life and in my clients. These collisions are signal flares from within your system that something needs to be tended. The main way these inner wars manifest is through acts of self-sabotage and self-victimization.

The Healing Invitations of the Four Guardians of the Heart help the Mental Being and protective Parts discover that we now have a greater capacity to work with the potentially overwhelming information, memories, or emotions of the wounded Parts of us, therefore allowing us to fully tend to our system.

In the next two chapters, I will share more insights on how to talk to the Four Guardians of the Heart, recognize their Healing Invitations, and move through the impasses and inner wars in our protective programs to access our True Self. However, before we get there, let's start with an exploration and pulse check on your system's overall current relationship and immediate associations with the basic "idea" of the four survival patterns.

CHAPTER PRACTICE

In this reflection practice, completed in your journal or in contemplation, we'll allow your Mental Being to share its free form associations and feelings on the four patterns—*Child, Victim, Prostitute,* and *Saboteur*—to gauge our starting point awareness. This will establish a baseline before we start to connect with these Four as the main Guardians of our Heart Being.

Try not to look up definitions of these, just go with your knee-jerk reactions and personal associations. There is nothing you have to get right here. We will dive into definitions and build awareness in the next chapters. Try not to get ensnared by the wounded Parts held within these patterns during the following explorations. We are trying to stay big picture with these reflections. We will dive deeper into each of them in the remaining practices of this section.

How Do I Feel about the Survival Patterns?

Check-In—Take a moment to do a short Check-In and Body Scan to give yourself a baseline of what your current system feels like *before* you call forward one of the survival patterns. This yields a clearer picture of the messages from both the Body and Mental Beings when and if something shifts or changes (sensation- and thought-wise) during the practice.

The Child—Guardian of Innocence

When you hear the phrase, *Inner Child*, in general what thoughts come forward and how do you feel toward it?

What do you like about the idea of the Child pattern?

In what aspects of your life do you find it easy to connect with some of the characteristics of the Child—for example, childlike play, joy, and freedom of movement and expression?

The Victim—Guardian of Truth and Choice

What is your general reaction to and relationship with the word *victim*?

Do you feel that the word *victim* has been used (by yourself or another) as a tool for shame and blame? And if so, how?

Where can you see that the Victim pattern in your life has allowed you to seek and receive support?

Where can you see that the Victim pattern in your life has been shut down or misused, and how?

The Prostitute—Guardian of Worth and Integrity

Even though you might not know what this pattern entails, what are your general first reactions to acknowledging that you have a survival pattern called *the Prostitute* within you that governs your worth and integrity?

What associations do you make with the words *compromise* and *exchange*?

The Saboteur—Guardian of Our Power

What are the top ways you experience self-sabotage—i.e., backing off your inner guidance?

Do you find yourself procrastinating on or resisting actions that match your guidance? If so, what are some of the top ways and realms of your life in which you do that?

Now that you have a general idea of the difference between archetypal patterns and the Parts that are held within them, we are going to move into exploring the Four Guardians of the Heart in-depth: their main themes, how they run at their different levels, and how to identify and work with their Healing Invitations. By learning how to shift from seeing these patterns as the Four Horsemen of the Apocalypse to seeing them as the Four Guardians of the Heart, we gain the ability to remain connected to the Sacred Witness within, even amidst active survival and protective responses within ourselves and others.

Chapter Eleven

The Child and the Victim

The Child and the Victim patterns walk very close together in our system. Learning how to identify the traits of the Child and the Victim is an essential skill of the Sacred Witness because almost every witnessing we do will be holding a healing presence for the wounded Parts held within these two patterns to be seen, tended, and unburdened, thus opening us up to the ability to grow and integrate how we work with these survival themes in a totally new and supportive way.

In this chapter, we are going to explore how to identify and work with the traits, themes, and healing invitations that come from the Child and Victim archetypal patterns within us.

ARCHETYPAL TRAITS OF THE CHILD

The Child is the first survival pattern activated in our field in utero. The Child's biggest survival driver is needing to belong to survive. Therefore, *belonging* is a huge subconscious survival driver for the Child pattern—seeking it, opening to it, catering to it, and protecting it. The theme of belonging, and the adaptations and traumas we have experienced around this theme, constellates our *whole* system. The main survival driver of the Child will follow us throughout all the survival archetypal patterns and can override our ability to access true choice at any age and stage of our life.

In the Light, exploration, play, imagination, curiosity, and freedom of movement are some of the basic functions and gifts held in our Heart Being that belong to the Child archetype within. When we are a child, in an ideal world, these gifts are honored, nurtured, and allowed to support us *and* the adults around us too.

Here are a few key points about the Child archetypal pattern:

- **A Child, by its nature, needs a caregiver.** The child isn't designed to be in charge of caring for, nurturing, or protecting itself. The child is driven by the survival need and desire for belonging and protection. Because the child is not burdened with the responsibilities of caretaking, it is free to be in innocence, open to exploring their world and connecting with all that is.

- **A Child, by its nature, has no real power.** The ideal of a power differential is a very real phenomenon for the child. It can share thoughts and needs, *but* it isn't the adult, the Creator Being and decision-maker, in the relationship. The Child cannot make things happen on its own. Ultimately, it is at the whim of the authority and control of people outside itself to meet its needs to be seen, felt, heard, and tended in the physical realm.

- **A Child is in the moment.** By its nature and stage of development, the consciousness of a child doesn't yet have a capacity for big-picture conceptualizations or time awareness. Children are in the moment and with whatever is present. They quickly release the past and don't have a solid framework for the future.

- **A Child can see, hear, feel, and interact with different dimensions.** The child has an innate knowing that Soul Beings are a part of every Being—plants, animals, insects, fish, rocks, trees. A child recognizes that everything has a Soul and they can connect with them because they are both speaking Soul, our true nature and original unspoken language. A child can dance with the elements—air, water, earth, and light. They don't have the mental constructs of separation and/or a belief system yet that humans are the only form of intelligence on Earth or in the Universe.

- **A Child perceives differences as beauty.** Children don't understand that differences are something that separate us, determine our value, or should be something to fear. In their innocent and Soul-Led way of being, children perceive every Being's uniqueness as something to celebrate and explore, understanding that difference is what contributes to the whole.
- **A Child has no Inner Critic.** This is one of the hardest aspects of the Child for us to connect with as adults: a child, in its true nature, does not have a harsh Inner Critic. They don't innately use shame and guilt to learn, adapt, shift, and change. Instead, they use exploration, trial and error, success *and* failing to help them learn, grow and change. Not having an Inner Critic also means that the Child, by nature, is willing to try. They can easily lean into the ideal of faith that it will all work out somehow, someway and therefore leap joyfully into the unknown.

Gifts of the Child

One of the other gifts of the Child is their own willingness to unapologetically be in their own glorious dance with freedom, play, imagination, love, and grace in a way that naturally invites us adults into remembering the same thing. Simply by witnessing them and opening to their wisdom, we can invite our system to heal some of the protective adaptations and restrictions we have developed that cover up our inner knowing and balance, which the Child naturally embodies.

A moment I shared with my youngest daughter, Willow, is one of my favorite stories about how a Child can help us remember our own joy and light. She was seven years old and we were down at the natural swimming hole on our property. This swimming hole is a magical place surrounded by amazing outcroppings of larger rock faces with little caves in them, which the flow of the creek has created over hundreds of years. This section of the creek has a natural bend in it with a wonderful little basin, deeper eddy and natural swimming hole, adjacent to the flowing part of the creek. In the eddy, a few parts of the rock floor come up to form a shallow bench. Willow once asked me what the Creek and Water's names were. I guided her to ask for herself! After connecting in with the water, rocks, and trees surrounding the banks of the creek, she proudly exclaimed the Creek's name was Bob! Bob is magical. Bob is home to wonderful little schools of small fish. The surrounding trees, along with the rock walls and floor, add to the mystical nature and support the whole system.

This particular day, Willow and I were down at Bob on a hot summer day. Henry, my husband, and Savannah, my older daughter, were coming down later after wrapping up their day's activities. Dancing to the music playing from our outdoor speaker, Willow was swaying on the large rock floor in the middle of Bob a couple feet below the surface. She called to me to join her. I felt my Inner Child calling me to leave my chair in the middle of the creek and dance with her. I waded across the swimming hole to join her. As I waded through the water and started to dance, I could feel Parts of me wanting to resist joining her and fully allowing my body to move and dance with her, the water, the air, and the trees. These Parts were looking around, almost as if making sure no one was looking. Other Parts were judging my dancing and even judging how Willow was dancing. Tons of voices were at tug-of-war within my system. I honored them all, took a breath, and reminded my system that I can dance, I can laugh, and I can enjoy connection with Bob, Willow, and all the amazing

Beings dancing with us. The worried, resistant Parts of me calmed down, and I was able to open up to the gifts of the Child. Together we danced, twirled, and splashed in the water. A few dragonflies and butterflies even joined in!

Then it happened. I heard the sound of my husband's truck coming along the edge of the hayfield to join us at the swimming hole. Instantly, I felt the desire to stop dancing, retreat to stillness, and regain the seeming safety of my chair. Willow caught my hesitation, grabbed my hand, and said so beautifully, "Mom, you don't have to stop dancing just because someone else is here."

In that moment, I looked at my gorgeous daughter—her hair soaking wet and her little spindly body reaching out to call me back. Luckily, my own Inner Child was healed enough to allow me to see the little wounded Child version of me in my mind's eye. She was lost and believed it was not safe at all to be seen. She wanted to dance, to laugh, to sing, to play, but she was scared and holding all the memories of being wounded when she was in her innocence and glory. In my Heart, I smiled at the little wounded one. I silently promised her I would connect with her again in meditation. I promised her I would listen to the wounds and scars she held and help her heal and rejoin my Heart. But for right then, I invited her to stay and dance with Willow so she could see that things could be different now. She was safe—she now had me to protect her—and she could laugh and play.

This moment stays with me even today because it was such a beautiful example of how Willow, in all the glory of the Child, gave me a gift, no strings attached, just by being herself. She did not have any shadow or unhealed Parts gripping at her to take on another role beyond the Child. I didn't ask her to serve as a shadow rescuer, healer, or caregiver. She was able to just BE a child. Her being a child provided me an opportunity to see and call forward a sweet and tender healing without burdening her in the process. Her pure joy, playfulness, imagination, and freedom opened a doorway for me to remember what it was like before the Inner Critic and Judger took over. I was able to explore freedom of movement throughout my Body Being. I was able to make a conscious choice to connect with the seen and unseen worlds. This innocent invitation from Willow—"Come dance with me!"—provided me an opportunity to heal Parts of me that were lost. That is the power of the Child when it is open to its inherent gifts and the light it brings.

Wounds Held in the Child

We all have an inner Willow in our hearts—a version of us that guides us into remembering the zest and joy of our life and the Beings in it, from an innocent, pure-of-heart point of view. Unfortunately, for so many of us, that beautiful inner little one is often burdened by responsibilities, fears, and inner judgements that do not belong to the Child. Wounds, betrayals, and traumatic experiences have fractured off subsets of protectors and shadow roles that now burden our Inner Child.

For most of us, our Inner Child is bogged down with survival and trauma-based archetypal sub-patterns like:
- The Wounded Child—the child that has had their innocence taken advantage of and harmed in that process
- The Invisible Child—the child that felt as if they were never seen or heard, and therefore didn't have the connection and care they needed
- The Parentified Child—the child that was forced to take on independence and responsibility for their own care and/or care of the family before it was age-appropriate
- The Orphan Child—the child that felt abandoned, isolated, and alone without someone to belong to
- The Perfect or Golden Child—the child that felt they could

      not make any mistakes and were required to only excel and
      provide pride for their caregivers

These are just a few examples of survival-based sub-patterns we may adopt in order to meet the unique demands of our childhood environment. Each one of these Child archetypal sub-patterns comes with their own unique strengths and burdens. They have their own stories and range of how they operate in the Light and Shadow. Let's look at the example of the Orphan Child.

While the wounds of the Orphan Child are centered on a sense of loss and abandonment that create the survival driver to make it on their own, the strength held within that sub-pattern is an ability to break free from the family burdens and ties of Belonging that often bring the Child pattern into the shadows. Therefore, the Orphan Child in the Light is free to construct a family that matches their own values system and break free from unhealthy relational bonds that would normally hinder the Child through shadow loyalty and Belonging drivers. From this example, we see that the wounds and protective programs held with the Inner Child in all of us have the potential to bind up our system—body, mind, and soul—in reactive, fearful, and shaming responses, because they are lost in their own survival and trauma stories and adaptations. And, yet, they also have the potential to set us free into the Light.

Another common wounding of the Child happens when, at some point in our life, people tell us something like, "That is not true, that is childish, why would you believe that?" Some of us suffered from shaming and teasing if we shared that we could connect with the unseen world, for example. For those of us that could sense what another Being was feeling or thinking and shared that information, we were often met with their protective Parts that told us it wasn't true and negated our perceptions. Sometimes we experience being met with aggression and anger at different truths and invitations we offer others from a place of innocence. There are tons of reasons why we start to shut down our ability to connect with the Heart Being and its Four Guardians, thereby pulling back from sensing or having conscious connections to all that is within and around us.

For example, once I realized that most people didn't see, hear, or feel the way I did, I hid it from everyone. I didn't want to become a target for the people around me—both from people desperately wanting to take advantage of my abilities or those that were afraid of them because they challenged their belief systems or protective Parts in some way. I went so far as to mock and openly cut down any woo-woo type things, all while quietly being an Animal Whisper and Soul Whisper behind the scenes. For years, people thought I didn't believe in talking to animals, spirits, or anything. I was known as the science-based expert in my field. The desire to Belong created a barrier to sharing my True Self with others. However, that hiding came at a cost: I never felt truly seen by anyone. I was alone and I was the one that created the cage that separated me from them.

Roadblocks for Working with the Child Pattern

Before we dive into the Healing Invitations held within the Child pattern, there are a few pitfalls and common traps we often fall into when we start working with this pattern.

First, culturally, our Mental Being has received a few common concepts that do us no favors. The biggest one is that we try to force the Inner Child to "grow up." This is a slippery slope because the Inner Child pattern is separate from the other archetypal and developmental patterns that unfold through different stages of our development. Our Child pattern is necessary and needed for the time it serves as our main pattern. As we grow, we step into activating different patterns—the Young Adult, the Adult, the Provider, the Caregiver, and the Elder. Each one of these patterns is necessary for our development and the different stages of our life. *And,* the Child is there, only able to do what a child does. It doesn't grow up. It is what it is. Our Inner Child stays with us throughout our lives to help us remember the pure, innocent connection that we have to the world, ourselves, and our life! Sayings like, "When I was a child, I spoke as a child, I understood as a child, I thought as a child; but when I became a man, I put away childish things" cause us to abandon some of the very needed healing gifts that come from the Child.[1]

Another big stumbling block for us, in the beginning of starting to befriend this core Guardian of the Heart, is realizing that the Child pattern within us always remains whole and can help us remember the Light and gifts held within. This means that the Child pattern is not damaged or tainted by the wounds we experienced as a child. We all struggle to remember that the Child pattern remains whole within us because of *all* the wounded fractured child Parts and *all* the protective Parts they created to help us survive are held within this pattern too.

The biggest takeaway I ask my clients to remember when working with the Child is that experiences and adaptations needed to survive and seek belonging are literally what constellate how our system grows, organizes, and reprograms itself. This truth creates a *massive,* constant inner war between our Mental Being and our Heart Being, until we can help our Mental Being realize our Heart is not trying to expose ourselves to more harm—rather, it is trying to help us heal the wounded Parts so we can reorganize the system to have access to stronger, healthier ways of protecting ourselves. So, until we can help the Mental Being shift its survival point of view, we will have a whole host of Protectors that try to control and/or block the themes of the Child—restricting play, shaming innocence, doubting, and closing down our imagination, and controlling or tempering other wonderful gifts that our Child can bring to our life today.

HEALING INVITATIONS OF THE
GUARDIAN OF OUR INNOCENCE

Since the Child constellates our system, almost every Healing Invitation that comes forward from any of the Four Guardians is going to lead you back to healing a wound or survival program held within your Child pattern. This is because it is the unmet needs, fears, and wounds held within this pattern that literally creates the Mental Being Protective Parts you find within the other patterns. Therefore, if you are working on a Healing Invitation involving a core wound or block, all roads will lead to the Child and witnessing a younger exiled or fractured off Part of you that is heavily burdened with experiences that were beyond the capacity of the Child to work with.

The wounded Parts of us need a caretaker or protector—they need a parent. Because of this, the Healing Invitation of the Child is going to ask *you* to step into that role—to be the Guardian of Innocence for your system that was not able to be there for whatever reason before. This helps us recognize where we have wounded younger Parts seeking shadow belonging, caretaking, and illusionary innocence in a manner that is not aligned with our True Self. When we unlock the Healing Invitation of the Child, we become the active protector and the healing agent within our system. We therefore help free up the burdens holding our whole system hostage so that we can have balance between play and responsibility, belonging and independence, and innocence and discernment.

Willow, without even knowing it, offered me a spontaneous Healing Invitation that day at the creek. I was able to see the ways in which I had young wounded Parts of me blocking my direct access to the traits of the Child in the Light, including laughter, bliss, wonder, imagination, exploration, freedom of expression, and yes, innocence—in the ability to function without a harsh inner critic judging me. Additionally, Willow reminded me what it felt like to not be burdened by conscious thoughts of what it takes to belong in relationships. She safely assumed I would accept her no matter what, even if her innocent invitation challenged me or brought me into "looking silly," because she accepted me just as I was. The Child in the Light easily seeks connection because Belonging is something natural to all Beings. Therefore, it is not in its own pattern to be burdened by embarrassment, fears of humiliation, and shadow pride that come from the normal unfolding dance of connection. We are going to have moments of stepping on each other's feet, falling down, getting back up, and trying once more. The Child in the Light is not burdened by any of those fears, those burdens are held in the different survival patterns, mainly the Victim.

ARCHETYPAL TRAITS OF THE VICTIM

After the Child comes online, the next main survival pattern or Guardian that begins to support us is the Victim. The survival driver of the Victim reminds us that living on Earth is gritty—every Being can and will encounter harm, pain, illness, and suffering. Because the Child often doesn't understand what is happening or how to express itself when it is hurting, confused, scared, or upset, it needs a different pattern to help it. The Child often does not know how to reach out and seek caregiver support when they are experiencing disappointment, sickness, pain, and confusion that needs tending. The Victim pattern helps us seek aid for the wounded Parts of us. The Victim in the Light helps us witness ourselves and others when they are in need of care. It also helps us override any instincts the Child might have to hide or dismiss the support, due to shadow protective programs around Belonging. Therefore, the Victim's role is to help us realize that every Being needs care, support, and compassion.

A very interesting trait of the Victim is that the gifts and wounds held in the Victim are the same thing. In Shamanic Healing, they say *the medicine is in the wound*, meaning that what we need to heal is going to be found within the wound itself. The Victim, in its Guardianship role, guides us into witnessing our wounds in ways that help us discover the medicine held within.

We have been working with the Victim throughout this whole book. I started this book by sharing with you one of my own self-victimizing stories: that moment of overwhelming pain I experienced at twenty-three years old. The Victim in the Light reminds us that this moment was not born in isolation. Its roots began further back, and the medicine it was guiding me to was in unwinding the hidden impacts of the trauma and illness that caused me to lose connection to my own Body, Mental, Heart, and Soul Beings at thirteen years old. To deeply heal and move from sheer survival mode into living, loving, and leading my true life, I had to work with the Victim at every level of my being.

This Guardian of Truth and Choice invites us to step forward with the healing gifts of forgiveness, understanding, compassion, courage, and healing. The Sacred Witness cannot help us without our willingness to partner with the Victim in the Light.

Here are a few key points about the Victim archetypal pattern:

- **The Victim, by its nature, is not personal:** This means that the Victim (like all the archetypal patterns) is an impersonal pattern. While we deeply feel the impact of our hurts and wounds personally, this pattern reminds us that if we really zoom out and see the experience from an archetypal point of view, we are going to be asked to switch the statement, "why me?" to "why not me?" This fundamental switch in perspective is why the Victim is the Guardian of Truth. It takes us from only seeing things from the personal perspective to the impersonal perspective of "I'm not exempt from any of the broad range of experiences common to all Beings in Earth school."

- **The Victim engages us with acts of Care:** Because we will experience moments of harm, confusion, and pain, the Victim in the Light can compassionately and willingly witness and take us into action around tending our wounds and others' wounds.

- **The Victim provides us with Choice.** Because the Victim acknowledges that we are all going to be wounded—physically/emotionally/mentally/spiritually—and we will all need care at some point, it asks us to explore how, when, and what we are willing to tend and not tend. Once we can see that care is needed, this Guardian helps us move into motion, seeking, receiving, and taking actions to address, support, and act in ways that would support overall healing. Are we seeking and offering shadow protective stances and care that come from the wounded Parts, *or* are we stepping into action that is guided by our Heart Being? For example, do I allow the wounds of my past to create barriers for me, *or* do I work to acknowledge where I have choices and where I don't?

My Journey of Cultivating Medicine with the Victim

As I began the medicine cultivation journey guided by my Inner Victim, I started to understand what had happened and was still happening to me from that illness. But early on, I became lost in the whirlpool of *Why me?* I was also stuck in the trap of, *HOW could such a devastating event happen to me, at just thirteen years old? I was innocent and didn't deserve what was happening to me.* I bet you have wrestled with similar inner wars at different times. I felt betrayed by my body and mind. I also felt victimized by the Divine, this God thing, that *allowed* this to happen to me. I didn't want to ever feel weak and helpless again.

After Schedule died, I adapted a cold and separate persona that held every Being at a distance and didn't allow my Heart to be present at all. I took the wounding from my earlier illness and used it as a shield to create distance from me with the protective thought, *No one can understand what I went through.* The pain and isolation left me cut off from my Inner Bridge of Connection and from feeling connected to any purpose for my life. Lost and feeling totally alone in my basement apartment, a Part of me just wanted the pain to stop. A Part of me also wanted the world to finally *see* that I wasn't okay.

That Part of me was willing to die to finally be seen—because that was the wound that had never been acknowledged. Luckily, Baron was there and helped me to accept that he saw the pain I was holding. He was my Sacred Witness, reflecting and bearing witness back to me the pain I couldn't fully see myself. From that moment, I partnered with the Victim differently and I sought the medicine held within my wounds. I began the journey of learning how to witness myself fully. I realized that I needed to shift *how* I held my pain because it was not serving me.

I had to be willing to shift gears from *Why me?* and the belief that the universe had harmed me intentionally, to *Why Not Me?* The Victim squared up with me and asked:

Michelle, are you willing to learn how to shift your inner stance around the horrible things that happen, things for which you will never receive a sufficient reason? Harm happens, and Parts of you will never agree they should, and yet they *did.* Can you accept this? Can you accept that, in your search for meaning and reason, you are victimizing and ensnaring yourself repeatedly? If you can shift into acceptance, you will free yourself. You need to step into witnessing the Parts of you that are lost, trapped in the grips of the trauma. You need to learn how to build a bridge back to you and your life.

It was my Inner Victim in the Light that called me forward into the transformation I so desperately needed back then. It guided me through its gifts of Truth and Choice, allowing me to see and accept What Is, and that shift enabled me to find the choices that would truly liberate me from the trappings of past trauma. Through its compassionate care, the Victim's role was instrumental in helping me build the Inner Bridge of Connection.

Healing Invitation of the Victim: From Personal to Impersonal

The Victim walks you into the wounds and helps you call forward the medicine held within. To access the Healing Invitation though, we have to shift from the personal to the impersonal, something archetypes help us access, but Parts cannot.

In my journey, I had to be willing to shift into a more impersonal point of view first, accepting that what happened to me could happen to any Being. Once I was willing to honor that point of view, I could witness my past in a way that allowed me to be deeply open to true understanding of the wounds, from the point of view of the wounded Parts themselves. I was free to release any projections of shame, blame, resentment, and judgements of those experiences and of myself. This allowed me to open to the main Healing Invitation of the Victim, gaining internal and external support so the wounds could be fully tended and complete their circuit of unmet needs.

This completion of unmet needs allowed me to access the medicine within. As a result, I can now cleanly share this medicine with others in a way that allows them to use my stories as a Bridge of Connection to their own isolated and exiled Parts seeking support, care, and liberation as well. In this way, the Victim in the Light serves others just as the Child in the Light does.

WHY HEALING THE CHILD AND VICTIM ARE CRUCIAL TO EMBODYING THE SACRED WITNESS

Let's connect our work with these two archetypes to our primary purpose in this book—to embody the Sacred Witness. Why is healing our connection with these patterns of the Child and the Victim so important for embodying the Sacred Witness? Here are three main reasons:

One, to hold space with the Sacred Witness energy, you will most likely be holding space for wounded Parts held in the Inner Child or Victim, for yourself or another Being. IF your protective Parts still view the Child and the Victim as threats; and thus running them in the Shadow range, you will be flooded by the wounded Parts of you. They will kick you out of connection with your Heart Being, take over the driver seat of your conscious choice, and then either the wounded Child or Victim Parts in you will run the show. You will lose the ability to have Clean Compassion, curiosity, and witness clearly what is being asked to be witnessed.

Two, healing doesn't have to be *all* painful, serious, and somber. Laughter, joy, movement, and play are amazing healing tools! When we are in the role of the Sacred Witness, we might receive directions to care for the younger Parts of ourselves in different ways—such as to run, to skip, or bring in supportive laughter. There is a difference between avoidant play and humor and healing childlike movements bubbling up to give us buoyancy. And yes, you will be able to tell the difference once these patterns in you are able to run in the Light.

Healing is about remembering and restoring your wholeness. The aspects of imagination, play, connecting with the worlds we cannot see, seeing every Being as sacred, and having a voice to share those thoughts and ideas are required skills in the embodiment of the Sacred Witness so that you have the freedom within your system to see, sense, hear, feel, and know what is wanting to come forward.

Finally, this healing work lends you the ability to discern where the Inner Child and the Victim patterns in the Shadow are showing up in the different areas of your life and creating imbalances. Knowing how to recognize these patterns gives the Sacred Witness within you the ability to see where a burdened Child Part might be struggling with responsibility versus play, or innocence versus maturity and discernment, therefore re-victimizing you or the other. For example, as you are witnessing your system, you recognize the Child pattern in a shadow survival mode is present because you notice Part of you that is trying to seek caretaking when it isn't necessary. As you lean into this need, you witness a young exiled Part of you that felt it always had to take on the responsibilities of caring for self and others beyond what was age-appropriate if they wanted to be accepted into their family. This Part is tired and doesn't want to be responsible for anything else. As you turn to witness how this is showing up for you now, you currently see that it is expressing itself as a person seeking a caretaker and having others take responsibility for you in shadowy ways because that is how the system is seeking "healing" for that younger victimized Part of you.

I call this *Shadow Healing*, where we have Parts of us seeking from current relationships the support and care they needed *in the past*. Through the ability to witness and perceive your system through these different archetypal patterns, you can see the burdened Child patterns showing up in your current relationships in unhealthy ways that are causing you to victimize yourself and others with the unmet needs of wounded Parts of you. And now, because you have witnessed it, you can make a different choice!

Through the act of Witnessing how these different patterns within you, or another, are running you can access your greatest superpower—the ability to actively tend and heal the younger Part of you so that you can now rewrite and update the survival programming in your system to be in greater alignment with who and how you want to be *now*, instead of the past protective programs running subconsciously from the shadows.

CHAPTER PRACTICES

Because the Child pattern, and the wounds and protective Parts held within the Child, is *how* we unconsciously constelled our whole entire system, the practices of this chapter are designed to help you to explore, reconnect, and gain more comfort with the Child in the Light. Unlocking the gifts of the Inner Child is absolutely a key component of embodying the Sacred Witness energy.

As you can gain comfort and permission within your system to open to the Child as one of the Four Guardians of your Heart, rather than a wounded or protective Part of you that needs to just "grow up, suck it up, and change," your whole system will soften and gain more willingness and confidence to tend to the exiled and fractured off Parts of you that are held within these patterns.

Through these practices, you will also be walking with the Guardian of Truth and Choice, the Victim. These practices are going to call upon many of the skills we've been building throughout our journey together.

Healing Tips: Please note, these practices are meant as a place to get started. We are not able to cover ALL the practices one might use in healing the Inner Child and Victim in this book. If you are ready to dive deeply into this healing path, I encourage you to continue this Self-Work with the help of an appropriate mental health professional, Archetypal Consultant, spiritual coach/director, or other qualified professional of your choice.

Also, please note that these practices might seem very simple and even a bit silly at first, do not let that stop you from slowing down and really working with them. They are so powerful if you let them fully support you. From working with these simple practices, you will develop the ability to:

- Somatically notice when a protective response is being activated and sending you into a "triggered" reaction and response, instead of a Heart-Led action.
- Develop very real nervous system pathways and willingness to turn toward the trigger with curiosity and compassion, instead of falling into the flight, fight, and dorsal responses and the accompanying harsh inner shame and judgements.
- Start to fully tend the different Parts of you that were upset, nervous, or triggered so that they no longer are trapped in your system. Once these are released, you can develop *new* pathways and programs that are in alignment with your True Self.

This is why working with these Guardians and their healing invitations is the missing link in most Self-Work practices.

PRACTICE 1: ACCESSING INNER CHILD GIFTS OF IMAGINATION, PLAY, AND EXPLORATION WITH DEEPER SOMATIC AWARENESS

To start us off on our journey of befriending the Heart, I'd love to guide you into experiential connection with the Inner Child, one of the key functions and Guardians of our Heart Being. Unfortunately, far too many of us have had to dim and even shun this key pattern within us to survive or protect ourselves. Yet, the role of our Inner Child in the Light allows, opens, and invites us into working with play, joy, and imagination as healing tools for the Sacred Witness.

To serve as our entry point of exploring the Inner Child in the Light qualities, I would like to take us into a series of short guided meditations. We will bring in the Victim in our second pass through these meditations.

Check-In: Start with a short Check-In. Next, see if you can ask your Mental Being to step back and release its attachments to what you think you know about your system, just for a few minutes, so we can explore a few questions with a fresh sense of curiosity and a childlike perspective.

One: The Gift of Exploration

For a few moments, pretend you are seeing the space around you for the first time. Be curious like a child. Allow yourself to move around, explore, see, and touch things just like a child does when they are in a new space.

Side note here—notice if any old protective Parts pop up right now. It might be an Inner Narrator's voice that says, "Don't touch things, be careful, or don't look like you are too excited." In your journal, make a quick note of what different stories might be active. Let them know you will come back to them and explore their role and experiences a little more. But for right now, see if they are willing to step back and allow you to continue your practice of exploration to its fullest.

- What do the different objects or fabrics in your space feel like?
- If you move them around, what ways does the light change the object?
- Is there a smell to the space or any objects drawing your attention?
- What memories or senses become activated as you take in the different scents?
- Take a breath in through your month, what can you taste?

When you are ready, settle back into a resting position. Take a moment to check in with your Body about how it felt during that experience—open, happy, curious, nervous, critical, wanting more, something else? What was that like for you to interact with exploration and discovery?

Now, let that practice go if you can.

Two: The Gift of Imagination

We are going to visit another one of the Inner Child's gifts—the ability to see and walk in both worlds, via imagination.

Ask your Heart to guide you in remembering a time that your imagination was a doorway into interacting with the unseen world. Recall a time when you were able to interact and communicate with different worlds, dimensions, and types of Beings. Let your Heart start to guide you back to a time that you felt connected to the unseen world around you.

Maybe it was a plant Being that you could talk to. Maybe it was an animal, fish, or insect Being that you talked with and felt completely connected to. Maybe it was the companionship of an invisible friend or angel?

Let your Heart guide you to remember this connection to the Being and/or world it opened you to. If it feels good, let your Heart show you what that relationship was like.

- How did you talk and communicate with each other?
- How did you know that the other Being understood you and you them?
- What ways would you interact with this Being?

Soften and let your Body and your Heart Beings share with you what that relationship was like.

(Again, be mindful of any feelings or tugs of a protective story or Part trying to take over or cloud your remembrance. It might even be a wounded Part that has bittersweet memories of this connection. Let them know that you are aware of them and their desire to help you, even make note of them, then ask them to step back and trust you to tend them at the appropriate time so you can remain in this practice.)

Just like in the past, let's see if we can use imagination as a doorway to connection. Can you imagine that somehow this Being is still available to connect with you now, across space and time? What would you like to share with that Being right now? It might be offering love, gratitude, showing them around your space and introducing them to your life now, or some combination of these. See if you can allow yourself to open up the same type of communication and connection you had then with this Being now. What do you sense, feel, see, hear or know coming from them to you? Maybe they share love, gratitude, or even insights on what they are up to now.

Take a few moments to experience and explore this connection and sacred reunion.

When you are ready, thank this Being and your Heart for bringing that connection back to you in present time and let them know that you can continue your connection in whatever way feels appropriate in the future. However, for right now, say goodbye, call all your energy back to you, send all their energy back to them, and return to center.

Before we step into the next mini practice, take a few moments to explore what that experience was like for you. Again, notice any Parts of you that had resistance to allowing that connection to come forward or to move from a memory into current time. Remember that the mixed bag of emotions and Parts are all welcome. What was their worry about opening the doorway to imagination? What was your system's comfort level with opening a doorway to connection and exchange with that which is beyond the mundane world? Did it have fears or maybe a sense of doubt, guilt, or silliness? Protective Parts come in all different shapes and sizes and their jobs are varied. Just notice if any are/were present and what their role might have been with you.

Three: The Gift of Play

Let's now explore another gift of the Inner Child—Play.

Once again, ask all the Protectors that normally control how, when, why, and *if* you get to interact with the frequency of Play to give you space so you can simply observe what your frameworks for Play are for a few moments.

Invite your Heart Being to guide you to remember a time you felt free to play and explore. Let it guide you to a time that you let your body move you to interact and open to the world within and around you via this state of being that is Play. Notice what insights arise as you witness that time. What did that version of your body feel like? What were some of the emotions that were allowed to be present? Explore whether you notice the presence of any worried energy about being accepted, belonging, or doing something right or wrong.

Check in to what the Mental Being was doing during this memory.

If it feels good for you, explore making movements or gestures that might embody this Play energy. It might be a laugh, a smile, a sound of excitement, a movement through the body like a stretch, skip, or hop. Maybe it is allowing yourself to lay down with your arms and legs outstretched like starfish, just like a little child does in the grass or on the floor after playing. Again, explore what Play feels like.

When you are ready, come back to center. Once again thank any doubting, protective, and managing Parts for stepping back to whatever extent they did as you explored these different gifts of the Inner Child. Also, thank your Inner Child for coming forward and helping you remember.

PRACTICE 2: INVITING IN THE VICTIM, GUARDIAN OF TRUTH AND CHOICE

I invite you to go back through this whole series of explorations again, but this time with a focus on the places of micro-resistance that indicate the Victim's presence. We'll ask the Victim to be your chief guide as you explore re-establishing your connection with exploration, imagination, and play. Utilize these practices as a launching pad for Self-Work, helping you to start to heal and unburden the wounds and protective programs held in your system.

Invite the Sacred Witness, the Victim, and the Child to help illuminate any subtle messages coming from the Body and Mental Beings via working with an active Body Scan and somatic awareness to notice any subtle restrictions of movements, old stories, and other ways in which you find your mind or body trying to bounce you out of the practice.

For example, in the Exploration exercise, where you are exploring your space as if for the first time, you may find yourself wanting to reach out and touch an object. BUT you notice a little micro-hesitation in your arm when you go to reach for the object.

When that somatic awareness happens, pause the movement and allow yourself to scan your body. Be curious and let your Body Being guide you.

- What does your stomach feel like, your arms, your legs, and so on?
- Next, check in with the messenger of the Heart Being, emotions. What emotions are present, and what stories are attached to those emotions?
- Be curious about what clues you can use to discover any protective Parts held within your Victim.
- If the Body and Emotions Scans have guided you to a protective Part, such as one holding an idea such as, *Don't touch that, you will get yelled at*, ask, *What else is there?*
    - o For Example: You might see an image of your parents scolding you after you accidentally broke someone while exploring it. You have a couple of options:
        - First, acknowledge that you see this protective program and the wounded Part that created it.
        - See if that Protector is willing to step back to allow you to continue to explore and practice this remembrance, knowing that through this practice you are healing the wounds held in your Inner

Child and relieving that Protector from having to
restrict your movements

- However, if that Part doesn't give you permission
  and doesn't feel comfortable to step back, you can
  pause the practice and have a *Healing Interview,*
  which you learned to do in Chapter Nine.
- After that process, resume your exploration practice, repeating the movement or thought that
  accompanied the micro-restriction or movement,
  and see what is shifting now with that movement
  and what gifts of your Child and Victim patterns
  you are now able to access—perhaps more freedom
  of movement, trust in yourself, and compassion if
  you make a mistake.

Rinse and repeat with the Imagination practice and Play practice.

You might even combine these exercises with mindful nature
walks, expressive movement, and/or mindful dance where you are
pretending to dance with wind or trees or an animal companion like
a dog or horse. This would be a great place to intentionally bring in
somatic movement and notice where your system opens and flows and
where you notice a restriction or shut down of movement and flow.

Healing Tip: Repeating these practices in many different settings
helps to create a muscle memory willingness to be both in motion and
turning toward those little micro-moments of restriction and withholding with the curiosity and willingness to witness what is there
and tend to it. These three practices combined create the Bridge of
Connection to your Heart Being that you will need to work with yourself and others when you find yourself triggered, just like I did with
Willow that day at the creek. Because I had developed these pathways
through practices like these, I had the skills I needed already in place.
So when I felt the overwhelming wounded and triggered Parts of me

clawing at me to stay in my chair or retreat when I heard the engine of my husband's truck coming through the field, I was able to stay in connection with my Heart Being whispering, *You are fine—laugh, play, dance, you are going to be okay.*

I invite you to stay with these practices, they are absolutely one of the best ways I teach my clients to rebuild willingness and a felt sense of safety to stay embodied when experiencing different triggers, allowing the Sacred Witness within to help you hear the sacred messages of the Body, Mental, *and* Heart Beings.

Practice 3: The Child in the Light Guided Journey

The Child is an integral aspect of our system. Therefore, to help you continue to reconnect with this Guardian, let's continue to explore the Light aspects of the Child through guided meditation. Please note that this guided journey can feel bittersweet. We are going to consciously welcome the Child to our Wise One Team, through its role as a Guardian, not a wounded Part of us. That means your Victim will be there holding sacred space for you in this meditation, helping you tend to this aspect that might be heavily burdened with wounded Parts. The conscious choice to open to the Child can be freeing *and* it can also highlight grief arising from the moments when, as a child, we didn't have the luxury of accessing our Child's gifts for whatever reason.

If it feels good to you, see if you can allow Grief and its Protectors to pull up a chair and be held by the Guardian of Truth and Choice, so you can allow your whole system to acknowledge that wounds are present *and*, through non-dual thinking, so is healing. You can have Parts of you that are wounded, in the process of healing, and healed all at the same time. You can cultivate a current-time connection to the Child, and also let your system know that we are not trying to replace or reprogram our Inner Child. Bringing this guide onto our Wise One Team is not about ignoring any of the unhealed fractured off young Parts held within your Child. We are bringing in the Sacred Witness to serve as a guide as you restore your system by finding and healing those wounded young Parts.

Check-In: Take a moment and drop into a Check-In via your Body and Emotional Messenger Scan. What sensations, images, and/or emotions are present—opening, tension, excitement, worry, flashes of you as a Child? Again, this might be a mixture of bittersweet energy.

What about your Mental Being—what thoughts, stories, and Parts can you feel present? Call forward your Healing Room. Invite any of those Parts to step into the Healing Room to gain support while we explore the pattern of the Child in the Light.

Sacred Witness: Call forward the Sacred Witness within, ask for support for your whole Body Being and create an orb of healing light and support to surround you.

Heart Being and the Guardians of the Child and Victim: Invite your attention to flow back to the Heart space. There, sense, feel, see, hear, and know that within your Heart is a doorway to the nucleus of your system, the interior of the Heart. At that doorway or gateway are the Guardians of the Heart. Notice that these guardians protect your sacred light and the connection to your Soul Being. See if you can walk through the gateway. Once on the other side of the gateway, notice what the landing looks like. Here, you might sense a beautiful meadow or secret garden open only to you and your Wise One Team. It might be a cozy room or a secret place between the dimensions. Take a moment to explore this space with all your senses.

Reflection and Remembering: Next, notice that there is a beautiful light from a sacred pool of water, which forms a reflecting pool. You walk toward the edge of the water and peer in. The surface of the water begins to show a scene. As you peer into the water, a beautiful child appears and motions for you to see all the gifts within them.

Let your imagination reflect in the waters—do you see laughter, joy, wonder? Let your Heart show you what is revealed in the water.

You might see a child swinging on a tree swing, or talking to the wind or the fairies. You might see a child captured by the awe and curiosity of the light dancing on the walls from a prism's reflection. You might see a child staring up at the stars, imagining the life held within each of them. You might see a child starting a wonderful two-way conversation with an animal.

Perhaps you see a child who notices that another child is sad, feeling left out at the playground. Upon seeing this, the first child walks over and asks the sad child if they want to play. The sad one smiles and reaches out a hand to join the first. Together, they return to play and laughter.

You might see a child who is scared or upset. Then you see a beautiful mystical parent coming to tend to them, listen to them, help them feel safe again, and make sense of what scared them.

You might even see a child's wonder and awe at watching the snowfall and the light shimmering off the thousands of crystals calling her into a magical fantasy world.

Take a moment to allow the reflection pool to share what your Heart Being would like you to witness and remember is possible.

Reclaiming: Next, explore what energies you would like to reclaim at this time from the Inner Child, The Guardian of your Innocence. See if any lost or stifled gifts of the Child are ready to infuse back into your whole Being—the desire to develop more laughter, curiosity, playfulness, joy, connection?

Know that you can come back here anytime you need help remembering these pathways of joy, light, fun, imagination, hope, freedom of movement. You can use this sacred reflection pool to help you remember and witness anything you need support with.

Thank the Water and your Heart Guardians for supporting you during this meditation of sacred remembrance. Thank this gorgeous Child for coming forward to help you reconnect with their innate patterns.

When you are ready, turn and walk back through the gateway of the Heart. As you do so, know that healing strands of grace are tending you and your whole Body Being, as well as your timeline, to help support and bring healing wherever and whenever it is needed. Trust that your Sacred Witness and Wise One Team know exactly where to send this healing energy. If you want, you can also direct it to any areas—physically, emotionally, mentally, and spiritually—you feel guided to as well.

Closing: When you are ready, take three centering breaths. On the first inhale, call all your energy back to you from where it has been, across space and time, and as you exhale blow out with sound—blowing yourself back fully into your body. With your next breath, breathe in love and compassion for your whole Being. And as you breathe out, exhale all that is no longer serving and that which you no longer need to carry with you. On this last breath, inhale peace and exhale worry and fear.

Take a moment to stretch, feel into the space around you and feel your hands and feet by wiggling your fingers and toes. Come fully back to the present.

And so it is, Peace, Peace Peace.

I invite you to continue developing compassionate curiosity toward the ways you manage the gifts of the Child—exploration, imagination, and play—in your life.

Hopefully, what we are doing through the process of Self-Work, is to un-blend the shadow Parts held within the Child and the Victim so we can access our true guidance. Through this work, we get to consciously know what triggers the different wounded stories that our Child and Victim carry that were never tended to fully and witnessed. Once we can begin to see, sense, hear, feel, and know how these two Guardians work together, we are able to catch when we are operating from a wounded Part and unlock the medicine held within us. This allows us to consciously parent our Inner Child, allowing ourselves more freedom in our choices and actions so that we stay in alignment with our Heart Being. The same goes for all the four survival archetypal patterns.

Up next, we are going to awaken and befriend the two remaining Guardians of the Heart, the Guardians of our Worth and our Power.

Chapter Twelve

The Prostitute and the Saboteur

Similar to the Child and the Victim, the Prostitute and Saboteur archetypes run closely together like a duo in our systems. Where the Child and the Victim mainly focus on negotiating our relationship to belonging, need for care, and seeing different levels of truth and choice, these two—the Prostitute and the Saboteur—invite us to look deeper into what is actually driving our choices, encouraging us to recognize the reality that we ultimately need to meet our own needs and claim our true power.

Once we accept that we have self-agency and different levels of responsibility in meeting our own needs, we can establish *how* we want to meet those needs and *how* we want to be in connection with ourselves and others in that dance. The Prostitute archetype correlates with the Heart Guardian of our Worth and Integrity, while the Saboteur archetype relates to the Heart Guardian of our Power. These two, in balanced relationship to the rest of our systems, are crucial to our capacity to engage our Heart Being for the greater purpose of embodying the Sacred Witness.

In this chapter, we'll explore how you can identify the traits, themes, and healing invitations of the Prostitute and Saboteur archetypes, our Guardian of Worth and Integrity and our Guardian of Power, respectively.

ARCHETYPAL TRAITS OF THE PROSTITUTE

First and foremost, this archetype doesn't refer to the physical act of prostitution, rather to the ways in which we exchange our valuable resources with others. Thus, all Beings, regardless of gender, have this archetypal energy running within them. The Prostitute, as a survival archetypal pattern in the Light, understands that to survive we must eat, have shelter, wear clothes, and so on. This Guardian is incredibly down-to-earth, real-world savvy, and understands that we must meet our basic needs first and then we can focus on any personal preferences and desires second. As a survival pattern, it reminds us that the biggest assets we have are our time and our attention. The Prostitute governs how we manage, allocate, and exchange our time, talents, and treasures with ourselves and others.

Thus, our Guardian of Worth and Integrity is a part of almost every decision and choice we have. When it is running in its Guardianship in the Light, it supports us in discovering and aligning our actions with our true values and is the keeper of our internal Code of Conduct. In the Light, it helps us honor and respect ourselves and others as we engage in healthy compromises that fully honor ourselves as well as the other. When the Prostitute energy is cut off by protective Parts and running in shadow survival levels, the system prioritizes following choices that are protecting the wounded, exiled Parts held in the Child over your own personal or Soul-Level Code of Conduct. Shadow survival choices might look like this pattern encouraging us to exchange or compromise on our personal integrity in order to gain belonging and get someone to care for us. Boundaries, boundaries, boundaries are the name of the game with this Guardian—within us and with others. More on boundaries in the coming chapters.

Here are a few key points about the Prostitute archetypal pattern:

- **The Prostitute engages us in the Dance of Relationship.**
  Every connection we make internally and externally comes

with requests, giving, receiving, yielding, leading, and compromising. These actions create a dance of connection and relationship with ourselves and others. The Prostitute is who we work closely with in the fourth Pillar of our Bridges—Connection. During these dances of Connection, we are continually engaging in verbal and non-verbal exchange, communicating our desires, wants, wishes, fear, likes, dislikes, and needs with ourselves and others. The question the prostitute is constantly bringing forward in these exchanges is: *Will expressing my True Self in these moments be safe, be helpful to my overall wellbeing, or will it cost me in some way that will be harmful?* Meaning, can I match my actions with my Heart's guidance, *or* do I have another survival need that is trumping that guidance from a wound held within the Victim and/or the Child?

- **The Prostitute invites into understanding what has Authority within us.** This Guardian is our internal checks-and-balancer. It asks us to look at the choices we are making and why. If this Guardian believes we can make a choice in alignment with our Heart's Guidance, we get the green light in our system to open to the fifth Pillar of our Bridges—Purpose—and the ability to follow and align with our own inner *why* and Code of Conduct as the main governing authority within us. However, one of the main components we explore with this Guardian is our own personal hierarchy of needs and how those govern our choices, for better and worse. Meaning *that if* we feel that our Code of Conduct and Heart's guidance is going to clash with a survival need, we will give the authority of our choice to another Protective Part of us or another outside Being.

Gifts of the Prostitute

When this Guardian is able to help us claim and remember that our true worth is always present, we gain consistent access to our Inner Bridge of Connection. We have a willingness within us to follow and align our actions and choices with our Purpose, i.e., Heart and Soul's guidance. From that willingness, we step into Connection with self and others from a place of understanding our worth and having integrity to hold ourselves accountable to the guidance we receive through the Purpose within. Because we are committed to following our guidance and we understand our worth, we are willing to follow up with our actions and can have inner faith in our ability to course correct as needed with love and compassion, thereby establishing Self-Trust and Self-Respect. This Guardian helps us discover that unlike the Child, we can esteem ourselves, granting ourselves Self-Worth. The Prostitute is also our Guardian of Integrity. Integrity means that we have the ability to match our values with our actions, even when we feel pressure to act out of alignment with our values.

When we understand our true worth and values, we can fully consent to giving and receiving love, igniting our system with passion, joy, and desire to create. The Prostitute helps us answer the questions we will meet each time we pass from pillar to pillar along our Bridges. For example, at the big choice point between the Pillar of Choice and Willingness and the Pillars of Connection and Purpose, this Guardian invites the Mental Being to trust that our Heart and Soul's guidance does include survival-level care—however, from a place of understanding our true worth instead of a compromising shadow stance that gives authority to a wounded or protective Part. Therefore, we can take the leaps of faith to believe in ourselves to create, grow, and open to new experiences with our Heart Being present.

Wounds Held within our Prostitute

The Prostitute archetype is a primary survival pattern because it recognizes that we have to make certain negotiations in life in order to procure the resources we need to survive. In shadow, this archetypal energy compels us to compromise some essential aspect of our Being and/or our values to get what we think we need in life.

The wounded and protective Parts of us that are held within the Prostitute pattern relate to our own sense of unworthiness and unhealthy moments of relationship. The wounds and protective programs held within this pattern can drive us into self-victimizing compromises and giving ourselves away. For example, you receive a simple request from a co-worker, "Wow you make such amazing treats! Can you make them for the office again for the next staff meeting?" Your Prostitute in the Light might initially remind you, *You don't really have to say yes to making snacks again if you don't want to.* The Body Being shares, *I'm tired and need a break this weekend.* You hear your Sacred Witness say, *You've done it the last three meetings and while it isn't an insane cost, you really don't have the time without it creating a lot of extra pressure on yourself.* You decide to say no.

Then a protective Part pipes up, *You can't do that! They like your treats and value you for them. If you tell them no, they might get mad and take it out on you somehow. Remember the last time you said no, your boss didn't let you share your thoughts during meetings after that.* Then a Part held in the Victim chimes in, *Yeah and you didn't understand what was happening and felt totally shunned by the rest of the team. It wasn't until you brought treats for the next meeting that everyone started listening to you again.* Cue a flashback of a wounded, young Part flooding your system with a time you felt wrongfully excluded because you said no to a request as a child. The Guardians of your Heart are drowned out by those Parts and you shift your answer to, *Okay I know my body needs a rest, but I have to do this; if I don't, they might get upset and take it out on me. Maybe I can say no next time.*

It is easy to see how subtly and quickly we negate our own inner guidance and default down to hidden shadow drivers and protective mechanisms held within the Victim and Child that cause us to abandon our true worth and inner guidance.

Healing Invitations of the Guardian of Our Worth and Integrity

This Guardian speaks in whispers, inviting us to be curious about the true motives of our actions. It asks questions such as:

- What is governing my different choices?
- Am I making a choice that matches my real values and my worth?
- In what ways am I resentful of my choice?

These questions can lead us into discovering hidden needs within our actions, thoughts, and behaviors. For example, you might find a wounded, young, or protective Part that is lost in scarcity and questioning your worth as a valuable team member, getting you to undervalue your time. Or maybe you discover a wounded Part that doesn't understand that you have the right to value your own needs as much as someone else's, and therefore will never allow you to express your own needs in connections, but rather constantly defer to the other's needs and desires. I'll share another example of what the Guardianship of the Prostitute can look like once you meet its dynamic-duo partner, the Saboteur.

ARCHETYPAL PATTERN OF THE SABOTEUR

After the Child, Victim, and the Prostitute activate within our system, the Saboteur is next to come online. The Saboteur is one of the most misunderstood patterns of them all. This is because we typically experience the Saboteur only through the common behaviors held in the survival level of this pattern, such as procrastination, avoidance, self-victimizing justifications, harsh inner critics, and shadow excuses for why we are not matching our actions with our inner guidance and whispers of our Heart Being. The Saboteur's main goal in the Light is to make sure we are ready to fully claim our choice and therefore hold the internal sense of empowerment it will take to be true to that choice. The Saboteur is like our final cumulative exam before we can graduate into claiming our innate power within. It asks you to do one final reflection of all the survival patterns to ensure you are ready to step into greater self-agency, responsibility, and empowerment.

Another reason the Saboteur is an often-misunderstood survival pattern is that it can show up when we are making choices that are not in alignment with our True Self and are disempowering us. My friend calls this "running down the wrong road faster." The Saboteur can sometimes act like the universal caution sign trying to get us to slow down and revisit our choices before we keep acting out of alignment with our True Self and guidance.

Here are a few key points about the Saboteur archetypal pattern:

- **The Saboteur is a signal we are close to empowerment.** When we catch ourselves having saboteur self-talk, such as: *I'll get to that tomorrow,* or *I don't know if I can really follow through on that goal,* it is a sign we are at a threshold moment in our own evolution. We are close to reclaiming more authority over ourselves and our life. This Guardian only comes forward in our system when we are ready to shift into a new stage of power, consciousness, and self-agency.
- **We often don't believe we are ready to leap.** The Guardian of Power is connected to our Heart and Soul Beings. It is connected into our divine timing and potential, things to which we are often not consciously connected. Therefore, it

has faith in our abilities beyond what our own Mental Being can access. For that reason, it often asks us to leap into the unknown. As you might recall, the Mental Being can only project into the future that which we have experienced in the past. It really doesn't like to try something new for which it doesn't have a solid point of reference. Because of this gap between what our Mental Being might feel we are capable of and what our Heart Being is calling us to believe about ourselves, we end up with a division between our mind and our heart. We then tend to stall out and self-abandon.

However, if we can see that behaviors that feel self-sabotaging are actually a sign that we are at the edges of our Mental Being's comfort zone, then we can remind ourselves that we actually *do* have the power to leap, we just can't always see it. This means our Heart knows we have the power within because it is an innate aspect already held within us. This Guardian is asking the Mental Being to pass the baton of our survival over to our Heart, which has a greater range of Knowing than the Mental Being does.

Gifts and Wounds of the Saboteur

Like the Victim, the gifts and wounds held by the Saboteur are often the same thing. The Saboteur's ways are initiatory: meant to prepare us for liberation from the protective survival levels of our Mental Being and open to the true protection of our Heart and Soul Beings. It is through the wounds of regret, disappointment, frustration, doubt, inner criticism, and fear that we open to the medicine and the antidotes of these wounds. Think back to my story with Diesel. It was the fear of regret that caught me, helping me realize I was sabotaging my own connection with Diesel due to hidden fears and pain that I wasn't aware of. So, the Saboteur's fear and potential regret served as a doorway into healing and empowerment. The Saboteur facilitated my access to the real desires coming from my Heart Being.

HEALING INVITATIONS OF THE SABOTEUR

The wounds of disempowered choices always leave us burdened by resentment and regret. This type of wound tends to compound itself with more shame, blame, and harsh self-judgements piling up. For example, when we know we heard the inner guidance of our Heart Being inviting us into a choice and we don't do it, we will have internal discomfort around that choice point. This isn't to shame us or to punish us. This is because we potentially self-victimized ourselves from a protective program. This Guardian wants us to shift gears, and fully tend to release those protective programs so that we can be in true empowerment and free to match our actions with the whispers of our Heart Being.

The Saboteur running in the Guardianship of our true Power, helps us take the time to reflect on three very important points so that we are ready to claim and walk with true empowerment:

- One—Are you ready for the impact that your committed powerful action will have on your world and the people in it?
- Two—Are you okay if it doesn't go well or as planned? Are you going to lose power if that happens?
- Three—Are you willing to hold your power and stay true to it, or are you going to abandon it if someone challenges you?

Through reviewing these three healing invitations, this Guardian is asking us to pause, pull back the curtain on our own system, and really see what has true authority, and therefore power, over our choices: fears of humiliation and the drive to belong, *or* our own inner guidance and knowing? This is why learning how to work with the

Prostitute and the Saboteur together will get you further than working with them individually. When we can affirm these three questions, we have the internal alignment our survival system needs to trust in our own Self. From that Self-Trust, we are ready to leap forward into choiceful action based on true empowerment without the high risk of self-abandonment as the consequences of our choices unfold.

CASE STUDY—CHOICE AND SELF-SABOTAGE

Let's take these concepts into an example from my own life. While you read through this example, I invite you to sense into and write down some of your thoughts. See if you can identify the themes or clues indicating the presence of the four survival archetypal patterns. Again, by learning how to identify their voices, you can get to know them better in yourself as well.

A few years back, my Body Being shared that it needed me to stop drinking coffee for a bit and switch to a specific herbal tea in the mornings. This sounds like a pretty simple shift. However, I found myself sabotaging my own guidance. I could stick with drinking the tea for a day or two, then I would back slide into drinking coffee again.

After about a week and a half of struggling to match my own guidance, I was curious what was happening. I briefly thought it was because of the caffeine, however that didn't feel true. I also had a lot of inner discouragement and harsh inner judgements going on. Such as, *Wow Michelle, this isn't that hard, why can't you just do this? You just need to make yourself do this!* When I found myself slipping into self-talk that broke my own inner Code of Conduct, I knew I was struggling with something more than just wanting caffeine again.

I decided to drop into a Healing Interview with the Part of me that kept picking coffee over tea. I started by calling forward the guidance of the Prostitute and Saboteur to help me sift deeper in my system. When I brought up an image of me drinking tea in the morning, I felt a ton of resistance in my chest. I found myself holding my breath and bracing in my arms. I saw an image of my husband, Henry. As I got curious about why I was seeing an image of Henry, I felt a flush of anxiety and embarrassment roll through me. Part of me worried he was going to judge me for switching from coffee to tea. Additionally, I also felt an ache in my heart. As I opened to the ache in my heart, I felt a gripping fear that somehow my change would cause Henry to abandon his love and connection with me, leaving me totally alone.

I knew this strong of a response had to be coming from a wounded Part, and I asked for permission to work with that Part directly. Once there, I saw a very young, wounded Part. She was the source of the fear that shifting from coffee to tea would cost me a connection with my husband. She didn't want to be alone, and she believed if I stopped drinking coffee, he would really disconnect from me and leave. I asked her to share more about what created this belief.

She showed me a scene in which she asked to change what she ate because her Body Being just didn't feel good with it. When she shared this need, she was met with what she viewed as anger, shame, and eventually what felt like removal of connection from her family because she was sent to her room and told she was ungrateful. The following mealtimes, she felt that her connections to her family were more distant. Plus, she had to continue eating the foods that didn't make her feel good because her request was not understood. Therefore, to protect her, her system spun off a Protector that said, *Never again will I go against what others eat,* for my own safety and connection.

Fast forward, this Protector is now trying to stop me from changing my food habits. Why? Not only because it wants me to match my family, but also because my husband makes us coffee every morning and brings it to me with a kiss. It is a beautiful ritual we share. It is also one of the beautiful ways he shares and shows his love and connection with me. It gives me a way to return my own love and connection as we drink our coffee together and connect before we separate and dive into the day. This little wounded Part of me could feel his discomfort with my change in needs, just like she did when I was little. From this reflection, I realized that I had not directly shared with Henry why I was saying no to his cup of coffee in the morning. Instead, I had just shifted our ritual and was silently making my own cup of tea. Each morning, he was still making me a cup of coffee and offering it to me, and each morning I said "no thank you" and fixed my own cup of tea. This young Part registered Henry's flash of confusion and even a newly forming hurt Part in him at my seeming rejection of his offering. It was also catching my own fears of communicating my new needs directly with Henry because of a possible rejection of my needs, like in the past.

From the Self-Work, I was able to find the Healing Invitations of the Heart Guardians and heal this young, wounded Part. After I completed those healings, I shared with Henry that I was switching up my morning routine and why. I apologized for only now communicating this shift with him. I felt guided to tell him I wasn't rejecting him with my switch; however, this was what my Body needed right now. Henry laughed it off, said it was no big deal, and started to resume what he was doing. However, he paused mid-turn. I could tell he was realizing and processing that somehow this little thing was a big deal. He realized Parts of him had felt confused and rejected. He turned back to me and gave me a kiss. The next morning as I came into the kitchen, he greeted me with a cup of tea, a smile, and delivered it with a kiss.

By following the Guardians of the Heart and staying connected to the Sacred Witness, both my own wounds and Henry's, which he didn't consciously realize were there, were witnessed, tended, healed, and repatterned.

BRINGING ALL FOUR GUARDIANS
OF THE HEART TOGETHER

Take a few moments to reflect on this story and what we've explored about the four survival patterns (and Heart Guardians) of the Child, Victim, Prostitute, and Saboteur. Consider journaling on the following questions:

- What themes of the different Guardians could you track?
- What voices of the wounded Parts did you notice coming through my self-talk?
- What Pillars of Connection was the Sacred Witness working to re-establish during this chat? (see pages 390 to 392 for a refresher)
- How does reestablishing those Pillars of Connection allow different healing invitations to come forward?

Here, I'll offer my own reflections from my own point of view to help you learn how to identify the different Guardians, Parts, and Healing Invitations of the Heart Being:

Saboteur:

- Inner Narrator: *I should be able to do this, but I can't, what's wrong with me . . .*
- Theme: *Can I hold true to my inner willpower, matching my actions with the choices I hear from my guidance? Or is there another need running in the background that believes my survival would be threatened by this change in my diet?*
- Healing Invitation: To drop into a deeper reflection as to what is happening behind the scenes and what is causing my system to lose Willingness. Therefore, discovering what Parts are kicking me out of Connection and back into the Mental Being's ways of managing choice, instead of letting the Heart Being lead

- Pillars of Connection—re-establishing Trust and Respect: Do the repair within myself and recommit to show up for Self-Work with self-love, matching my loving Code of Conduct, then the system feels that I will have regard for myself

Prostitute:
- Inner Narrator: Willing to compromise my needs to match the wishes or beliefs of another
- Theme: Integrity and noticing when I was losing the ability to match my actions with my inner Code of Conduct, another survival need was overriding my own inner alignment
- Healing Invitation: To understand what hidden survival needs were causing me to act out of alignment with my inner guidance and knowing
- Pillar of Connection—Choice and Willingness: understanding and respecting that there is a reason my system is saying No, and a desire to seek understanding instead of bullying the system into a Yes

Victim:
- Inner Narrator: *You will be left if you stay with your own guidance.* Even a shadowy acknowledgement, *you are hurting someone else with your choice*
- Theme: Feeling the burden of self-victimization and removal of true choice for aligned action
- Healing Invitation: To explore the truth of what has control over my true choice and asking if that protective mechanism still holds true for me today
- Pillar of Connection—Connection: I am willing to sense, see, hear, and know what the different needs are in my system and the other's; I have a willingness to tend and be in dialogue with them

Child:

- Inner Narrator: *I'm helpless and have no real power or voice if I want to belong.*
- Theme: Powerlessness, feeling at the whim of others' systems
- Healing Invitation: To open to and reconnect with the exiled, wounded Part of me so they can be tended and therefore allow the *whole* system to change, rewire, and reestablish your Inner Bridge of Connection
- Pillar of Connection—Purpose and Values: Seeing the adaptations that were created and why, so I can tend the exiled Part and a new way of Being can come forward

In the above scenario, you can see that without allowing all Four Guardians of the Heart to help walk us through the different healing invitations, the hidden survival needs of protective and wounded Parts would continue to bully the whole system into believing it was weak or dig itself deeper into helplessness. Thus, I would have remained totally blocked from any healing messages from my system as to why it was fighting back on the food change and how to support it releasing that stance.

When we become more conscious about spotting the themes, language, and metaphors of the Guardians of the Heart, we can help the Mental Being and the protective fears within it naturally release blocking the Heart and Soul Beings' support and grant us more access to our True Self and inner wisdom.

CHAPTER PRACTICES

It's your turn to get to know and explore your last two Guardians of the Heart. There are two practices: the first helps you get to know how your personal Guardians of the Heart might talk with you so you can identify when you are working from a wounded or protective mechanism that is cutting you off from hearing or matching your true guidance. The second is a guided journey to meet all Four Guardians of the Heart and experience what it can be like to consciously work with them as helpful messengers instead of the Four Horsemen of the Apocalypse.

Healing Tips: Your system is dynamic and changes to match what you are being asked to interact with at any given moment. So just like how your access to the pillars in the Bridge of Connection change and shift, so does the level in which your system allows these Guardians to function as healing agents within your system. They can be overrun by shadow survival responses and Parts drowning out their guidance. They can also be running with no disruptions to their connections, sharing with you their true Healing Invitations and asking you to sense, see, hear, and know what needs to be tended within your system so that you can be in connection with your True Self.

Also remember, these patterns aren't here to make your life a living hell or because you are weak and running in survival mode. They are attempting to bring forward messages we need to address so we can shift from surviving into living fully in alignment with our True Self. They are asking us to see if our actions are in connection with our fifth pillar of connection—Purpose and Values—therefore helping us be in connection with our true power.

PRACTICE 1: HOW DO MY GUARDIANS TALK WITH ME?

I would love to invite you to explore a scenario in your life similar to mine, where you found yourself in a collision, a tug-of-war within your system, between following your guidance and how you're actually acting. The easiest way to find an inner war scenario is to think of when you have found yourself making statements like:

- Saboteur—"I am always self-sabotaging . . ."
- Prostitute—"If I don't do this, then it will cost me . . ."
- Victim—"Why does this always happen to me . . ."
- Child—"Ugh, I don't want to be the one responsible for . . ."

Once you have a scenario you would like to review, reflect in the following way on that scene via a Healing Interview with that memory, seeking insights and guidance using the same reflection exercise I had you do with my story.

See if you can identify the different Guardians trying to help you recognize that a hidden need within your system was causing warring agendas and what healing invitations might have possibly been trying to help support you to illuminate those needs.

- What Inner Narrator voices of the wounded Parts do you notice coming through the self-talk?
- What themes of the four Guardians could you track?
- What healing invitations of the Sacred Witness and your Heart Being are coming forward?
- What Pillars of Connection might the Sacred Witness be working with the Guardians to try and re-establish access to so you can work with your system differently?

PRACTICE 2: GUIDED JOURNEY—
MEETING THE FOUR GUARDIANS OF THE HEART

Let's directly meet the Four Guardians from the point of view of your Heart through a guided journey.

Check in with your system and when you are ready bring your awareness to your heart center.

Approaching the Heart center (the nucleus of you).
Imagine that as you approach your heart center, you notice that four guardians are protecting it.

Each of these guardians have a specific job and point of view:

Up first, you meet the Guardian of Innocence.
It is here to help protect and support your inner innocence, wonder, and ability to see beyond the mundane world. This Guardian helps you to see, hear, and interact with *all* the Beings and Souls you walk with daily, in both the seen and unseen worlds. This aspect of you knows the truth that animal, plant, nature Beings all have Souls and voices. It can help you remember to dance with the wind and play with the rain. It holds wisdom outside of knowledge and isn't bound by logic and reason. It is wild, untamed, and unbridled. It also holds a desire to connect, be loved, and give love in a beautiful, innocent way.

- Ask this Guardian now, What would it like to help you remember?
- Is there a gift or frequency this Guardian would like to give you now so that you can continue to explore and remember the gifts of your Inner Child?

Next, you meet the Guardian of Truth and Choice.
As you continue walking forward on the path toward your Heart

center, you meet the Guardian of Truth and Choice. This guardian is a sacred keeper of your Heart Being. It helps you see when something is out of balance, hurting, or needs to be tended. It helps you see through past limiting beliefs to the Truth of What Is. In addition to bringing your attention to tending what is in pain or out of alignment, it helps you see where you do have choices. It helps you realize that even in moments of pain or suffering you can choose *how* you want to receive support, how you want to react, and what choices to make in alignment with your Heart and Soul Beings, instead of which ones are more in alignment with wounded Parts cut off from your Heart. This Guardian is there to support you and help you support others when in need. It is there to guide you into remembering the greatest superpower you have—your free will and the ability to exercise it as a Being of Co-Creation.

- Ask this Guardian now what it would like to help you remember?
- Is there a gift or frequency this Guardian would like to give you now so that you can continue to explore and remember the wisdom of the Victim?

Next, you meet the Guardian of Worth and Integrity.

You walk forward on the path to meet the next guardian of your Heart—the Guardian of your Worth and Integrity. This Guardian knows the amazing gifts, talents, and treasures of your True Self. It knows the remarkable light within you and the gifts you have come here to offer the world. It knows and guards the love you have for yourself and others. This Guardian also holds within it your inner Code of Conduct—a value system that supports you in every choice you make and in how you show up for yourself and others. The values and their guided actions run from everyday choices to the larger Soul's values. It supports your willingness to follow your Heart's whispers and guidance.

This Guardian is there to help you remember your own innate worth and the essential worth of the Beings around you. It reminds you when you are making choices out of shadow scarcity, comparison, and a need to control because of fears and worries. It helps you step into the Dance of Connection from a place of love and respect for yourself and the Soul with whom you are dancing. It holds guidance for having healthy boundaries and making healthy compromises. It helps you remember that your true nature is loving, strong, and deeply honoring of self and others.

- Ask this guardian now, what it would like to help you remember?
- Is there a gift or frequency this Guardian would like to give you now so that you can continue to explore and remember the wisdom of the Prostitute?

Next, you meet the Guardian of Power.
You come to the end of the path and are right next to the doorway into your sacred Heart center. There you meet the final Guardian. This Guardian is smiling at you, welcoming you to sit down with it next to your Heart's doorway. Here, you may feel a sense of excitement and nervousness. The eyes of this Guardian bring forward a sense of great wisdom and love for you. This is the Guardian of your Power, strength, will, and conviction. This is the Guardian that helps you feel absolutely in alignment with your own inner guidance and wisdom, such that nothing can take that away from you. This Guardian looks back at the others and smiles. It invites you to do the same. It asks you a question: *Are you willing to walk on a path that is just yours?*
Then it shares the following:

> *This is a path that some will understand and some will not.*
> *If you step into connection with your Heart Being, it will give*
> *you guidance on what is true for you and ultimately what*
> *is universal truth. Sometimes that will match others and*

284

sometimes what you find, learn, and remember within will go against their beliefs. When that happens, people may not understand you. They may try to sway you to go back on the truths your Heart shared. They may be frightened and threatened by it. If you go forward, there is no way to unhear, unsee, or unlearn the truths you find within. You might be asked to release your attachments to a habit or relationship, or an old way of being that once brought comfort but is no longer part of your path moving forward. You might be asked to make a totally illogical choice for which you cannot see the outcome or chances of success. You will be asked to make choices based on faith in yourself and your guidance.

Next, it asks you: *What do you need to help you open that door and step into the sacred place of your Heart and open to its guidance?* The guardian smiles at you and is truly giving you an opportunity to look within and look back at the other Guardians for support and guidance.

If there is a specific question or prayer you have for this Guardian, bring that forward now or:

- Ask this guardian now, what it would like to help you remember?
- Is there a gift or frequency this Guardian would like to give you now so that you can continue to explore and remember the wisdom of the Saboteur?

Connecting with your Heart Being.

Now, if you are ready, turn toward the doorway of your inner Heart center.

Take a moment and see what you are being guided to do at this point. There is no right or wrong—if you are being guided to stay with the Guardians and continue to work with them, beautiful, that is exactly what your system needs. If you are being guided to step over the threshold into the sacred place of your Heart, beautiful as well.

Either way, take a few moments and be with your Heart Being, listen to it, explore it, see what sensations, thoughts, and messages are there within and around it.

Closing

Thank your whole system for its willingness to step into direct connection with your Heart Being and its Guardians.

If it feels good, let your system know that you want to continue to work with them, learn from them, and ultimately commune more and more with your amazing Heart Being and its Guardians. If it feels good, plan right now for when you are going to come back and be with them in a more intentional and dedicated way like this.

Take three cycles of breath to bring yourself fully back in the present moment and time.

Gently wiggle your fingers and toes and softly open your eyes.

Before dropping back into the rhythm of your day, I invite you to record a few highlights and insights you gained during this journey so you have them to revisit and build off in the future.

When you learn how to identify the main themes and Healing Invitations of your Heart's Guardians, you gain confidence in your ability to identify if you are running your actions and thoughts in alignment with the guidance of your Heart Being or in alignment with your survival and trauma adaptations and Parts.

The more you can maintain a conscious connection with these Four Guardians of the Heart, the more connection you will be able to maintain between your system and your Heart Being. This connection allows you to access the Sacred Witness within as a constant companion.

Now that you journeyed through awakening and befriending the Heart Being, our final stop on the journey of cultivating the Sacred

Witness within is to explore and awaken to the realm of your Soul Being. Here, we'll dive into the gifts of the Soul Being: Clean Compassion, Sight, Blessing, and Gratitude in our everyday lives.

Section Five
Awakening and Befriending the Soul Being

Overview

> *"One day I stopped, listened and heard*
> *a beautiful sound ... my soul."*
>
> —UNKNOWN

We are entering the final stage of our journey and pulling all the aspects of you together—your Body, Mental, and Heart Beings as a way to open and connect more deeply with the Sacred Witness energy within you via your Soul Being.

By now you have discovered that the Sacred Witness is not an outside form or Being separate from you. It IS you! It is an innate healing wisdom held within your Soul Being, which is also present within your Heart, Mind, and Body Beings.

Our Soul Being is constantly available to support and guide us. The trick is to help our whole system be willing to slow down and open to the beautiful sound of our Soul. The Soul whispers words of support, love, inspiration, and guidance. The Sacred Witness is so often our Soul's messenger, letting us know that something is cutting us off from our own inner Bridge of Connection.

Some people hear the word *Soul* and think it is something separate from them, out there in some distant part of the universe. Unfortunately, what the Soul actually is can be distorted by religious and dogmatic beliefs and teachings. I believe the Soul has no religion. It has no allegiance to a particular faith or view of what God is.

From my own personal felt sense and witnessing of the Soul Being, I understand the Soul as something very different from what most religions define it to be. I witness the Soul as an active part of us. The Soul is an integral part of what makes us, well, *us*. Each Beings' Soul has its own unique frequency, traits, and gifts. The Soul Being is the part of us not bound by the labels or filters of our ego-self, which is often taught to desperately cling to outside validation for a sense of worthiness. The Soul Being is the part of us that knows our intrinsic worth. Our Soul understands our capacity to give and receive love. It can freely give and accept compassion for our faults and suffering. It also holds loving and empowering boundaries with and for ourselves and others.

Our Soul Being can transcend the limits of our personal consciousness or ego mind and connect us to the wisdom and knowledge of the collective, the inner wisdom we have accumulated from *all* our experiences beyond this lifetime, and allows us to access the cosmic mind. Our Soul also links us to the Cosmic Heart and the limitless radical love and support that comes from that well.

BIG PICTURE CHECK-IN

In this final section on the Soul Being, we come to the final two stages of our road map for cultivating the Sacred Witness within.

I'd like to give you a quick recap of the healing skills you have developed so far on your journey as we awakened and befriended our Body, Mental, and Heart Beings:

- Stages 1 through 4: *Cultivating the Observer Self.* You're developing awareness around when Parts of you or another are needing something and recognizing that these wounded Parts might not know how to ask for help directly. You understand that when you are willing to Witness the wounded Part, a new way of being with yourself naturally emerges from the process of Sacred Witnessing, which is more in alignment with who you truly are.

- Stage 5: *Cultivating non-dual thinking and the ability to perceive beyond our attachments.* You have cultivated the ability to bring curiosity to often dueling Parts of you lost in their different trauma and survival adaptations, and can release yourself from shame and blame. You know that ultimately trauma or survival responses and adaptations are born from moments when the system was trying the best it could to survive, protect, and give itself a sense of control in the midst of no control or voice.

- Stages 6 and 7: *Cultivating the ability to understand and work with our own emotions and wounds in deep connection with our Heart.* You can work with the Four Guardians of the Heart to witness the survival stories and programs present within you, honor how they came to be there, and seek the Sacred Witness's point of view via Healing Invitations. This point of view provides you with options you might not have had access to before.

In this last section, we will look at the final two stages:

- Cultivating daily connections with the Medicines of the Soul that help us continue to grow and connect with the Sacred Witness within

- Realizing that the Sacred, the Divine, is within us and available to us all the time if we are willing to open

In this last section, we will be exploring how awakening and befriending the Soul Being is an integral aspect of embodying the key skill sets and "medicines" of the Sacred Witness. Over the next three chapters, we will explore:

- The Sacred Medicines of the Soul Being and how we integrate these medicines into our daily life

- How to access and offer other key Sacred Medicines of the

Soul—Clean Compassion, Gratitude, and the willingness to Bless our lives

- How to integrate all that you've gathered in our journey together so you can walk with the medicines of the Sacred Witness for the rest of your life

REMINDERS

As we enter the last stage of the journey, don't forget to bring the connections you have formed with your Body, Mind, and Heart Beings with you. We want to bring together all the aspects of you—Body, Mind, Heart, and now Soul—as they merge into the beautiful tapestry of you.

Let's dive into the final section, starting with awakening and walking with the Medicines of the Soul.

Chapter Thirteen

*Awakening the Sacred Medicines
of the Soul Being*

Now that you have a relationship with the Four Main Guardians of the Heart, it is time to step directly into exploring and cultivating the gifts and Sacred Medicines of the Soul Being. The medicines you can access through deeper connection with your Soul Being are an integral part of bringing the Sacred Witness teachings together as an active daily companion and support for yourself and others.

The idea of calling the gifts of our Soul Being our *Sacred Medicines* originally came from my shamanic trainings, based on the concept I shared when we talked about the healing invitations of the Victim— that the medicine we need to support ourselves is found within the wound itself. The healing Medicines of the Sacred Witness are always available to us because the Soul Being is a true part of us. We carry its healing graces, or Sacred Medicines, within ourselves at all times. The healing medicines of the Sacred Witness are not outside of us or something to which we need to be granted access from an outside source. We *all* hold the power the Sacred Medicines of Soul needed to be both our own Sacred Witness and to invoke the Sacred Witness in others.

Just as it did with the Guardians of our Heart, the Mental Being struggles at a survival level when we dare to claim our innate power and allow ourselves to embody the power of our Soul Being. The teachings I shared throughout this book have paved the way for our Mental Being's willingness to constellate a new way of partnering and connecting with the Sacred Medicine of the Soul Being in a liberating and clean way, free from the survival and trauma adaptations we so often filter our Soul's guidance through. But before we go any further, let's explore the main strategies the Mental Being employs to bypass our intentions to fully partner with the Soul Being.

OVERCOMING THE SEPARATION OF OUR SPIRITUAL SELF AND OUR DAILY SELF

At this stage of the journey, I always pause and caution my clients that they are reaching a critical tipping point. In the journey of awakening to the Sacred Witness within, we eventually hit a point where our system no longer wants to separate our "spiritual self" and our "daily self." This point emerges once we have cultivated enough trust and faith in our Inner Bridge of Connection. Once we hit this critical mass, we can feel, hear, and sense our Soul, present and whispering to us all the time. We have literally awakened the different healing medicines of the Soul Being. The Soul Being, the Sacred Witness, and the core medicines they offer us and others shift from being a comforting idea to being very real, tangible, and practical guidance. The Soul and all of its Sacred Medicines are designed to support *us in* our daily life. The Mental Being can no longer deny that these aspects of us are always present and available from within, just waiting for us to engage with them.

At this point, however, the Mental Being can set up some tricky protective stories in an attempt to by-pass our true connection with our Soul Being and its medicines because it is nervous about whether or not the Soul can truly meet our survival and personal needs and wants. Because of this, it is totally natural for the Mental Being to make one last ditch effort to by-pass true Soul Being connection. It does this by creating the illusion of separation between our perception of our daily self and our perception of our Soul Being.

Here are a few top ways our protective Parts try to by-pass

integrating our Self-Work (which you can easily call *Soul-Work* now) into our everyday life experience as a companion, which separates us from the healing power of the Sacred Witness within.

This Soul Being bypass can happen when Part of us is holding ourselves to the standard of spirituality shown in movies; where the heavens part, a singular moment creates a 180-degree shift in your life, and you now walk through life completely tuned in as an enlightened Being, perfectly and forever. While that version of Soul connection would be awesome (and if it happens for you, great), that isn't typically how it looks or feels. The reality of walking with our Soul Being as an active companion, instead of this weird separate balloon thing that just follows us around, is actually much subtler than that.

Another way our Mental Being tries to bypass the Soul Being is when a protective Part convinces us we have done all the mental work to understand the Medicine of the Sacred Witness and thus, declares you "enlightened." This protector convinces us we no longer need to stay in an active process of self-reflection and self-healing. I call this the "one-and-done weekend retreat trap," a favorite tactic of the Saboteur-in-shadow testing to see if you are willing to stay committed to true empowerment.

Further, we may have a Part holding the story that these two aspects of us—the spiritual self and earthly self—are too far apart; thus, it is better to keep them separate. This protector recognizes the beautiful moments of oneness, feeling the wholeness within ourselves, and glimpses of awakening to a different plane of consciousness in meditations as a real thing; *but*, it also sees that we crash land back into the harsh daily life of survival and living after those moments. When this happens, we feel the grit of the two extremes. Our Mental Being struggles to know how to bridge the two worlds and doubts that they even should be connected.

So, we leave our connection to our Soul Being—and therefore the Sacred Witness—to our time on the meditation cushion, on a spiritual retreat, and so on, not even trying to bring any of the insights we find in our Soul's messages into our daily life because it feels like too big of a divide. This protective response says, "I have my spiritual hat that I wear when I'm up to spiritual things, and then I have my daily life hat that I swap out for all the other times."

Another Mental Being trap that keeps us from walking with the Soul Being and Sacred Witness is getting addicted to the spiritual "high." This protective mechanism believes the union with their Soul is truly outside of themselves. When we fall into this trap, we are on a constant search for the ecstasy of union, and its accompanying high, with Spirit or the Universe, *outside of ourselves.* We do that massive spiritual by-pass straight into "all is one and therefore my life is the illusion." In this trap, we dishonor our own inner power, our physical life, and the reason for incarnating in general. We compel ourselves into a constant drive and need to keep searching for the feelings of union through an Outer Bridge of Connection instead of believing in our own Inner Bridge of Connection.

Lastly, a common Mental Being trap comes in comparison. This protective Part believes we will never have the connection with our Soul Being that others have or how we want it to be. The thought of not having that connection is deeply wrought with fear of disappointment and shame. In order to protect our personal Heart from that potential separation or future abandonment, our protective Parts numb our desire to continue and compel us to abandon any further connections and whispers of our Soul Being coming through. This by-pass holds us at the materialistic-stuff version of spirituality because it is not willing to risk the vulnerability that comes with a deep opening to our Soul.

Bridging the Separation: Cultivating
Your Personal Holy Trinity

To avoid falling into one of these by-passing traps, I would like to offer a different path. My offering is to take the healing tool box we have developed together as a foundation for continued expansion into your own inner workings. This means making a commitment to walk with our Self-Work or Soul Work as our sacred companion, continually addressing our fears, protective belief systems, and wounded Parts as they pop up in our daily life, which they inevitably will, *and* continually cultivating the Medicines of the Soul.

To fully embody the Sacred Witness, we need to walk with our Soul Being *and* our personal everyday Self as equal companions. I call this activating your own personal Holy Trinity within. Our personal Holy Trinity honors the three main aspects of us for their unique points of view, roles, and gifts.

The first aspect of the Trinity is your Personal Self, the "you" in this incarnation. This is the aspect of your Being here in this Earthly plane, in a body, in a limited life cycle. This part of your Holy Trinity honors your separate sense of Self from the whole, what some might call your *ego*. This aspect of you comes with its own personal sense of identity, needs, gifts, thoughts, desires, and challenges.

The second aspect of the Trinity is your Soul Self, which is the "immortal" you. This aspect of you extends beyond the personal Self. The Soul Being holds within it experiences from different incarnation cycles, both here on Earth and other planes of existence. This part of you can also access the impersonal essences and traits that are also "you" and are available to all Beings—such as the Sacred Witness.

The third aspect of the Trinity is The Divine, which is the "you" that is not separate from the whole—you are a part of it and it is a part of you. This aspect acknowledges that there is something beyond the personal and immortal versions of you, one that encompasses the larger organic creation of All That Is, of which you are a part.

Together, these aspects create the Law of Three—the Law of bridging together two seemingly opposite and conflicting points of view with the support of a third point of view that allows for creation and manifestation of union and resolution. Together, these three aspects of you create the pathways you need to fully activate non-dual thinking and free your Mental Being from struggling with what could be conflicting stances.

Sometimes it feels like our personal Self and our Soul Being are waring forces. The Soul is free from earthly limits and survival needs. The personal Self, which we might call the *ego*, is bound by the rules of Earth, life and death cycles, and the need to survive by eating, drinking, caring for its bodily needs, and so on. The Soul drives us toward connection and to seek union with the greater parts of ourselves. The Ego drives us to meet our basic needs to survive and thrive within the Earthly plane.

Which one wins? A third aspect comes in to support us—the Divine—the cosmic heart and intelligence that works outside the viewpoint of the other two, in an impersonal realm. The Divine offers all aspects of us a container big enough to hold the potentially warring perspectives together in a new form—the form that knows it can simultaneously honor and be all things. We can thrive within our lives *and* be in deep union with our Soul and the Beings around us. We don't have to deprive the human side to know the Soul and Divine sides, and we don't only tend to the human side and dishonor the Soul and Divine aspects of ourselves.

SEEING THE MEDICINE WITHIN

Ultimately, this journey is about embodying the Sacred Witness energy as a core aspect of who you truly be. The Sacred Witness is not a separate aspect of us that we can only call on when we are struggling. Instead, it wants to be a daily companion, ever available to support us in all walks of our life. When we can walk with our Soul Being as an integral companion, we gain greater access to the full range of medicines held within ourselves as a Sacred Witness.

Throughout our journey together, we've been cultivating the Sacred Medicines of the Soul. One Sacred Medicine, and core skill of the Sacred Witness, we've been developing is the Medicine of Sight and Vision. In working with the Body Being, we began to develop the Observer Self—the ability to perceive what is happening within our Body Being as a Sacred Messenger. You began to perceive your own physical system with the "eyes" of the Sacred Witness, releasing your attachments to perceiving your somatic sensations from the sole perception of your Mental Being protectors or wounded Parts.

The Medicine of Sight and Vision builds on our Observer Self capacity, bringing it into an expanded willingness to guide us through all aspects of our lives.

The Medicine of Sight and Vision is the ability to *cleanly perceive or see,* with both our human senses *and* our Soul's senses. When we walk with Sight, we can interact with all the worlds and dimensions, the seen and unseen, the outer world and our inner world, the Parts of us that are lost, and the Soul traits and gifts in us, waiting to be called forward. The Medicine of Sight and Vision allows us to see through illusions of separateness, suffering, pain, and dualistic thinking and allows us to envision something new.

With this Sacred Medicine, we begin to *see* beyond the filters of survival and trauma adaptation and actually perceive and interact with what is present. Sacred Sight is something we can utilize both within and outside of ourselves. When we open to the visionary nature of the Sacred Medicine of Sight, which is our ability to see through the eyes of the Sacred Witness, we can release our attachments to the filters that create a skewed perspective of Self, Others? and/or this world. When we walk with Sight—we have the powerful ability to "see" the projections of the false selves and perceive what is truly present and trying to come forward.

The Medicine of Sight is the foundation from which you begin to open to, develop, and cultivate other Medicines of the Soul, which I will describe briefly here. The Medicine of Understanding, for example, helps us identify needs within ourselves or another and release our own thinking around how to best tend those needs. This medicine instead opens us to *guidance* on what wants to come forward to tend those needs. When we seek understanding from the Soul Being level, we are willing to see all the types of messengers our system might use—such as Body Being sensations and postures, Mental Being protective patterns and parts, and the Heart Being's invitations to lean into the discomfort and tend, instead of numbing or turning away.

Another Sacred Medicine of the Soul is Forgiveness. This medicine allows us to see when we are trapped in webs of shame, blame, wanting something to be different than what it is or was, or wanting something or someone to pay a price for harm that was inflicted. We can see where and when we are losing energy to past choices and judgments. The Medicine of Forgiveness allows us to bring our conscious choice to healing, forgiving, and tending the wounded parts so we can release the stranglehold the past has on our present and future.

Further, the Sacred Medicine of Courage helps us hear the whispers of the Soul, guiding us toward committed correct action that helps us break free from old ways of being, thoughts, actions, behaviors, habits, and postures that are no longer serving. Courage helps our Mental Being release the reins of shadow fears and step into the unknown, willingly trusting the guidance and support of our Heart and Soul Beings.

The last Sacred Medicine we'll explore here is the Medicine of Healing, through which we can call forward the laws of wholeness, transmutation, balance, alignment, and transformation. When we are activating the Medicine of Healing, we embrace our Wholeness. The Sacred Witness energy allows us to perceive from a different point of view that honors the wound *and* calls forward the medicine within the wound.

As you can tell, the Sacred Medicines held within our Soul Being are vast and many. All of them begin to open to us through the foundational Medicine of Sight. In the next chapter, we'll explore three more Medicines essential to deeply connecting with the Sacred Witness within—Compassion, Gratitude, and Blessing. Let's first pause and reflect on our relationship to our **Soul Being and the Medicine of Sacred Sight.**

CHAPTER PRACTICES

Allowing the Soul Being and Sacred Witness energy to be with us at all times helps to bridge the potential separations our protective mechanisms have created. When we activate our own Holy Trinity within—allowing our personal Self, our Soul, and the Divine to all be present within us—the fear that somehow a part of us will be harmed or abandoned once we connect to our Soul Being begins to fade, because we are honoring all aspects of us. We can trust that we can hold the Parts of us that are scared of our Soul and the Divine in a way that accepts them instead of shames them. We can also shift gears from needing to have something wrong in order to open to our guidance of our Soul and instead realize we can be in connection with all aspects of us all the time, during the amazing times and times of loss or confusion.

The two practices for this section are designed to invite you to explore your Mental Being's willingness to open even more to trusting your connection to your own personal Holy Trinity within and allowing your Soul and the Divine to be more a part of your personal Self. The first practice is a series of reflection prompts designed to help you begin a dialogue with your system on how it feels about opening more to your Soul's presence. The second is a practice that helps you engage with, interact and expand the Observer Self to include the Soul's Senses—the Medicine of Sight.

PRACTICE 1: HOW DO I FEEL TOWARD MY SOUL BEING?

Let's first start with an exploration and pulse check on your system's overall current relationship and immediate associations with the basic idea of the Soul Being and how it can support you as a daily companion.

Check-In—Take a moment to complete a short Check-In and Body Scan to give yourself a baseline of what your current system feels like. This allows you greater access to the Body and Mental Beings' messages when and if something shifts or changes, sensation- and thought-wise, during the contemplation practice.

Reflection Questions:

General Ideas:

- When you think of the idea of your Soul, what comes to mind?
- What does it mean to you?

Body Being:

- Where do you feel your Soul Being in relationship to "you," in or around your body?
- How does your Body Being feel about the idea of connecting deeper with your Soul Being?

Mental Being:

- What do Parts of your Mental Being think about the idea of allowing your Soul Being to guide how you perceive your inner and outer worlds?
- Do any Parts of you have concerns or worries about allowing your Soul Being to have an equal voice in your system? If so, explore what might be behind those fears?

Heart Being:

- How do the Four Guardians of your Heart Being feel about allowing more access to the perceptions and guidance of your Soul Being?
  - o Child
  - o Victim
  - o Prostitute
  - o Saboteur

PRACTICE 2: EXPANDING THE OBSERVER SELF WITH THE MEDICINE OF SIGHT: OPENING TO YOUR SOUL'S SENSES

Now that you have had the opportunity to explore how your system feels toward the Soul Being, this practice helps you open to exploring *how* your Soul Being talks with you and how you experience it.

*Please note this practice is not a one-and-done. By repeating versions of this practice throughout your day in different circumstances, you will cultivate a closer and more active connection with the Medicine of Sight, allowing you to Witness yourself across the three Levels of you—your Holy Trinity—in your daily life.

Also, please call forward the Gift of Imagination you developed in the last section with the Child to be with you during this practice. You truly might not know or have a vision of your Soul Being's point of view. Or, if you have experienced sensing via the Soul Being before, maybe a new or expanded way of working with Sight might want to come forward now. Give your Mental Being permission to allow your Heart and Soul Beings to take the lead and let you sense, see, hear, feel, and know from a new point of view, from your Soul.

Step One: Body Being Check-In: Allow yourself to settle into this moment. Gather a baseline of your five physical senses:

- What can I see in this moment?
- What can I hear in this moment?
- What can I taste in this moment?
- What can I smell in this moment?
- What can I feel interacting with my body at this moment?

Step Two: Call forward the Soul Medicine of Sight: Now, invite your field to bring in the Medicine of Sight so you can do the same check-in again, but from this Soul Sight perspective, allowing you to access the senses of your Soul Being.

Step Three: Soul Senses Check-In via the Soul Senses: First, ask your human senses to soften and release their very concrete way of interacting with the world around you. Take a few breaths and invite your human senses to step back, allowing the Soul's senses to come to the forefront.

Ask your Soul's senses to share their point of view:

- What can I see in this moment if I soften my human eyes and open to my Soul's eyes?
- What can I hear in this moment if I soften my human ears and open to my Soul's ears and hearing?
- What can I taste in this moment if I soften my human sense of taste and open to my Soul's sense of taste?
- What can I smell in this moment if I soften my human sense of smell and open to my Soul's sense of smell?
- What can I feel and sense if I soften my physical felt sense and open to my Soul's felt sense?

Step Four: Soul-Led Sight: Next, ask your Soul Being to help bring your awareness to what else is present. What are you noticing and sensing in this moment? *It might be a slight flutter in your chest or gut. It might be coming through as a sense of fear and apprehensions with protector stories such as "what if I can't connect" or "what if I can't control it, am I safe . . ." It might be coming into deep warmth, an inner sense of peace, and being held within your field. You might be greeting yourself with open arms or a sensation of love. You might be seeing the Soul of the Beings around you if you are looking at a beloved companion animal, child, tree, or partner.*

Whatever is coming forward is beautiful and perfect for you at this time.

Step Five: Closing: At this point, we are not asking our system to fully disconnect from our meditative state of being open and available for insights and guidance. However, we do not want to walk around our daily life in a full-blown channel state either. I like to ask my Heart and Soul to adjust the level of my Soul Senses or Sight to match what is optimal for me as I move into the next cycle or aspect of my day. That way I remain open to the Sacred Medicines available and with me throughout the day.

I often close with a blessing such as:

> *I ask to sense, feel, see, hear, and know that all aspects of me are present at this time in whatever level is optimal for me. I ask my energy to come home, home into my Body and home into my Heart. I ask for my thoughts to be in alignment with my True Self and remember that they are part of the cosmic mind as well. I welcome the support of my senses—body and soul—to be with me, as well as my Wise One Team, as I move throughout the day. And, so it is.*

Healing Tip: Remember how I encouraged you to not get disappointed if you have a hard time learning the language of somatics when you dialogue with the messages of your Body Being? Opening to the Medicines of the Soul Being follow the same guidance. Your Body and Heart Beings already have these pathways within them. They have most likely been lying dormant or severed from your own conscious connection by protective Parts of your Mental Being (driven to help you survive, gain belonging, and have a sense of control). Therefore, take your time with this practice and try not to get discouraged if it feels like radio silence from your Soul Being at first. You most likely have a Protector that is nervous about re-establishing your conscious awareness of how your Soul perceives the world.

Deepening the Practice: As you work with this new expansion to your Check-In, you might want to add in the mantra—"Soften and Open." This mantra, mixed with your natural breath cycle, can invite your system to remember and open your awareness to both the seen and unseen worlds. Remember, the intention of accessing the Soul's perspectives and insights isn't about leaving your body so that you can experience your Soul. Your Soul is already within you!

Instead, this practice is about connecting your personal Holy Trinity within—you, your soul, and the Divine. The only place you can directly interact with all aspects of Self is within you, through your Body and Heart. Using the mantra "Soften and Open" invites your Mental Being to trust in your ability to include the expansion of *all* your senses while staying connected to the Now-moment.

Also remember, this isn't about purifying yourself to become worthy of this connection. That isn't necessary; you are always worthy of connecting with your Soul and the Divine: period. It is more about the Parts of you that are scared, nervous, and over attached to the idea of the Soul and the Divine as unattainable, instead of integral aspects of you, which are always within you. Plus, it isn't about losing yourself and dissolving your ego structure; they are essential aspects of *you*. True embodiment of the Body, Mind, Heart, and Soul is allowing and honoring *all* aspects of you.

In the next chapter, we'll dive deeper into three more core Medicines of the Sacred Witness—the Medicines of Compassion, Gratitude, and Blessing—and how to bring them into our daily lives. We'll explore key skills and practices that will help you fully awaken and befriend your Soul Being, thus opening to the Sacred Witness within.

Chapter Fourteen

Cultivating Clean Compassion

In this chapter, we are going to explore one of the Medicines of the Soul that I believe is an absolute key skill in embodying the Sacred Witness: the ability to walk with Clean Compassion. I have waited until this point in your journey to present the concept of Clean Compassion for a reason. If I had brought forward the Soul's level of compassion at the beginning of our journey, your Mental Being and its host of protectors would have really struggled to believe there was a "clean" way to bring compassion forward as a committed action instead of a "nice" idea or thought. As you will learn in this chapter, *compassion* is a verb, not a noun.

As a starting point, let's revisit what I shared about Clean Compassion in the beginning of the book.

> The Sacred Witness has what I like to call Clean Compassion. They are able to allow the other to be themselves without trying to consciously or subconsciously rescue, take on, over-empathize, and/or project their own feelings onto the other (or that which they are witnessing). They are able to simply be with and honor the other's truths while holding their own internal and external personal boundaries. They are deeply committed to their own Self-Work and to bringing awareness to any Parts of them that might awaken while in the act of Sacred Witnessing, so they do not self-abandon or override the innate healing wisdom of the other.

And to help flesh out this idea of Clean Compassion a bit further, I also previewed Soul Being-level compassion when describing the sixth and seventh stage in our road map:

In Stage 6 and 7—we are able to stand with the point of view of the True Self (which you now know is connecting to your Holy Trinity—you in this incarnation, your soul, and the Divine). We allow ourselves to shift from being emotionally manipulated and blended with Parts of us that are wounded, scared, fearful, resentful, and looking to derail us from healing or growing as a way to survive and protect ourselves. When we can shift from the point of view of our wounded Parts, we open to the energy of our True Self and the innate healing power of the Sacred Witness—curiosity, understanding, kindness, caring, compassion, and a desire to support the Self and others without sacrificing Parts of ourselves or any other Being in the process. When we can stand with the point of view of the True Self, we naturally take that ability and bring it out into our daily life—living and breathing with our practices as an integral part of us.

In this chapter, you will have the opportunity to free up the host of shadow protectors and survival programs that may currently be skewing the Medicine of Compassion (i.e., Clean Compassion), shifting this Medicine from a "nice idea" to actively infusing Clean Compassion into how you approach every choice and action you take throughout your day to be in alignment with your True Self.

The Difference Between Sympathy, Compassion, and Empathy

Before diving into defining Clean Compassion, let's pause and explore a couple definitions first. Unfortunately, we often totally mix up and blend empathy, compassion, and sympathy together. They really are very different concepts.

Sympathy is defined by Webster dictionary as a noun—from the Greek *sympathēs*, meaning "having common feelings." The Oxford dictionary describes sympathy as having feelings of pity and sorrow for someone else's misfortunes. I like to expand on these to define sympathy as offering care and support to another based on our own projected sense of what they are experiencing because we have been through a similar past experience or could imagine what that experience would feel like to us.

Empathy refers to actively sensing into another's experience as if from their point of view. I define empathy as the ability to literally feel, sense, see, hear, know what another is sensing, from *their* first-person point of view. It is not sympathizing. True empathy is an embodiment of what you are witnessing as if it is happening to you—*but* from their point of view and sensing, not your own. Additionally, empathy doesn't actually include feeling a sense of kindness toward that sensation nor a desire to care for anything. It is a sheer technical term to describe that someone is literally experiencing what they are witnessing as if it is happening to them. However, during and after that empathic transmission, our caring Parts *may* kick in and we experience a desire to help support, console, alleviate and tend to the situation or other(s)—but this is not a required part of empathy.

Here's an example of the difference between empathy and sympathy. Say someone stubs their toe and you want them to know you understand what it feels like to have a stubbed toe. So, you bring to mind a time that you stubbed your toe. This opens you to the ability to sympathize: *I can understand what you are going through because I have experienced something similar.* However, this is not empathy. Why? Because true empathy would mean that through my empathic connection with you (which is happening through the Heart Being via the Law of Sensing), as you stub your toe, my physical body registers and has the actual experience of what your body is sensing and experiencing, without any of my own filters. I don't need to go stub my toe, remember a time I stubbed one in the past, or imagine what it would be like to stub my toe; I am directly experiencing *your* experience of stubbing *your* toe.

Empathy means to literally experience and sense what another is experiencing in a carbon copy. To muddy the waters worse, another thing happens as a side effect of empathy when we truly find ourselves in an empathic response. While my system is mirroring what I am empathizing with, my system is also having its own internal response to those sensations in my body. This means, within my own system, two points of view are colliding at the same time—the carbon copy of your experience and my own reaction to feeling what is happening within me.

Hang with me a few more moments on these definitions because you will see *why* I have developed a distinction between Messy and Clean Compassion.

Compassion is its own separate inner state. In addition to sympathy, it adds one's desire to understand and help alleviate another's distress because one doesn't want another to suffer. The word compassion roots back to Latin, meaning "to bear, suffer," or "to suffer together." It is defined by emotional researchers as a feeling present when we are confronted with another's suffering and feel motivated to relieve that suffering. Oxford dictionary defines it as a noun as well: "sympathetic pity and concern for the sufferings or misfortunes of others."

Mindful's website (which has a Buddhist background and undertone) says:

> Compassion helps us connect with others, mend relationships, and move forward while fostering emotional intelligence and well-being. Compassion takes empathy one step further because it harbors a desire for all people to be free from suffering, and it's imbued with a desire to help.
>
> Compassion is simply a kind, friendly presence in the face of what's difficult. Its power is connecting us with what's difficult—it

offers us an approach that differs from the turning away that we usually do.

They go on further to say:

> *Self-compassion is the art of granting these traits to ourselves and having the same compassion that we have for the suffering of others for ourselves as an act of self-healing, love, and opening a link to a felt self of inner happiness—when we are trying to honor and tend to our suffering parts versus fight them, shame them, or hide them.*

Therefore, when we pull all of these separate yet intertwined concepts into the Medicine of Compassion, we all almost always end up with a mixed bag of imagining the pain or suffering of another (sympathy), experiencing it within ourselves (empathy), and having a desire to release or alleviate that pain (compassion).

This might sound like an amazing thing, which it is. However, the question is not whether we are moved to support the release of suffering within ourselves or another. The big questions are *how* are we stepping into compassion, and *what* aspect of us is driving our bus when we are expressing Compassion toward ourselves or another. This makes all the difference between following the promptings of our Soul Being, via Clean Compassion, or getting hooked by shadow Protectors forcing us into actions based on what I call Messy Compassion.

The Difference Between Clean and Messy Compassion

Here are a few tricky issues with compassion, sympathy, and empathy based on our definitions above.

- Sympathy—When I'm sympathizing with you, I'm projecting my experiences and how I felt or think I would feel onto you and offering you a version of support from that point of view—that is, what I believe would be supportive and good to me in that situation.

- Empathy—I feel, sense, and experience what happens to you within my own system, as if it is me. Therefore, if I want to feel different, you need to feel different too.
- Compassion—Compassion, by itself, means that when we are witnessing the suffering of another, *and* we are feeling a need to act toward alleviating? that suffering, because we are suffering with them—what happens to one happens to all. If I feel happy, you have to feel happy too. If I'm sad, you have to be sad too. If I don't want to be sad, and you are, I need to help you not be sad so I can avoid my own sadness.

Can you see the potential problems here?

When you combine these three together (like we have all done), you end up having a hidden protective scenario like this: *I am holding the suffering of you as me; therefore, alleviating that suffering is something I must do if I want to alleviate the suffering in you and me, so we can all feel better.*

But what if the suffering you are witnessing, either in your own life or another, is an integral part of the healing? What if a Being likes or wants it? What if they want help to alleviate the suffering, but they do not want to be responsible for the actions needed to shift the circumstances creating the suffering? What if there is a bigger thread working through the suffering that is needed to liberate a Being into deep healing? What is our responsibility to try to alleviate and what is not? How do we hold the act of Compassion and *not* step into the modes of fixing and alleviating based on our personal projections and discomforts? How do we hold Compassion and open up to guidance around what is for the highest good and benefit for all? How might we embody what Mindful captured when stating, "Compassion is simply a kind, friendly presence in the face of what's difficult. Its power is connecting us with what's difficult—it offers us an approach that differs from the turning away that we usually do."

The answer to *all* those questions is the beginning of what I call Clean Compassion.

Clean Compassion means: I can witness. I can honor and stand with the pain, discomfort, and suffering and not turn or shy away. I can be with what I'm witnessing, and not shame it or make it feel bad for me seeing and opening toward it. Also, I don't push what is being witnessed to change so that I can have a more comfortable experience with it. I'm willing to hold healthy boundaries with myself and with others as guided by the Sacred Witness and my Soul Being.

When I can choose Clean Compassion, I am not placing *any* agenda on what or whom I am holding compassion for. I don't feel compelled to shift, change, fix, or save any Being. I am simply with them, from a neutral point of view. From that neutrality, I am open to being guided by what is in the highest good and benefit for all—including myself.

Messy Compassion means I'm all shades up in protective shadow fixing, rescuing, scapegoating, agenda-pushing; shadow savior roles; shadow stories of the Victim, Child, Prostitute, and Saboteur; having empathy without boundaries; blurred lines; and so on. When I am practicing Messy Compassion, I'm driven into choices from protective and wounded Parts of me, which is bad news bears and creates potential for more harm than good, to myself and most others as well.

Can you think of a situation where Messy Compassion has gotten you to overstep, ignore, or otherwise break from your own inner guidance, only to then foster resentment and the feeling of being used or underappreciated on the back side?

Now can you think of a time that you had what I call Clean Compassion?

Here are a few traits of Clean Compassion:

- The willingness to see as many aspects of any given situation as we can. We are able to hold space for the Parts of us that are upset, mad, hurt, nervous, scared, feel abandoned, or have righteous anger, *and* the Parts that can understand the other—the pains, traumas, and Parts that are creating their actions. We can see the different stories (flight/fight, shutdown, and Sacred Witness), see the different Parts and their roles, and be able to do that without siding with any of the stories, Parts, and so on.

- Works with the Medicines of Sight and Understanding by being able to perceive, honor, and respect all the different wounded Parts present (seen and unseen). This means I'm not marginalizing or over valuing any one "wounded" Part over the other. I'm not going to discount or dismiss a wounded Part by saying, *Well, that was rough but it's over now so it isn't that big of a deal, let's just move on.* Or other such statements.

- Holds the yes-ands, by allowing two or more conflicting points of view to exist at the same time. We can hold a neutral point of view that validates the wounded Part *and* can see, sense, and hear the guidance on how to support *all* parties for the highest good and benefit, and invite them into true empowerment and healing.

- Understands and is willing to act in alignment with how you are being asked to show up. Clean Compassion has built into it the invitation to step into committed action or not based on what your guidance is, versus trying to just alleviate suffering at all costs. This means that sometimes saving, bending to the will of another, and so on are *not* really compassionate responses. Those types of shadow drivers are often survival and trauma responses. Clean Compassion means we have the ability to transcend any potential survival responses that are triggered in us while witnessing pain and suffering and instead, respond in alignment with the Soul of the witnessed Being guiding us.

Clean Compassion is a verb—an action—a choice we have to continually make in each moment. It actually walks hand in hand with incredibly fierce, beautiful, and strong healthy boundaries. So, let's explore healthy boundaries together next.

HEALTHY BOUNDARIES

Once again, let's start with a common definition. Oxford dictionary defines boundaries as "a line that marks the limits of an area; a dividing line and a limit of a subject or sphere of activity." We can take this definition into the realm of personal development and growth to say that personal boundaries are a "line" that marks the limits of our own person—physically, emotionally, mentally, and spiritually. It is something that indicates a sense of Self.

Then, what are healthy boundaries? Healthy boundaries have to do with honoring the limits of what is Self—physically, emotionally, mentally, and spiritually. In ideal circumstances, we teach kids about personal space. We let them know that they have a personal hula hoop around them and to honor their hoop and others' by seeking and giving permission to each other to enter that bubble or not. But how do we teach emotional, mental, and spiritual boundaries? *And* what level of responsibility do others have in maintaining and honoring our boundaries?

I'm going to warn you that Parts of you may not like my answers.

I have come to understand a Soul-Level truth: healthy boundaries are an inside job. No one is responsible for them but me. If I hand responsibility for my personal boundaries to someone else and say,

"Here can you hold this for me, reinforce it for me and make sure it remains strong?" that is not a healthy boundary. A statement like that, implied or direct, is creating a parent-child relationship with someone. Yes, when we were younger that was the correct equation because we did not have the freedom or capacity to see, set, and enforce our personal boundaries with another one hundred percent of the time. However, as adults we do have that freedom and capacity. Whether someone respects our boundaries or not is really not the essence of a healthy boundary. The question is: Do you respect and honor your boundaries? And if you do, what actions are you willing to take to match that boundary or value in your everyday life?

Bottom line is that we would love for everyone to respect our boundaries and honor them for us because that way we don't have to spend energy reminding them of our boundaries—and what I call our Code of Conduct—nor do we need to exert energy to enforce our boundaries with consequences. While it makes *life so* much easier when someone else honors and holds our boundaries for us, it isn't their job—it is ours.

STEPS FOR CULTIVATING CLEAN COMPASSION

The inner archetype responsible for aligning us with the Medicine of Compassion is the Prostitute—the Guardian of our Worth and Integrity and the team leader for Clean Compassion. Remember, the key to helping this pattern within us step into the Light are boundaries, boundaries, boundaries. But what guides our boundaries? How do we decide what they are and how do we differentiate between a healthy boundary and a shadow-based boundary? If we are going to develop Clean Compassion and have and hold healthy boundaries, we first need to establish our own personal Code of Conduct, a set of values aligned with your Heart and Soul Beings, instead of potential survival and trapped trauma-based programs.

Reclaiming Your Inner Code of Conduct

Because the Prostitute's main job is to help you act in alignment with your internal Worth, it governs your "rules of engagement" with yourself and others. These guidelines create what I call our Code of Conduct. Our inner Code of Conduct is the value system through which we engage the Medicine of Compassion. *If* we have protective Parts overriding our Soul-Led guidance, we end up in Messy Compassion—abandoning or violating our Code of Conduct by folding or fawning, based on past survival and trauma adaptations prioritizing belonging, illusions of safety, and unhealthy compromises, which ultimately victimizes ourselves and/or others.

To identify the survival or trapped trauma reasons we compromise our Code of Conduct, we need to look at the different exchanging and/or serving Parts and roles we agree to that often lose balance very quickly—the slave, servant, caregiver, good son/daughter, and so on.

I understand the slippery slope of these roles all too well. I personally have been on a deep and long healing journey around balancing a main protective survival pattern within me that I call the Indentured Servant pattern. When this Protector is running unconscious in me from the base level of survival, *everyone* and *everything* is my master. In the past, the wants and needs of others constantly overrode any of my own.

The first time I saw the Disney movie *Aladdin*, with Robin Williams, I cried when the Genie was talking about how he wanted most to be set free from his role as genie. He would give anything to not have to say, "Poof, what do you need? Poof, what do you need?" The Genie was dreaming about the ability to say *no*. He longed for the freedom to match his own inner guidance—to choose when, where, and how he interacted with and helped people. "Oh, to be free!" was his prayer when Aladdin asked him what *he* would wish for.

While you may not have a Protector in a servant or other service-oriented pattern, I'm sure you can relate in some way to the burdens, experiences, and drivers that the Genie was talking about. We all have a version of this within our inner world for survival protection. So many of us were taught Messy Compassion and sloppy boundaries growing up, because they were the exchanges we had to make to belong to our family units and tribes. Here are few versions of what I'm referring to:

- To be a good family member or friend, you need to sacrifice yourself or your personal boundaries for the other.
- To be a good person, you need to forgive and forget about any boundary violations.
- To sacrifice is to be humble and good—God-like.
- To love is to allow the other to hurt or own you in subtle and not-so-subtle ways, because that is what a loving, caring person does.
- If someone is uncomfortable or mad, at or around you, it is because you either did something to *make* them mad or upset, or didn't do something to fix it.
- If someone asks for something and you say no, then you don't really love or respect them.
- If someone needs something and you have it and don't give it to them, that makes you a bad selfish person.

The list can literally go on and on with how we have been ingrained to believe that holding a boundary or staying true to our own inner Code of Conduct is actually a *very* selfish, rude, and non-compassionate thing to do. Conflicting with all these beliefs, we are also taught that if we don't have boundaries, we are a weak person. It is literally darned if you do, darned if you don't, which is a special kind of crazy-making in our systems.

If we let the wounded Parts of us or another person be the "master" of our actions and of how we try to engage the Sacred Witness within, we will end up abandoning the clean versions of the Medicines of the Soul and instead drop into messy versions of shadow protection and control with them. We end up running patterns such as the Martyr, Toxic Codependent, the Vampire-Blood Donor relationship, acting as the Evil King or Queen to protect ourselves from feeling or working with pain and bigger emotions, and so on. When we allow our wounded Parts to dictate our actions, based on survival needs of seeking belonging and shadow exchanges for safety at all costs, our wounded and protective Parts literally enslave our system, preventing us from having true freedom of choice to match our actions with our True Self.

Luckily, we have been working on healing and liberating these wounded Parts from their survival and trauma adaptations this whole journey, so that you can now open up to your true Code of Conduct and release any shadow codes that were robbing you of your true Soul-Led choice.

Restoring the Power to Say: Yes, No, and Maybe

The second step of cultivating Clean Compassion is releasing the myth that saying "yes" is compassion.

The truth is that sometimes the most compassionate guidance we get is to say "no." When we are in the act of utilizing Clean Compassion with ourselves or someone else, we might receive guidance from our Heart Being such as, *I know that they look like they are "drowning" right now. However, they are right where they need to be. They are exploring how to find their inner strength and resources. Don't jump into action and rescue them right now.* However, if we feel that saying "no" to someone's request is going to make them mad, and we have a wounded Part insisting that *If someone is mad at us, they will no longer accept us we will not belong and therefore not survive*, that guidance is going to set off major danger alarms within our Mental Being, which have the potential to override the guidance of the Sacred Witness within.

In this case, we will not be able to hold ourselves in alignment with Clean Compassion, which might be inviting us to say to our friend, "I hear that you are really struggling right now. I don't think I can fix it for you; however, I would love to be a sounding board to help you explore what options you might have."

Our shadow survival "serving" Parts try to get us to say "yes" to whatever requests come our way. They also try to get us to compromise and respond in ways that match what others' protective Parts want, even if it doesn't match our inner guidance or theirs. However, with healthy boundaries that match our Code of Conduct, we can say "no" as a whole sentence if guided. No more explanation. No more justification. However, to liberate a Clean Compassionate response from our wounded Parts, we need to be centered and *clean* with our guidance.

Here's a hitch: You might never know *why* you are guided to say "no" to a request. Yes, I just took it one step further—you might never know why you are asked to hold a boundary. This part of Clean Compassion drives us nuts. *We love to know why!* We want to be able to justify why we are holding a boundary, because then our Inner Bridge feels secure with a strong Respect Pillar: the ability to make sense of a request and have it feel fair and just. We believe that any justification we can provide to ourselves and others is going to keep us safe, because they will feel respected in our actions. We mistakenly believe that if others can make sense of our boundaries, they will offer respect in return, and stop pushing on our boundaries. We think the "why" will ensure that the other person will agree to our boundary and, even better, pick it up and hold it for us, because that is what happens in a secure connection.

We hope they'll say, "Oh wow, I totally get why you are saying 'no' to this request now. I apologize and accept your 'no' now, because it makes sense to me and I honor it. No hard feelings, request withdrawn." Not, "I see why you are saying 'no,' but I really don't care. I want this. My needs and wants are greater than yours so ..." Slippery, slippery slope my friends, to rely on the Outer Bridge with another to support our own inner connection to true guidance and safety.

Because people's Mental Being protectors naturally push back on boundaries that would challenge their ways of operating, and we have our own protective Parts that are *very* uncomfortable with that, most of our systems have figured out really savvy, hidden ways to set and hold boundaries for us from the shadows. Here are some of the top hidden ways the system helps set shadow-based, messy boundaries for us. (And yes, I know these because I have done them too, so no judgment.)

- Illness—*If I'm sick, people back down their requests*—this includes physical, emotional, mental, and yes, spiritual illness and dis-ease.
- Busyness—*If I don't have time for one more thing, you can't ask me to do anything else.*
- Harsh personas or "identity Parts"—Parts make it appear you don't give a darn. I'll let you insert most of these patterns on your own but here are a few—the narcissist, the a-hole, the bully, the uncaring/pragmatic one, and so on. These are adaptive shields and Protectors.
- Hermit and other isolation-adaptive shields and Protectors—*If I withdraw from connection, no one can ask me for anything.*
- Helpers for Hire—Superhero, Wonder Woman, Counselor, Healer, and so on. These Parts have you literally saving the day for everyone. While this might not feel like a shield, it is because the real boundary it creates is a protection from real intimacy. Ideally, boundaries open us to deep vulnerable connections. But these helper Parts provide a shield of the "having a job" in all connections, which keeps emotional intimacy at bay because they are literally separating friendship and vulnerability from their ever-on "work mode."

Walking with Clean Compassion means we are going to have a real line of Sight in our field for these types of wobbles. The best way to see these wobbles is through working with your four Guardians of the Heart the way we explored in Section four—learning how to identify their themes and recognize their healing invitations to address the wounded Parts that would drive you into Messy Compassion based on old trauma and survival programming. When we do this, we reestablish a true yes, no, and maybe within our system, reestablish our true Code of Conduct, and are therefore willing to move into connection *and* be in alignment with our Heart and Soul Beings, because our "why" is solidly connected to our True Self and not our wounded or protective Parts.

Choosing Clean Compassion

The third step to cultivating Clean Compassion is a willingness to follow the guidance of the Sacred Witness within. Just because we can see and hear our true inner guidance, doesn't mean we are always able to follow it. The Medicine of Courage helps our Heart and Soul Beings set the tone needed within our system for our Mental Being to take the leap and follow how we are being asked to partner with the Medicine of Compassion.

The best example I have to show this in action is when I work with a client who is really struggling. I can feel *all* their unmet needs and wounded Parts pulling at me behind the scenes, without the client having any conscious awareness. They have Parts that want me to save them and poof, take away *all* their issues—physically, emotionally, mentally, and/or spiritually. They have young Parts seeking approval and belonging due to attachment wounds. They have protective Parts that are scared, frightened, trying to hide, and don't want to be exposed or seen. Other Parts are pissed as hell at me, wanting to lash out and beat me up because they are angry and looking for a target to unload on. Plus, all of my client's Parts are talking to my Parts, of which I'm both conscious and unconscious.

How do I show up as the Sacred Witness to create a sacred, safe healing space for my clients and myself?

I use *all* the steps of embodying the Sacred Witness we have spoken about up to this point:

Inner Bridge of Connection: This is the hardest part of walking with Clean Compassion. I lean into my Mental Being's willingness and ability to stay connected to my own Soul Being and Sacred Witness within, and not the unhealed wounded Parts' desires and needs, both of my client *and* of my own system. This is quite difficult in the beginning. The good news is that it gets easier the more trust and faith you build in your Soul's guidance over your Mental Being's limited survival and trauma adaptation points of view. Here are those five pillars again, in this context of Clean Compassion:

- Trust and Respect—Pillars one and two; Activating the Medicine of Sight; The Observer Self - Being able to perceive and partner with the wisdom of my Body, Mental, Emotional/ Heart Beings to track and see as many of the active Parts as possible, internally and externally; and making a commitment to see, hear, feel, or know the guidance coming in from my Heart and Soul Beings and their Healing Invitations.
- Choice and Willingness—Pillar three: Am I willing to follow the guidance of the Sacred Witness and stay true to my inner Code of Conduct? The biggest stumbling block to Clean Compassion is not being willing to step into action with it. Are we willing to have the push and pressure on our field (both internally and externally) of the unhealed Parts? Even with that push, can and will we still match our actions with the Code of Conduct coming from the Guardian of our Worth and Integrity?

Additionally, Clean Compassion helps us remember to call forward Non-Dual thinking and look for all the different Parts of us that might fall into the traps of needing to offer advice, save, fix, or stop the perceived suffering in yourself or another. It helps us hit the pause button on reacting automatically, slow down, and take an Exit Ramp if we find ourselves stuck in an old protective, black-and-white story. We can realize that we have well-meaning problem-solving and other caretaking Parts causing us to abort our true connection to our Heart and Soul Beings because they are trying to manage and protect us and/or the other, leading us into actions that are based in Messy Compassion.

- Connection and Purpose/Value—Pillars four and five: Once we decide to match our actions to our own Heart and Soul Being's Code of Conduct, we can offer Clean Compassion—love and understanding to all the moments that created these habits and ways of interacting with suffering or discomfort within or around us. *And* we can decide to act in a way that honors the True Self, both within *and* with others. We give ourselves permission to not fix or save the other just because there is "suffering." We willingly soften our attachment to the perception of "suffering." Instead, we offer the most amazing gift of all—Sacred Witnessing—deep listening and presence that doesn't assign judgements. Sacred Witnessing then organically leads to aligned Soul-Led healing actions within ourselves and others.

CHAPTER PRACTICES

I have two practices to help you cultivate the skills of Clean Compassion. The first is exploring and beginning to create your own Inner Code of Code, reclaiming and establishing your Pillar of Purpose and Values. This Pillar allows us to seek and receive insights and guidance on what our Code of Conduct is so that we can quickly recognize when we are sliding down to default survival and trauma adaptation ways of being.

The second is a set of reflections to help you engage with a felt sense of the Medicine of Clean Compassion, bringing it to a struggle point in your current life.

PRACTICE 1: DEVELOPING
YOUR INNER CODE OF CONDUCT

In this practice, we are going to establish Step One of Clean Compassion—having an internal Code of Conduct that governs our ability to match our actions with our inner value system.

Think back to Chapter five. During those practices, I asked you to set up a loving intention and Code of Conduct around how you wanted to engage in your Self-Work (page ____). Now, I invite you to expand those intentions out to how you would like to engage with your life and others.

Healing Tip: Remember, *be kind* to yourself during this reflection exercise. Values or a Code of Conduct are living, breathing guides that can help us make daily choices (big and small) in greater alignment with who we truly be. I like the image of the North Star or a compass, tools for helping us stay on track and in alignment with our True Self. When we can begin to allow our values to guide our current responses, we are no longer bound to other, "false" versions of us we created in order to survive, protect, and give us a sense of control. Instead, we have a guiding force to helps us adjust our actions to match our True Self.

Check-In—Take a moment to do a short Check-In and Body Scan to give yourself a baseline of what your current system feels like. This allows you to have a clearer picture from both the Body and Mental Beings of their messages when and if something shifts or changes, sensation- and thought-wise, during the contemplation practice.

Reflect and Journal: Establish your own inner Code of Conduct. The following questions are designed to help you build your own Code of Conduct, which can serve as a compass for you, your intentions for how you want to show up for yourself and others. Once you set your intentions, you can use them as a daily guidance system for the Medicine of Compassion on what choices you make and how you are willing to walk with your Purpose and Values.

- List three feeling states you would like to walk with every day.
  Example: *I want to feel connected to a state of love, joy, harmony, sincerity, courage, Clean Compassion, happiness, freedom, honor . . .*
- List three feeling states you would like to embody in your interactions with others.
  Example: *My intention is to match my values of*
  _____*with the different actions and connections I make throughout the day.*
    o *Deeply honoring another Being's sentience.*
    o *Embodying the Medicine of Clean Compassion—remembering that something created both my actions and theirs.*
    o *Pausing before reacting. I want to remember to pause before I respond to any triggering interactions and be*

committed to taking an Exit Ramp, to support my own
system in responding from a place of connection to my own
Heart Being's wisdom, not my protective or wounded Parts.

o Remembering that healthy boundaries are my responsibility.

Now that you have a short list of your intentions of *how* you want to
feel internally with yourself and externally with others, you have the
bare bones of your Code of Conduct.

PRACTICE 2: ALIGNING WITH CLEAN COMPASSION

During this practice, you are going to take the bare bones of your
Code of Conduct and build into it a plan for how you can course correct when you struggle to maintain Clean Compassion.

Check-In—Begin, as always, with the short Check-In practice from
page 389 to provide you with a baseline of how your system is responding to each reflection question.

Reflections

- List three ways you know you struggle to maintain healthy
  boundaries.
  Example: I struggle to hold healthy boundaries when:
  - *I believe someone else is not going to respect my boundary for
    me, therefore leaving it up to me to reinforce the boundary*
  - *When I feel that someone is going to be disappointed in me*
  - *When I know that someone is going to be mad or upset*

- List three ways you can support yourself when you find your-
  self acting outside your Code of Conduct and lost in Messy
  Compassion.
  Example - *When I realize that I am lost in engaging with Messy
  Compassion I can:*

- *Remind myself to deeply honor the other Being's sentience— remembering they have their own thoughts, emotions, and desires that do not have to match my own*
- *Remember that Clean Compassion doesn't involve judging— remembering that something created their actions and to pause before I respond to any triggering interactions*
- *Remember that messy compassion often means there is an unmet need or fear in my own system and that I might need to do a Healing Interview with the Parts of me that are guiding me to respond that way*
- *Remember that healthy boundaries are my responsibility and not theirs*

- List three ways the Sacred Witness within can get your attention when needed.

  Example: When I _____, I know that the Sacred Witness is trying to get me to pause and check in:
  - *Feel a tap on my shoulder*
  - *See the image or hear the voice of the Sacred Witness avatar that I created in Chapter Two*
  - *See the image of a stop sign or an exit ramp*

- List three ways you can ask for your Soul Being's support when needed.

  Example: I commit to seeking the advice and support of my Soul Being in my Daily Life by:
  - *Setting a daily check-in and reflection time to open to any insights and messages I might have blown past throughout the day*
  - *Creating a daily or weekly Healing Pause Practice, during which I consciously allow myself to check in and see if my actions are matching my guidance or not, leading to Healing Interviews and course corrections as needed*

Now that we have discovered a core skill set of the Sacred Witness, the power of Clean Compassion and how engaging this Sacred Medicine is connected with our own inner Code of Conduct, we can now allow our Soul Being to help us consciously set intentions around how and with whom we want to be in connection.

Cultivating Clean Compassion opens us to accessing cleaner versions of the Medicines of the Soul Being, which are needed to deepen the pathways of partnering with our Soul's guidance, values, and Healing Invitations that come through this aspect of us.

In the next chapter, we will build off this foundational Medicine by exploring the final three key Medicines of the Soul—the Medicines of Gratitude, Blessing, and Joy.

Chapter Fifteen

Medicines of Gratitude, Blessing, and Joy

Having the Medicine of Compassion running through us in a clean way and in alignment with our true Code of Conduct opens us to working with three additional Sacred Medicines we need to fully embody the Sacred Witness as a core healing aspect of us. These are the Medicines of Gratitude, Blessing, and Joy.

Just as we found with the Medicine of Compassion, these two medicines can be heavily distorted and burdened by protective Parts and programs in our system that cause us to interact with them in very messy and detrimental ways. In this chapter, we will be exploring how to support our systems in breaking free from these unhelpful ways so that we can walk with the clean versions of these Sacred Medicines and further unbridle the Sacred Witness within.

THE SACRED MEDICINE OF GRATITUDE

Gratitude **is defined in the** Oxford Dictionary as "the quality of being thankful; readiness to show appreciation for and to return kindness."

As a Medicine of the Soul and healing tool of the Sacred Witness, Gratitude is an action that brings a healing presence to our daily life, by honoring our life and what we are cultivating within it. When we walk with the Medicine of Gratitude, it helps us actively turn toward what is happening in our life with clean awareness and awe—being thankful for that which is already in our life, having appreciation for what we are in connection with, and gratefulness for what will be co-created and called into our lives by and for ourselves and/or with others in the future.

A crazy number of scientific studies show that gratitude is literally a "medicine" that can bring harmony and balance back into our physical, emotional, and mental bodies. Many traditional Western medicine doctors actually recommend and prescribe keeping a gratitude journal as a way to help reduce blood pressure, improve sleep, and even address chronic illnesses, mental health, and other conditions.

Difference between Messy and Clean Gratitude

I love gratitude journals and practices. However, I also see a hidden self-victimizing shadow phenomenon that can happen when people develop a Gratitude practice. This forced or "messy" version of Gratitude is actually incredibly harmful. I have witnessed in myself and many clients that gratitude practice can actually gaslight our own systems, forcing an idea that we are or should be happy and joyful at all times and things aren't "that bad." What often happens as we start to work with Gratitude is that we have protective Parts of us that can actually learn to use the idea of "gratitude" to subtly shame ourselves for what we have, and to bully ourselves out of some of the "down" or unhappy feelings or attitudes we have toward certain aspects of our lives.

Per usual, I want to be really clear about the tricky traps of working with the Soul Medicine of Gratitude so you don't accidentally find yourself bound up in them too.

Messy Gratitude

Have you heard someone say something along the lines of, "Well, you should be grateful for what you have, some people have nothing," or "Be grateful it is only _____ that is happening to you right now, because you could be experiencing _____or have lost so much more?"

Statements like these are actually coming at Gratitude from Messy Compassion. Such statements are actually using shame and guilt to get us to honor what we have; therefore trying to force us into feeling something other than what different Parts of us might be experiencing.

It might seem harmless to give these types of so-called pep talks to our system. However, they are harmful in the long run and don't do much to help us in the short run either. This type of practice or thinking cultivates shame and a psychic undercurrent of fear of loss, scarcity, shadow pity, comparison, and trying to force our system into "looking at the bright side." It is a subtle way of dismissing Parts of us that might be upset or being harmed by something. They marginalize the wounded Parts' points of view in our system, which is Messy Compassion. Messy Gratitude leads us to shun and ultimately dishonor Parts of us and their point of view, which exiles their real needs. As you know, when we exile Parts of us it causes a whole host of issues—physically, emotionally, mentally, and spiritually.

A Messy Gratitude practice essentially tells Parts of us that they are wrong and shouldn't feel the way they do. It causes you to lose your Inner Bridge of Connection, because it doesn't Respect that a Part of you feels as if something is off, lacking, wants/needs support, and/or to be tended to. Therefore, it isn't truly connected to the voice of your Sacred Witness within. Instead, a Messy Gratitude practice is run by shadow Mental Being protectors trying to convince aspects of you that their view point isn't valid or real, and should be dismissed because "it isn't that bad" or "it could be worse."

Also, to be clear, I'm not saying we need to give the wounded Parts of us free rein to take out our whole system and set up base camp in their wounds. Doing so would not be a Clean Compassionate way to tend to them; because that, too, would dishonor your whole system. Instead, we want to honor them and let them have a chance to share what their needs are with healthy boundaries so they can release their pain and we can channel of the Medicine of Gratitude in a clean way.

Cultivating Clean Gratitude

To understand Clean Gratitude, let's feel the difference between the following two approaches to Gratitude practice. At the end of my meditation time, I invoke the Medicine of Gratitude in one of two ways:

Option 1 –I'm Grateful for the people I have in my world. I'm asking today for the Sacred Witness within to help me remember that when I'm triggered, upset, or annoyed today—that it is a gift to have my life, and the people in it. Some people don't even have others to get annoyed with, or are struggling to simply be alive. Help me be Grateful for what I have and remember this truth. Thank You, thank You, thank You—and so it is.

Option 2—Today I'm grateful for the people I have in my life. I have the opportunity to be with them, give and receive love and support, and be in the dance of connection with them. Even though at times I might be upset or stressed out by others' actions, I am grateful I get to be in the dance of connection with them, and my life in general. We bring a richness to each other's lives and I'm grateful for that.

I ask for my Sacred Witness's support today to help me stay connected to the Medicine of Gratitude in my tone, body, thoughts, and Heart as I interact with the people, Beings, and experiences I encounter today. I call forward the Medicine of Sight and Vision to remind me that I can clear my perceptions of the fog of past pains and wounds that might cloud my ability to perceive clearly when I feel triggered. I ask for the Medicine of Compassion to remind me that Protectors might try to override my true choice or cut me off from being in the current moment with someone.

I thank the Sacred Witness for reminding me that I can remain balanced and open to being Soul-Led, instead of manipulated by the wounded Parts of me in those moments. I ask for Gratitude to walk with me today so I can remember, when I am pulled into an automatic past reaction, that this is a beautiful gift for me. In that moment, I have the opportunity to heal, in a loving and compassionate way, a piece of me that has been lost. I'm grateful for the support I feel coming forward now and I know will be with me throughout the day to help me recognize and hear those moments within the vastness of my inner world. Thank you, thank you, thank you—and so it is.

What feels different between these two approaches to a Gratitude practice?

The first one carries an element of shame. As I move throughout my day, any time I have a feeling tone or a flare of an emotion, such as irritation, anger, or disappointment, a Part of me would shame me for having that thought or emotion. It would use the words "should" or "ashamed" and would beat down any Part of me feeling anything out of alignment with the "gratitude" it *should* be channeling.

The second version carries an acknowledgement that life is a very mixed bag of experiences and emotions. With a Gratitude practice grounded in Clean Compassion, we recognize that, in some moments, it will be easy to work with the Medicine of Gratitude and, in other moments, it will be much harder. Once we can honor that life will be a mixed bag of likes and dislikes, the Medicine of Gratitude helps us see a moment of dissonance within our day as an opportunity to create more harmony, balance, and ultimately choice within our lives. We can therefore deeply honor what is present in our lives.

Additionally, we would miss many Divine gifts hidden in the everyday mundane moments of our day if we were resisting being fully present in our life. These little gems of Light are so often lost in the hustle and bustle of the consumer world we find ourselves in now. The Medicine of Gratitude reminds us to see beyond the illusion of normal life and open to the magic and grace flowing *through* the ordinary, thereby helping us cultivate genuine delight. Gratitude opens us to seeing the little portals of love, magic, and gifts of the seen and unseen that can come when we walk with an open channel to the senses of our Soul.

Like the other Medicines of the Soul, Gratitude invites us to walk with non-dual thinking to both tend the wounded Parts *and* celebrate the awesome aspects of ourselves and our life with unabashed joy and love. It allows us to be truly present and excited about what we are interacting with, even if other aspects of our life or another's life are less than desirable.

Additionally, Clean Gratitude helps us step out of another tricky trap of shaming ourselves for what we are Grateful for having in our lives. True Gratitude allows us to compassionately honor the experiences others might be having, which may be opposite of ours. It also helps us honor the gifts another Being's experience might be inviting them into, without condemning ourselves for how our abundance and joy might be manifesting differently compared to theirs.

The Sacred Witness within utilizes Clean Gratitude as a Sacred Medicine because, through it, we bring a willingness to engage deeply with our life and interact with what is present in it. This opens our access to one of the most powerful Sacred Medicines of the Soul: the Medicine of Blessing.

The Sacred Medicine of Blessing

When you think of a blessing, what comes to mind? Most of us are taught that the act of blessing is used to grant or ask for something. For example, "Please bless my day for good fortune." Or "Please bless my friend with safe travels today." However, this version of Blessing is only one small aspect of the Sacred Medicine invoked in the act of Blessing.

Messy or Conditional Blessing

As you might expect, there is a messy version of this Soul Medicine. The messy version of Blessing links expectations, attachments, desires, fears, and conditions to that which we are directing our blessing. I call this the vending machine effect. Remember back to the good old vending machine: you put your money in, picked the code that matched the product you wanted, and then waited for the machine to move that product forward and drop it down to you. It was a transaction. The expectation is that as long as you have the correct money to put in, you can direct the machine to give you what you want.

In this metaphor, a conditional blessing would be:

- The money equals the resources of your time, intention and attention, which you use to activate the blessing.
- Selecting your desired item equals a Part of you becoming attached or deciding what outcome you believe will make the blessing come true.
- Pressing the buttons is setting the expectation of how that blessing is going to come back to you, often with a very savvy hidden condition of "I want this *or* something better"
- And the machine *should* give it to you. The blessing should be delivered back to you as desired because you agreed to the set exchange of this "price" for this "blessing".

There are huge issues with this version of blessing. If the blessing doesn't come forward in a way that matches or is even better, the assumption is that you or the Being that you are blessing did something wrong. This brings us back to hidden shame, blame, resentment, disappointments, and getting all shades of burdened with victimizing *Why?* questions, which ultimately strip us of our inherent worthiness to invoke *or* receive a blessing. Again, this is a very slippery slope that takes us further outside of balance, worth, and Clean Compassion.

Ultimately, what happens with this version of blessing is that we end up "cursing" ourselves or the other with resentment and shadow judgments, which separate us from the true Blessings that could be present.

Cultivating True Blessings

Truly channeling the Medicine of Blessing will always include:
- acknowledging the inherent worth and light of all involved in the Blessing
- offering and welcoming LOVE toward all:
  - L—letting it be
  - O—opening to what wants to be present with you
  - V—willingness to be vulnerable and connected to your Heart and Soul Beings
  - E—willingness to experience all the emotions, thoughts, feelings, and Soul-Led guidance present
- offering Gratitude toward and acknowledging that so many different levels are present and active, which you might or might not see
- willingness to welcome a channel of love that honors the inherent wholeness of that which is being Blessed.
- rooting in non-attachment, meaning that to truly Bless

something we go hands off on any expectations of how, when, or what that Blessing will produce or create

When we consciously Bless ourselves, something, or another Being, we allow the unconditional love and healing power of the Sacred Witness to flow from us, through us, and to another.

Remember, in the act of Sacred Witnessing we are not pushing our energy, desires, thoughts, or outcomes of what would be best onto another *or* ourselves. That would take away their free will and sovereignty. It would also be channeling so-called support from our Mental Being or personal Heart's desires, which doesn't necessarily fall into alignment with Soul-Led support. Therefore, in the act Sacred Witnessing in the Light, we are not attached to a specific outcome or expectation of what the Medicine of Blessing should look like as it unfolds.

When I feel the clean version of the Medicine of Blessing organically bubble up and flow through me, I Witness a deep sense of honoring Self and Others, rooted in each other's inherent worth and wholeness. The act of honoring another's wholeness and divine nature opens a pathway for them to remember their True Self. This remembrance of their own innate wisdom and truths within their own system organically activates a deeper connection to their own inner Healer and love force within.

The gift of Blessing our Actual life

The Medicine of Blessing means that I am willingly present, open, and honoring my life—the good, the bad, and the ugly. I don't try to gaslight myself, edit, or shift it from What Is. When I walk with the Medicine of Blessing as an action and part of my inner Code of Conduct, versus a static idea or concept, I release my need to brace against or ignore aspects of my life I wish were different. My Inner

Bridge remains fully active, letting me have connection to my Soul's guidance and the Sacred Witness all the time. This helps me willingly step into action with the aspects of my life I might have shied away from in the past. I believe in myself and my ability to shift, change, and work with what is present. A willingness to Bless my life invites me to surrender my struggles and my cursing and wishing away the things in my life I don't have the ability to control, influence, or change at that moment.

The Medicine of Blessing helps us feel centered as we surf through life's ups and downs. I can be present with the experiences that I *love* and want to last for eternity, while also Blessing a flow of love to the opposite experiences that I completely dislike and totally wish were not present. For example, as a person who has walked with traumatic experiences, abuse, long-term life-threatening illness, and chronic conditions, I spent a lot of my time wishing that illness wasn't a part of my life. I would look at others who seemed to have naturally more coherent baseline nervous system functioning and struggle with envy and longing to have their experiences of being in a Body and not mine. I walled off needs, dreams, hopes, and desires as a way to protect myself. Who wouldn't?

But eventually I realized that I was wishing and cursing my life away. I was hiding in the "good work" of being a healing practitioner and teacher. I had a very "messy" way of working with all of my practices; instead of meeting my life with them, I was escaping into my coping mechanism of meditations in some very destructive ways. I was hiding in my protective Parts' strategies of isolation and separation and avoiding my vulnerabilities. I was deeply rooted in Messy Compassion, running from healthy boundary work, and calling forward messy "no-worries" Gratitude in a super shadowy way. I was hiding from the ups and downs and the messy parts of life. I had a smile plastered on my face that didn't match my inner world. In truth, I was at war with my life, the connections in it, and the requests of the Sacred Witness whispering for me to find true balance and healing.

To really Bless my life, I needed to make peace with the experiences of my life. I needed to release my desire to know why horrible things happened to me or others. I needed to release my righteous anger at a "god" that allowed such pain and suffering to be present within one of his "kingdoms." I needed to release the belief that humans constantly hurt everything and everyone because that is part of their make-up. In order to connect with the Medicine of Blessing, I needed to surrender the driving question of the Victim in the shadow, *Why is this or did this happen?* and open to the liberating questions of the Guardian of Truth and Choice—*What is happening or working its way through at this moment? How am I being asked meet this moment in the most balanced and helpful way?*

The Grace of Blessing asks us to open our personal Heart and Mental Being to the Soul's whispered answers to these questions:

- What is calling for my attention right now?
- What is wanting to be created in this moment?
- What is here for me to perceive in this moment?
- What am I open to and what am I bracing against?
- What am I trying to run from or resist? What is driving that response?

When we catch ourselves in a shadow response that doesn't serve or match our Soul-Led choice, instead of running to *Why is this happening to me?* the Medicine of Blessing asks us to switch to, *WHAT is up right now, within me or another, that needs tending to so I can meet this moment from a stance of true choice, rather than wounded and survival Parts automatically taking over?*

To walk with the sacred Medicine of Blessing at its fullest capacity, without hidden expectations and attachments, we have to put down the *Why* questions. Surrendering the need to have a reason affords us the ability to Bless each moment just as it is and not curse it. The act of Blessing the moment opens a sacred dialogue that can unbridle the highest good and benefit for all—ourselves included. As we move into the practices, you will have an opportunity to open to the Medicine of Blessing, putting down the need to know why and opening to what is wanting to be seen, felt, and heard on an even greater scale.

THE ACT OF BLESSING CULTIVATES JOY

Before we get into our practices, let's explore the ultimate consequence of walking with the Medicines of the Soul we've explored in this section. Joy is the natural by-product of walking with the Sacred Witness energy as a daily company. Joy is accessible as a state of being when we have a deep inner-felt sense, knowing, and belief in our ability to resource ourselves internally or externally to walk with life's ups and down no matter what. Walking with the Sacred Witness and having a willingness to Bless our lives, allows us to fully embody experiences having of joy, laughter, love, and the magic of our physical *and* unseen worlds, dancing together moment to moment.

Joy is not just a feeling. It is an inner state of beingness. The authentic Joy that comes through the Sacred Witness's weaving of all the Medicines of the Soul creates a deep inner acceptance of life's ups and downs. In addition to the wonderful moments, there will be moments of gritty raw experiences no matter *what* we do. Therefore, we release ourselves from the massive burdens of perfectionism and shame when we find ourselves meeting inevitably imperfect moments.

We can hold onto moments of connection, happiness, awe, wonder, bliss, and celebration *no matter what* we are experiencing because we truly know that no matter what comes into our sphere of life, there is support, guidance, a way to meet each moment from a place of believing in our own innate ability to handle that moment, *and* a way to *thrive* during and after that moment as well.

The Sacred Witness truly opens us to non-dual living, allowing us to hold laughter in our hearts along with the capacity to hold and tend sorrow, loss, and grief. We carry a lightness within our heart and mind, along with the strength to witness deep suffering. We can feel an authentic smile bubble up on our face as we allow tears to flow as needed.

The Sacred Witness energy serves as a gateway to truly being and living. The willingness to be in our lives as they are gives us freedom to choose how we want to meet the different moments of life and what we want to co-create within it—fully living, loving, and leading our lives in alignment with our True Self. To me that is JOY! It is way beyond excitement.

A wonderful example of living as the Sacred Witness in connection with Joy can be seen in the interactions between the Dalai Lama and the late Archbishop Desmond Tutu. (If you haven't seen any of those videos, I invite you to search for and watch a few of them, especially of them recording the *Book of Joy*.) Both of them know great suffering and have had great weights and responsibilities placed upon them to be the Sacred Witness for their people and those who look to them as Teachers. Their personal traumas and expected roles of support for so many could be seen as a burden, or could hold them apart from connecting with the everyday moments. However, when these two were together, they bubbled over with laughter, joy, connection, openness, and LIFE! When I watch them, my Soul reminds me this is the true nature and rhythm our Soul Being is trying to bring to us. When we work with our Soul, we can access vast capacities for compassion, courage, joy, and activism. We can meet the harsh moments of life and also dance with laughter, play, and companionship.

CHAPTER PRACTICES

Below are three practices designed to help you cultivate and open to the "clean" versions of the Medicines of Gratitude, Blessing, and Joy.

PRACTICE 1: DEVELOPING A CLEAN GRATITUDE PRACTICE

In this practice, you are invited to develop and step into action with a Clean Gratitude Practice, starting with making a "list" of what you are grateful for.

Healing Tip: Be on the lookout for Healing Invitations from the Four Guardians of the Heart as you are making your list. *If* and *when* you find yourself adding something to the list and you feel a twinge of guilt or shame attached to it, it feels like you "should," or you're forcing yourself to add something, pause and drop into a Healing Interview with that Part.

Let's look at an example. Say you write in your journal: *I'm grateful for the ability to flip a switch and have electricity.* And as you are writing it, a Part of you feels guilty for being born into a life, or into a country, that has easier access to electricity. That thought is the messenger of the Victim. Lovely. Ask, *What Part of me is holding that point of view?* See if it is able to release it and step back, or if it is caught in a thread of unworthiness, shame around not honoring this privilege of your incarnation, or the like. Is it coming from an exiled Part of you that felt the shame of not having electricity at some point for whatever reason?

Use the tools you have been given to help heal and release as much Messy Compassion and Gratitude as you can. It might be as simple as holding a moment of love and light for those that are not able to experience a similar reality on a regular basis.

Remember the Soul, the Divine, the universe, does not want us to suffer because others are without or have a different set of life experiences. Instead, I believe they want us to honor the gifts we have and be guided into actions of loving, joyful service to support others.

Step One—Check-In: call forward or connect with the Body Being, Mental Being, Heart Being, Sacred Witness, and the Medicines of the Soul.

Step Two—Develop a List: write down a stream of consciousness list of what you are grateful for in your life right now.

Step Three—Committed Action: After creating the larger list, bring Gratitude into a daily practice by selecting one or two items from the list for which you would like to consciously cultivate gratitude throughout the day. Write it down in your journal. You could even add the words to your home screen on your phone or on a sticky note at your work space to remind you throughout the day.

In the morning, ask for the Medicine of Gratitude to be with you throughout the day as a Sacred Guide. List the one or two things you would like focus your appreciation on throughout the day. At the end of the day, reflect on three things from your day that brought you into a deeper level of living, connection, and/or healing opportunities with the item(s) you picked at the beginning of the day. Offer deep love and respect for those things and release the rest.

PRACTICE 2: CULTIVATING AN
OPEN CONNECTION WITH BLESSING

Before we can fully open to the Soul's Medicine of Blessing, we need to reflect on how and when we disconnect from and block this Medicine from being our daily companion. Remember, the Medicine of Blessing calls forward *all* of the Medicines of the Soul to work together in harmony. Please bring all the following skills we have developed on this journey into these reflection practices:

- Look for the different Heart Guardian Healing Invitations
- Sense into the Somatic messages of the Body Being
- Allow these sensations to guide you into finding the trapped messages of the Heart Being via the emotions held within the protective or exiled Parts of you
- Establish a willingness to slow down and open to Clean Compassion and Sight to help you identify and answer the worries and fears of the Mental Being's protective system that are blocking your Inner Bridge of Connection and the Medicine of Blessing

Step One—Check-In as you usually do.

Step Two—Seeking Awareness via Sight and Vision: Ask for the Sacred Witness within to help you perceive any and all blocks to Willingness that are causing your Connection and Purpose Pillars to feel shaky or cut off, therefore preventing you from deeply Blessing your life:

- In what ways am I bracing against my life right now?
- In what ways am I "cursing" my life or the life of another right now?
- In what ways am I trying to run and flee from parts of my life right now?

- In what ways am I stuck in the energetic realms of wishing for change but not allowing myself to fully hear the guidance my Heart and Soul Beings are sharing with me, including meaningful action steps to shift my life circumstances so I can be more in alignment with my True Self instead of my protective programs?

Step Three—Open to Exploration: Invite the Sacred Witness to help you explore one aspect or response above. Take the answer to the question into a Healing Interview to see what might be active and needing attention within your system.

We'll use this example: *I'm bracing from holding a healthy boundary right now with my partner because I don't want to be the one to hold it. He should hold it because he loves me.*

In the Healing Interview, I find parts of me that say: *My partner should know that I have this need. I want them to meet it for me, without me having to ask. Because I shouldn't have to ask. I feel like if I have to ask, it shows they don't have true regard for me. I'm angry at him/her for not honoring me. Because I'm angry, I am punishing them by withdrawing from our connection.*

Then I discover: *While there is an active voice of the Victim here, the main Guardian I'm perceiving and feel is driving this block is held within the Child. There is an exiled Part of me trying to hide from my responsibility for reinforcing the boundary of _____. I just don't want to do that.*

I also realize I have lost my full Bridge of Connection at the Respect Pillar—therefore I'm not Willing; I don't want to Connect to myself or my Partner, and I know I'm not matching my own Purpose and Values via my Code of Conduct, but I can't bring myself to change my actions or feelings.

I feel guided to drop into a deeper exploration of the Respect Pillar because I notice the feelings of disrespect and them not having regard for me is the most charged issue and is holding me from a Willingness to access any potential Choices and Connection.

Holding a Healing Interview with this young exiled Part, I

discover—*I have always had to be the one to set and hold boundaries. I have had to do this since I was so young, but I was too little. It shouldn't have been my job. No one ever saw my needs. I just kept waiting and wishing the people around me would just see me and figure out what I needed. I was so little; I didn't know what I needed. It was their job to know what I needed . . . but they never figured it out.*

In addition to the young Part, I find a Protector that doesn't want me to be the one to speak and enforce my needs, because it is still wanting and needing the other to do it for me. That way this young Part will finally feel safe, held, and tended to.

Step Four—Opening to the Medicine of Blessing: Invite in the Medicine of Blessing, a simple prayer, to help you to begin tending and shifting the illuminated areas that need support.

This is an example:

I'm grateful for my system's support in finding the Parts of me that are inserting my wounded, younger Parts into this now-moment with my partner.

I ask for the Medicine of Blessing to come forward and help me honor both myself and my partner right now.

I ask for Blessings of Understanding to come to us both during this rupture. I know that through this moment I have an opportunity to shift and heal an exiled Part of me and call forward my true inner strength and voice.

I invite the Medicine of Sight and Vision to be with me. Help me see with the eyes of my Soul what is present and wanting to come through.

I ask for the Medicine of Compassion to pour through me so I can make any corrections needed from a place of love and Clean Compassion.

I ask for the Guardians of my Heart to guide me to see any additional places I'm hemorrhaging my power from these past pains, fears, and traumas so that I can tend those and step into the dance of connection with myself and my partner in alignment with my True Self.

And so, it is.

Step Five—Committed Action and Closing: Before closing this reflection practice, take a moment to pause and engage in an inner dialogue with your Sacred Witness and the Four Guardians of the Heart on how you can shift your actions, internally or externally, to step back into the dance of connection with yourself and/or the other from a place of balance with a full Inner Bridge of Connection to your Heart and Soul's guidance with you online.

PRACTICE 3: WILLINGNESS TO FLOW WITH BLESSING AND JOY

Offering light, love, blessing, gratitude, and joy to ourselves and others is somewhat effortless when we feel that life is going well. However, what about the so-so moments or tough times of life? This final reflection invites you to gain a heads-up on what Parts and Protectors might need support to as you continue to cultivate the Sacred Witness within and gain more access to the healing Medicines of the Soul.

Step One—Check in as usual

Step Two—Reflections: Explore the following questions in your journal.
- When and where do I offer light, love, and joy to my life with ease and where do I withhold it?

- When do I easily connect with the inner state of joy and when do I struggle to honor its presence?
- What type of protective mechanism do I have around allowing myself to fully feel joy?
- How do I allow myself to see the sacred truth that joy is always present within me, even when parts of my life feel unfair, troublesome, painful, and tough?
- Do I allow the Sacred Witness to help illuminate the ways I'm bracing, hemorrhaging, or hiding from my own full beautiful life?
- Can I unbridle my Heart and Soul Beings even more? So that I am freer to step into living and leading my life from the point of view of, *What wants to be created through me today?* versus *What is wrong,* or *What do I need to fix before I can feel joy or happiness?*
- Can I release my need to know "why" and open to What Is?

You now have the core Medicines of the Soul available to you through the Sacred Witness within: the Medicine of Sight and Vision, which open you to the Medicines of Understanding, Courage, Forgiveness, and Healing. From these, the Medicines of Clean Compassion, and Gratitude, and Blessing activate Joy, Love, and the healing power of the Sacred Witness within and through you at all times.

So where do you go from here? The answer is very simple and yet also may feel intimidating. Where you go from here is *out into your life!* Living, breathing, and being with the Sacred Witness within to unlock the Blessings, Love, and Beauty that want to be born through you in every moment. I have one final stop on our journey—outlining a daily practice for embodying the Sacred Witness and one final blessing to be with you on your journey.

Conclusion

In our final chapter, I want to help you hold the vastness of the ground we covered together during this journey. So often, change is incremental and we do not always see how far we have come. Additionally, at the end of every deep immersion retreat, my client typically asks, "Where do I go from here? How do I continue to cultivate the seeds that I planted and started to grow?"

The answer is to gather the key principles and skills we have gained on our journey together into a framework that can be brought into our daily life. This framework will bring everything together into one daily practice—truly allowing you to embody, walk with, and BE the Sacred Witness.

WEAVING IT ALL TOGETHER

Before I share with you a final practice and framework that pulls it all together, I would like to pause and have you reflect on the all the areas we have explored throughout our journey together. Then we'll explore where we go from here.

Reflection—Revisiting Your River of Life

I invite you to pull up your memory (or even the reflection journal pages if you have them) from one of our very first reflection practices, called "The River of My Life," from Chapter Three. During that journey, you reflected on all the different twists and turns and experiences you have had with the energies of the Sacred Witness prior to starting this book. That meditation ended by inviting you to explore thoughts or themes happening in your life that were calling you to awaken to and embody the Sacred Witness within.

Invite the Medicine of Sight and Vision to help you call forward an image of that version of you. Really try to sense, feel, see, hear, and know that version of you from the beginning of this journey. What thoughts, worries, burdens, hopes, and desires was that version of you carrying with them?

Now see if you can follow them through time as we walked through each section, each reflection, and each practice. What shifted and awakened within you each step of the way as you:

- Discovered the strengths and traits of the Sacred Witness?
- Awakened to the Wisdom of the Body Being?
- Better understood the Mental Being and its role as your fierce Lone Wolf Protector?
- Awakened to the Heart Being and its Four Guardians of the Heart?
- And finally awakened to the Soul Being and cultivated its many Medicines?

Further . . .

- How were you able to feel and interact with the Sacred Witness coming forward in each of the practices, as it helped you lean into the raw or hidden places within?
  - What hidden strengths and awareness came through during the different sections?
  - Now that you have this robust knowledge of the Sacred Witness and the Medicines of the Soul, looking back, can you feel the presence of these Medicines throughout your journey co-creating a sacred space for healing? And if so, how or when?

Now, witness yourself moving through time fully to come face to face with who you are in this moment. Witness as they merge into one: the One you began this journey as, and the One you are now, in this moment.

- What changes and shifts can you feel you have embodied along this journey?

Where would you like to go from here?

Take a moment and sense into where you would like to go from here.

Imagine there is a sacred garden of you, or a flower, or tree of your True Self that is starting to take root and bud. The seedlings need support in order to continue to take root and grow to their full potential.

What intentions can you set that will help you continue to tend to the new growth you found on this journey?

Is there a section or practice calling you to revisit and continue engaging with them? If so, which ones? What might want to be created through revisiting that part?

CULTIVATING THE BRIDGE OF CONNECTION AND THE MEDICINES OF THE SACRED WITNESS— A FRAMEWORK FOR A DAILY PRACTICE

As you can tell by this point, I *love* the word *cultivating.* I love it because it invites us into remembering that we need to be an active partner with preparing, planting, tending, and growing whatever we are connected to. I have used this word throughout our journey because the Sacred Witness within is not experienced once and then instantly becomes an active part of us forever. The process of embodying the Sacred Witness within is an ever-growing connection we must *cultivate*. During this journey we have planted the seed, and it has begun to take root. However, to truly cultivate and embody the Sacred Witness within our life to its fullest potential, we need to provide this connection with conscious support and ongoing tending.

The Sacred Witness and the Medicines of the Soul want to breathe with you, walk with you, and be with you throughout your daily life. The last practice I have for you is about how to use the Inner Bridge of Connection every day to help you continue reclaiming your True Self and growing your ability to channel the Sacred Witness within.

When you hit a speed bump in the road of life (no matter how big or small), this is a simple exercise and framework you can use to stay connected to your own innate healing power and remember the Sacred Witness is there to help you step into conscious Choice.

(I have also included these key concepts in quick reference version in the appendix on page 386)

When triggered or feeling lost, drop into the following process:

- Check in and call forward the Medicines of the Soul and the Sacred Witness to help support you.

- Next, close your eyes and pull up the image of your Inner Bridge of Connection and its five main pillars: Trust, Respect, Willingness/Choice, Connection, and Purpose/Values.

- Run through them and see which ones feel like they are shaking or have taken a "hit."

- Invite the Sacred Witness to help you connect with the Medicine of Sight and Vision on what needs to be seen, felt, and heard.

- Scan the Body Being again—where do you feel that Part in or around your body? What Somatic messengers (sensations and/or emotions) are present with it?

- Check in with Mental Being—What protective mechanisms or shadow survival programs might be present, running in: Flight, Fight, Shutdown (including Fawning and Folding), or Freeze.

- Ask your Four Guardians of the Heart—the Child, Victim, Prostitute, and Saboteur—to illuminate what Healing Invitations are present. (The ones connected to the sensations you found in the Body's messages, leading you into the Mental Being and the different protective fears, worries, belief systems, and Parts, might be present and running.)

- (*This is a big one*) Check for Willingness—Calling forward the Medicines of Clean Compassion and Gratitude: Does the system *trust* you and give you permission to tend the wounded Parts that are present? If so, call forward a Healing Room. Bring forward the Medicine of Blessing to help weave together *all* the Medicines of the Soul through the act of Sacred Witnessing.

- Witness the Part via a Healing Interview. Allow it to share its perspective, experiences, fears, and insights.

- Re-establish your Inner Bridge of Connection—What does that Part need from you so it can heal and release the pain, suffering, and trapped trauma it has been holding for so long?

- As guided, offer the Medicines of the Soul—Compassion, Gratitude, Blessing, and Love—to your whole system and affected Parts. Call forward any and all support it needs. This support can come in the form of an element (earth, air, water, fire, light), a guide, your Soul, the Divine, whatever feels best and most supportive. Ask that support to come and help unwind, clear, and release that which is no longer serving.

- Check back in with the Body Being as the Somatic messenger of what is happening within your whole system. How does it feel? Is it ready to reclaim and recall more of who you truly are, now that the trapped trauma or protective program has been released? If so, what is it now ready to reclaim and access from your Heart and Soul Beings—a deeper felt sense of love, a sense of courage, clarity, discernment, joy, laughter, understanding, something else?

- Allow those frequencies to flow within and through you, rebalancing, tending, and restoring greater access to your True Self.

- Pull back up the Inner Bridge of Connection through the Medicine of Sight. How does it look now? Does it need anything else? If it does, answer its requests to the best of your ability. *(Note: this might be a willingness to come back and continue working on this issue in following meditations.)*

  Walk over to the Purpose/Value Pillar. Ask what actions and new thought patterns need to come forward so you carry this healing back into your life and to whatever caused the "shake-up" in your field and self.

- Last step—taking committed action, based on the guidance you received, and establishing a strong Inner Trust Pillar. We strengthen our own Inner Trust Pillar when we can say what we mean and mean what we say. If you want the system to truly Trust that you can now protect yourself from this state of Soul-Led conscious choice, based on your true Code of Conduct, you must consistently step into actions with what has been illuminated during your daily practices. Remember to have kindness and compassion with yourself if you find yourself falling back into an old habitual trauma response.

Simply circle back around and do the required repair work with yourself and those involved and start again.

At this point, you have gained tools, practices, and frameworks you can use in your daily life. You also have the ability to step into committed actions that align with the guidance you receive in working with your Inner Bridge of Connection.

This is the power of the Embodied Sacred Witness. No matter what is happening, you have a way to hold and meet each moment from the point of view of conscious choice, freer from the burdens of the past.

This is the starting place to living, loving, and leading your authentic life. From here, you can open even more to unbridling your Soul and Connecting with JOY!

FINAL HEALING TIP

Remember, it is not a question of whether support is present or not. The bigger question is, "Am I willing to open to the support of the Sacred Witness within me?"

When we can begin to consistently open to the Sacred Witness, we offer light to ourselves and others—even when we feel sad, angry, mad, disappointed, and so on. When we do this, we activate all the Medicines of the Soul—Compassion, Gratitude, Sight/Vision, Blessing, *and* their natural gift: Joy! We honor life. We honor each of our individual unique, beautiful, messy lives and the lives of every Being within it.

Afterword

I truly believe that each and every Being has the power to call forward the Sacred Witness within themselves so we can personally and collectively liberate ourselves from the burdens of trapped trauma and survival adaptations.

I'm not naïve. Much work must be done in this world to reduce suffering, pain, wounding, and what causes them. Whole systems and ways of being have to change: education systems, commerce systems, ways of living as beings of consumption, environmentally, in community, and so on. If we want to survive as a species, as a community, and not to mention live on Earth in general, there is work to be done.

However, if we want to bring that great outer work forward, it starts close in. It starts with our inner landscape and our relationship with ourselves and our lives. It starts with breaking up the legacy burdens that bind us and cut us off from true choice. It starts with healing the parts of us that are fawning, folding, and freezing because of our trauma and survival adaptations in the presence of someone else's unhealed Parts, which might be trying to dominate and control. It starts with self-liberation, self-empowerment, and radical self-healing. From there, it naturally flows out to the other; and from the other, it flows out into a revolution of love, empowerment, respect, stewardship, and deeply honoring all Beings, which creates and drives new ways of living. When the healing power of the Sacred Witness ripples out to create revolutionary new ways of beingness, it will be beyond what you could imagine.

Remember way back at the beginning of this book, I mentioned that I spent the first ten years after Baron helped save my life searching outside of myself for purpose. I was caught in the trap that so many of us fall into at the beginning of our "awakening" journey—trying to justify our life and the suffering we have been through. My main driving inner thoughts and point of view was, *There must be a reason why I have suffered and why I was saved all those times. There must be something BIGGER I'm supposed to be doing with my life, otherwise I wouldn't have been saved.*

While these types of beliefs sound like a good thought process, it was actually crushing me silently from the inside out. I was stuck in a loop of having to *earn* my right to life and having a *reason* for my suffering. Therefore, if I found myself in suffering, I was enduring the suffering for a blessing yet to come. I wrote off my physical pain as a side effect of "being of service" and "being granted life by the Universe." I used all the different skills of mindfulness I learned at the beginning of my journey of awakening to the Sacred Witness to totally cut off from my body even more—by-passing the "density" of Earth School to stay more and more in the energetic world. I surrounded myself with doing the "good work." I was literally on a mission—a spiritual warrior designed to help people heal and help liberate their minds and hearts.

While the first ten years of my journey brought me into so many different learning and expansion opportunities, I was unconsciously skewing the teachings to give me permission to avoid and dismiss my actual daily life. I didn't tend to many experiences of my own earthly life. I was by-passing life because I had a *huge* number of protective Parts that still didn't really want to connect to this plane because honestly, I overall still didn't like it. I didn't understand it. I was angry at the idea of a "Divine intelligence" that created what felt like a horrific, unfair, torture chamber.

Ten years into my journey, Parts of me really still viewed humans as one of the worst inventions this "God" thing could have created. To me, humans were generally these beings that were asleep, victimizing and hurting each other left and right because they were hurting, and really not aware of *all* the Beings around them as unique sentient Beings worthy of joy and happiness just like them. I believed humans as a whole just consumed everything, and were hopelessly lost in their own pain, suffering, and illusions of what life was. While some humans were exceptions, they were far and few between. I struggled to be in the presence of humans, let alone my own self.

I had begrudgingly accepted the narrative of a spiritual warrior. However, I was not willing, therefore I wasn't truly connected to my Heart and Soul Beings and was mostly working through my Mental Being. I was still somewhat cursing the life I had been sentenced to live. I was only at ease when I was out in nature, with horses, and/or helping humans heal (mostly through working with horses and nature). I had disdain for playing the "games" of acceptance and belonging with humans and within myself. I was trying so hard to honor the journey that Baron had set me on ten years earlier.

However, in truth, I was doing the work I was doing *not* because I was honoring my Soul and my life, but because I believed this God thing majorly messed up. I had a protective Part of me that was on a crusade to change the tide and therefore justify *why* I was still alive and present in Earth School. This Part had a strong belief if I had to be in this torture chamber of Earth School, I might as well try to help as many people as I could during this life's sentence.

I took a Shamanic teaching I learned to heart, in a very limited way:
> *If all the fish in the sea left this planet, the Earth would die. Or if all the winged birds and insects left this planet, the Earth would die. Or if all the four-legged land animals left the planet, the Earth would die. Or if all the trees and plant beings left this planet, the Earth would die. However, if all humankind left this planet, the Earth would flourish.*

The teaching is inviting us to remember that humans are given the gifts of blessing, creation, and manifestation. We are truly Beings of Co-Creation. We need to be good stewards of the gift of creation by learning to bless, partner, and work with land, the water, the natural rhythms and cycles of life, and of all our brother and sister Beings that call this planet their home. When we are asleep, disconnected from the guidance of our Soul (spirit), we are a threat to ourselves and others, slipping into use of our co-creative abilities for destruction and harm. Our gifts of creation can either support life or take life. Which will we choose?

SECOND AWAKENING TO THE SACRED WITNESS

During my first ten years of Seeking the Medicines of the Sacred Witness, I had healed and liberated myself from so many protective programs and trapped traumas. However, underneath, I was still viewing Earth and my life as a mistake—blocking the true Medicines of Sight and Vision, Compassion, Gratitude, Blessing, and Joy from fully helping me find a way to accept and willingly *be* with my full life.

In my early thirties, I had another significant spontaneous awakening to the Sacred Witness within that jolted me into seeing a massive Healing Invitation to deeply look at and heal the way I was operating with resistance and withholding Connection with my Heart and Soul Beings.

I had just had my first child and I realized that because I viewed my life as a "sentence" that needed to be endured, I wasn't really present in my life. Therefore, if I wasn't really present in my life, I couldn't be present for my daughter as I wanted. By contrast, I had seen that when I was with a horse or witnessing another Being that was working with their own healing, I was as present as I could be. I was open to connection, I was open to fully hearing and working with the whispers of my Soul and theirs. In those moments, I soft-ened my intense driving need to get something accomplished or to just endure whatever I was experiencing and would organically drop into my Body Being, soften my protective Parts, and willingly follow the Sacred Witness to guide me to meet the needs of the other as we worked toward a goal of wholeness.

One morning after I had just finished nursing my daughter, I was looking down at this little Being I was blessed to steward. In a flash, I realized that I couldn't stay with my current way of working with Earth School. As I asked for the support of my Soul Being to help me soften and heal my protective attachments to these beliefs, I heard the words of an old Christian belief system that I absolutely despise—*original sin*. A huge flash of anger flew through me. I pretty much demanded that spirit explain why in the world *those words* would come to me at *this moment*. The idea that a precious new life was born already tainted, already unworthy of Divine love? Nope and nope. I never got that one. It was so crazy to me and not at *all* what I had personally seen, felt, and witnessed coming from the Soul. But looking down at this beautiful little Being, I told Spirit it better have a very good reason for bringing this totally crazy teaching into my awareness. I then saw that teaching from a different point of view.

As I was looking down at my little daughter in my lap, my Sight shifted to perceive a film pushing on the outer edges of her aura. Her aura was struggling to hold this film off and I could see that some of it was leaking into her, shifting and changing her field. Spirit showed me that the film was made up of *all* the protective projections—from me, from my husband, from our lineages, from the collective consciousness, of our beliefs (positive and negative) about the world. My own limited beliefs and unhealed Parts were pushing on her field. I saw a vision of my own and others' jaded thoughts of Earth school trying to skew her innate ones.

My own Mental Being was broadcasting an energetic signal, telling her she would have to abandon her own beautiful, clear feelings of love and acceptance to craft similar beliefs that matched and mirrored mine so she could be accepted and belong. I saw how my own anger and wounded Parts were going to cause similar attachment wounds and protectors in her. I realized that the burden of "original sin" is not that we are all tainted from the very beginning of life and need to earn our way back to heaven (which is totally not sound and not true, in my opinion). However, it actually acknowledges that all the pains and survival adaptations that I (and others she would interact with) had up and running would be passed on to her to accept *if* she wanted to survive and be accepted into *our* tribe. That was the "original," the starting place of her first trauma and survival adaptations. It started the moment she was conceived.

A silent prayer for help suddenly burst from my Heart, just as it had with Baron those years earlier. *Help me heal my wounded Heart. Help me heal my anger. Help me bring the same love I have for the "natural world" to the "human world" and to my life. Help me shift, heal, and create a new way to look at and walk with this crazy human life thing.* I also asked for her Soul to help Bless her and shield her from that which is not truly hers to walk with in this life, while I healed my side of this equation, reducing the "film" that was pushing on her field and asking it to abandon her own knowing to match mine.

Then, I said this prayer aloud and called on the Sacred Medicine of Blessing—

> *Grant me and Bless me with the strength to see humans with a loving Heart. Grant me the ability to see life, including my own life, with a loving, open Heart. Help me to understand the Divine with an open and curious Heart. Help me to see the world through the eyes of the angels and the Divine, so that I can learn how to be in my life from a place of presence, honoring, and blessing it, versus enduring and cursing it. Help my Heart soften and release the point of view that Earth is nothing but a life sentence I simply need to endure so that I can be free again. Help me learn to be free, now, within this life, so I can help her see that she is free and not condemned to a life of just surviving and enduring. Help me open to loving and blessing my life so I can help her love and bless her life too.*

This organic invocation of a new relationship with the Medicines of the Sacred Witness came from a completely ordinary moment of looking at this precious little child before me. Calling forward the Medicines of the Sacred Witness, with the intention to consciously work more directly with them, relaunched me into the second part of my seeker's journey with a new North Star—to find a way to live, love, lead, and Bless my life. As I cultivated my connection with the Sacred Witness even more, I became more willing to connect with, open to, and support all aspects of myself, and therefore all aspects of the other.

I would love to say I stayed awake from that moment on. However, it was much more a process of discipline, searching, disappointment, falling asleep again, having my life shake me awake again, and so on. I'm a pretty habitual person. The old habits didn't fall away quickly. The universe has helped snap me awake over and over. I can honestly say that now I'm way more present and empowered, living life in deep alignment with who I truly want to be.

The way I do it is through everything I have shared in this book. It is through being willing to see what is calling to be seen, releasing my attachments to limiting perspectives and points of view, and allowing the Sacred Witness within to help remind me to Bless my life and that which is in it—both seen and unseen. I have a commitment to daily practices and Soul-Work that provides me with the space for reflection and communion with my Soul and Sacred Witness. I have committed to maintaining my Inner Bridge of Connection to help me stay aware of my needs. I have committed to allowing the Sacred Witness to help me stay in connection with the diverse dimensions I'm walking with daily—physically, emotionally, mentally, and spiritually. It's an ongoing practice for me—the way I invite this to become an ongoing practice for you.

CLOSING BLESSING

I would like to leave you with one last Blessing for your journey ahead:

Blessing for Courage, Love, and JOY!

Today as you meet your life, I ask for you to feel connected to the Medicines of the Sacred Witness, which is always with you.

I ask that you remember you are an amazing Being of light and love.

I ask that you walk with your Sacred Witness as your main inner companion—helping you see, sense, hear, and feel the Healing Invitations that come forward throughout the day. They are there, helping to bring up that which has been bound up. Inviting you to turn toward them, with the presence of the Sacred Witness. Helping the trapped traumas and pains be seen, tended, and healed so that you can show up for your life—present and open to Joy in the dance of connection; receiving, giving, and dancing with the promptings of your Heart and Soul Beings.

If it feels good to you, join me in saying this Blessing:

I Bless my life. I Bless the small moments of simply breathing in and out, of sitting with a cup of tea, of smiling at a stranger, of walking past a tree that offers the air I breathe and helps stabilize the ground I walk on. I Bless the Beings in my life that I love and cherish and offer the Medicine of Gratitude to them. I Bless all the Parts of me, the ones I love and the ones that I struggle to hold with Clean Compassion and Understanding. I know there are wounded Parts of me hurting and I ask for support on how to meet those Parts and soften my judgments of them so I can walk with them in a healthy and supportive way.

I Bless my past and offer love to it. I ask for support in softening any resentments and charged feelings I have toward different past events. I know that I am whole, just as I am—imperfections and all. I'm not broken. I'm not damaged. I am worthy. I offer the Medicines of Forgiveness to the aspects of me that have or are currently acting from a place of survival or unconscious trauma responses.

I open to Medicine of Sight and Vision from my Heart and Soul Beings, to see those adaptive mindsets and have the courage to change my actions to match my Code of Conduct.

I believe in my ability to sense, see, hear, and know when I'm being pulled into old survival responses and ask for the Medicines of Courage and Compassion to flow through me in those moments so I can pause before reacting from a place of being asleep and automatic survival responses.

I'm grateful for my willingness to show up for myself in this beautiful healing way. I ask for support in continuing this willingness and self-love throughout the day.

I open to support at this time and ask for these Medicines to flow through me to any areas of need within and around me now.

Thank you, thank you, thank you—and so it is, peace, peace, peace.

It has been a privilege and honor to walk the path of embodying the Sacred Witness energy with you, and I offer you Light, Love, and JOY as you continue on your journey!

Michelle

Gratitude and Acknowledgments

This book has over twenty years of experiences and connections to give thanks to. I offer a blessing of gratitude to clients, family, friends, teachers, mentors, and coaches. Each and every one of you are my guides and sacred teachers in the art of embodying the Sacred Witness within.

I would like to take the time to honor and thank a few that came together specifically to help me fully birth this project and bring it forward for you.

To my Spiritual Director, Lorena Williams, thank you. Your help and support cannot be measured as a Sacred Witness for me as I walked my journey of becoming devoted to the art of embodying the Sacred Witness. Through your sacred listening and questions, I have been able to open to the subtle metaphors and invitations of each of the teachings I have shared throughout this book. Also, thank you for holding space for me behind the scenes as I struggled with stepping more into the role of Teacher and Sacred Guide in the Healing and Spiritual Arts. Your support over the years has provided me with a wonderful template of the healing power of the Sacred Witness.

To Mary O'Malley, thank you for being a Sacred Witness to so many of us. Your body of work is born from the journey of healing and awakening and helped serve as a Sacred Witness for me during my own journey. Thank you as well for your belief in this book and its message! You are the perfect Being to write the foreword, creating the invitation for us be with what is. Deep Bow of love and gratitude to you for your journey and your willingness to share the fruits of it with myself and others.

Additionally, I would like to thank the interior and cover design team and other artists in their own right that helped bring this book forward. The Book Designers (Ian and Alan), you gave this book the look and feel of welcoming and blessing that it was calling for your work on line editing was amazing, giving the writing its final walk through before coming to life. I am extremely grateful that you were willing to share you expertise and guidance to help bring this book and its companion, *The Sacred Witness Oracle Deck and Guidebook*, into full form! Your support on the final touches of this work gave it the final structure it needed to support others.

To the Unbridled Change team, past and present. Your dedication, heart, and willingness to be on the crazy ride that happens as I follow my intuition and guidance is amazing! Since I founded Unbridled Change in 2008, it is because of the belief and support of both staff, contractors, volunteers, and supporters that I have been able to cultivate the body of work that is shared in this book. Thank you for being you and embodying the healing power of the Sacred Witness within.

To my family, your support and love has allowed me to grow and embody more of who I truly be! Without you I would not fully understand the depths of what I teach. Thank you for being willing to walk with me on this crazy journey that is our life.

To clients, you are my Sacred Witness. Each day I am honored to learn from your courage to lean into the pain points and open to the wilds of your own inner world. It is a gift to witness the Medicines each of you have as you walk with love, compassion, wisdom, and acceptance in every session.

To my beloved "other" Being Companions, I honor and give you gratitude. Your guidance, Soul's presence, and unwavering love and belief in us is amazing. I hope to continue to be a Guide for you and to help other Beings begin to sense, see, hear, and know the brilliance of your sentient light.

To all the supporters and those that backed this book and its companion, *The Sacred Witness Oracle Deck and Guidebook*, thank you! I was honored. and humbled by the support that poured forward. Together we collectively raised the funds for this project suite and additional resources that are helping support Unbridled Change's scholarship and horse funds so that we can continue to provide sliding fee scales for our services and programs along with high-quality care for our horse partners.

To you, reader, I send my love and gratitude. This is a journey of love, compassion, healing, and empowerment. Because of your willingness to step into love, you are also gifting love and compassion to everyone your life touches.

As the light from this work blends and weaves into the light of others, together we can bring the healing that we all so desperately need forward.

Blessings and love—Michelle

Notes

Section One Overview
Epigraph: Sheree Bliss Tinsley, "Medicine Woman's Prayer" (https://www.shereeblisstilsley.com/).

Chapter One
1—In addition to sharing my story of illness at thirteen within this book, I also share parts of the story in one of my other books, *The Horse Cure: True Stories Remarkable Horses Bringing Miraculous Change to Humankind* (Trafalgar Square Books, 2019).

Chapter Two
1—An Exit Ramp is a term I developed to help us remember to consciously pause and shift from protection responses to connecting with our conscious choice. When we take an Exit Ramp, we are willing to create a wedge of awareness that recognizes we are running from a protective Part, hit pause, and step out of a trauma response. Exit Ramps allow you to move toward curiosity to witness what is happening in your system and the present moment and invite you into consciously tending the different aspects of you. I share more about building Exit Ramp in Chapter Six.

Chapter Three
1—I first heard Richard Rohr's states for developing the inner witness during a conference called "Laughing and Weeping" in 2009 with Russ Hudson, co-founder of the Enneagram Institute. You can purchase a recording of this talk from the website for the Center for Action and Contemplation: CAC.org.

2—When we allow our practices to breath, move, and speak with us through our everyday life, that is what is called the "The Fourth Way of Living". The concept of allowing our life itself to serve as our spiritual practice was coined as the Fourth Way and first shared by the modern founder and teacher of the Enneagram teachings G.L. Gurdjieff in 1912 at a talk in Russia.

Section Two Overview
1—Epigraph—Meggan Watterson, *Reveal: A Sacred Manual for Getting Spiritually Naked* (Hay House, 2013).

Chapter Four
1—Epigraph—Pat Oden, *Sensorimotor Psychotherapy: Interventions for Trauma and Attachment* (Norton, 2015).
2—Bessel van der Kolk, *The Body Keeps the Score: Brain, Mind, and Body in the Healing of Trauma* (Penguin Books, 2015).
3—The concept of grounding includes more than aligning your subtle energy bodies, meridians, and or polarity of your field. When we are struggling to accept aspects of our lives, or ourselves, our system protectively starts to disengage its subtle energy bodies, flip our polarity, and begin to reduce our innate connection with our own life force energy, the Earth's energy, and the "space" we find ourselves in. While I teach and support people in helping strengthen and improve the flow and connections of their energy bodies, I have found that the missing link to helping interventions "hold" lies within supporting a Being to open to the Medicines of Acceptance, connection, and willingness to be with themselves just as they are, even if that is a work in progress. We also need to consciously *want* to connect to our life and everything in it, just as it is.
4—The practice I share here is a version of "Orienting and Felt Sense" a common exercise in somatic work developed by pioneer Peter Levine.

Section Three Overview

1 - Epigraph—Gurudev Sri Sri Reva Shankar, https://wisdom.srisri-ravishankar.org/13-uplifting-quotes-from-gurudevs-commentary-on-bhagavad-gita/.

Chapter Six

1—I derived and developed the Bridge of Connection after years of working with clients and myself in healing complex attachment wounds and ruptures. I pulled together key concepts and insights that I discovered while studying and training in: Somatic, Trauma, and Attachment Work (see list in Section Two of Resources); the Developmental Stages of Growth; the Transitions Model by William Bridges; and the stages of Self-Awareness and Spiritual Development via Richard Rohr, Caroline Myss, Carl Jung, and other mystics. You can learn more about how to learn and train in this model via my website UnbridledChange.org.

Chapter Seven

1—The framework of Healing Interviews is derived from a process in Parts Work called unburdening. The original framework was developed by Richard Schwartz and can be found in many different IFS-related books and resources, including Frank Anderson's book *Transcending Trauma: Healing Complex PTSD with Internal Family Systems* (PESI, 2021).

Chapter Nine

1—The original founder of the five stages of grief is Elizabeth Kulber Ross, her work can be found at ekrfoundation.org. Ross originally developed her work and stages of grief as they applied to terminally ill people through her work with hospice patients. The stages were designed to help the person work through their own imminent death and the changes that they would experience as they walked through the final stages of life. Later, her work grew to be applied to support anyone that was walking with a death in their own lives.

2—David Whyte, "Start Close In" from *Essentials book* (Many Rivers Press, 2020), see Appendix A.

3—This is an original mantra that I developed to help connect myself and clients with the true essence of love in action. You can use this mantra to help remind you that love is not just a feeling but a verb and action that we can consciously engage and partner with at any time.

Section Four Overview
1—Epigraph—Sri Ramana Maharshi, *The Collected Work of Ramana Maharshi* (Sopia Perennis, 2006).

Chapter Ten
1—I'm a graduate of CMED, an online school for Professional Certification in Archetypal Consulting run by Caroline Myss. I love her model for working with our personal archetypal patterns via the Archetypal Wheel. You can find out more about her work with archetypes and other spiritual awakening and development via her website at myss.com. In addition, I offer programs that support clients in discovering their own archetypal patterns and how to work with them for personal and spiritual development. You can find my programs at my website unbridledchange.org.

Chapter Eleven
1—Corinthians 13:11. *The Holy Bible*, English Standard Version. (Crossway Bibles, 2021).

Section Five Overview
1—Epigraph—opening quote—unknown.

Chapter Twelve

1—Mindful.org staff wrote a beautiful article, "How to be More Compassionate: A Mindful Guide to Compassion." Within this article, I found one of my favorite definitions of compassion. You can find the article at https://www.mindful.org/how-to-be-more-compassionate-a-mindful-guide-to-compassion/.

Resources

If you want to go deeper into the major healing modalities and themes we explored in this book, I invite you to explore the following resources. These are also sources that informed and supported my understanding as I developed *Trauma Informed Enlightenment*. The list of influential teachers, visionaries, and studies of different healing and spiritual modalities that contribute to who I am as a person, practitioner, and teacher are vast. I deeply honor and am grateful for their willingness to share the wisdom of their paths with so many, including myself.

Section One—Sacred Witness
See Notes for information on additional sources for the stages of developing the Sacred Witness.

Section Two—Body Being
There are some amazing teachers in Trauma Informed work and how it impacts the body, mind, heart, and soul. Here are some wonderful teachers to start with that have an abundance of free resources, books, and other offerings:

Somatic Work:
- Peter Levine is the founder of Somatic Experiencing and the orientator of the practice, "Orienting and Felt Sense" that I share in Chapter Four. You can find more of his work and resources via his website: somaticexperiencing.com.
- Pat Odgen is the founder of Sensorimotor Psychotherapy and you can find more about her framework and offerings via her website: sensorimotorpsychotherapy.org.

- Susan McConnell combines her expertise in Somatic Work with IFS and shamanism, providing a wonderful blend of Western practices and ancient wisdom. Her website is: embodiedself.net.

Polyvagal Theory:

- Stephen Porges, *Our Polyvagal World: How Safety and Trauma Change Us* (Norton, 2023).
- Deb Dana, *The Polyvagal Theory in Therapy: Engaging the Rhythm of Regulation* (Norton, 2018).

Trauma Work and the impact of trauma:

- Bessel van der Kolk, *The Body Keeps the Score: Brain, Mind, and Body in the Healing of Trauma* (Penguin Books, 2015).
- Bruce Perry, *The Boy Who Was Raised as a Dog : And Other Stories from a Child Psychiatrist's Notebook—What Traumatized Children Can Teach Us About Loss, Love, and Healing* (Basic Books, 2007).
- Bruce Perry and Oprah Winfrey, *What Happened to You? Conversations on Trauma, Resilience, and Healing* (Flatiron Books, 2021).
- Dan Siegel, *Mind: A Journey to the Heart of Being Human* (Norton, 2016).
- Gabor Mate, *The Myth of Normal: Trauma, Illness, and Healing in a Toxic Culture* (Avery, 2022).
- Richard Schwartz, *No Bad Parts* (Sounds True Adult, 2021).
- Sarah Petyon, *Your Resonant Self: Guided Meditations and Exercises to Engage Your Brain's Capacity for Healing* (Norton, 2017).

Section Three—Mental Being

Attachment Work:

- Dan Siegel, *The Developing Mind: How Relationships and the Brain Interact to Shape Who We Are* (Guilford Press, Third Edition, 2020).

Section Four—Heart Being

Archetypal Work
- The works of Caroline Myss: Specifically, *Sacred Contracts: Awakening Your Divine Potential* (Harmony, 2003) is a wonderful resource for how to begin and work with her model, and more about her perspective on the four survival archetypal patterns and their role as Guardians.
- Carl Jung's work is also very helpful for additional support around archetypal work, shamanic work, and dream work. A place to start is his book, *The Archetypes and The Collective Unconscious* (Princeton University Press, 1981).

Section Five—Soul Being

Shamanic Healing
- Sandra Ingerman—www.sandraingerman.com
- The Grandmothers, via Grandmother Flordemayo's teachings—www.grandmotherflordemayo.com
- Arnold Mindell—www.aamindell.net
- Misa Hopkins—misahopkins.com

Further Soul Support
- Dalai Lama, Desmond Tutu, and Douglas Carlton Abrams, *The Book of Joy—Lasting Happiness in a Changing World* (Random House, 2016).
- Mary O'Malley, *What's In the Way is the Way: A Practical Guide for Waking Up to Life* (Sounds True, 2016).
- Sarah Petyon, *Affirmations for Turbulent Times: Resonant Words to Soothe Body and Mind* (Norton, 2021).

Appendices

Appendix A

START CLOSE IN

by David Whyte

Essentials book, published in 2020 by Many Rivers Press. Shared with permission from David Whyte and Many Rivers Company, LLC, Langley, WA, www.davidwhyte.com.

Start close in,
don't take the second step
or the third,
start with the first
thing
close in,
the step
you don't want to take.

Start with
the ground
you know,
the pale ground
beneath your feet,
your own
way to begin
the conversation.

Start with your own
question,
give up on other
people's questions,
don't let them
smother something simple.

To hear
another's voice,
follow
your own voice,
wait until
that voice
becomes a private ear
that can
really listen
to another.

Start right now
take a small step
you can call your own
don't follow
someone else's
heroics, be humble
and focused,
start close in,
don't mistake
that other
for your own.

Start close in,
don't take the second step

or the third,
start with the first
thing
close in,
the step
you don't want to take.

Commentary from David:
This poem was inspired by the first lines of Dante's *Comedia* (known also as *Divine Comedy*) written in the midst of the despair of exile from his beloved Florence. It reflects the difficult act we all experience, of trying to make home in the world again when everything has been taken away; the necessity of stepping bravely again, into what looks now like a dark wood, when the outer world as we know it has disappeared, when the world has to be met and in some ways made again from no outer ground but from the very center of our being. The temptation is to take the second or third step, not the first, to ignore the invitation into the center of our own body, into our grief, to attempt to finesse the grief and the absolutely necessary understanding at the core of the pattern, to forgo the radial and almost miraculous simplification into which we are being invited. Start close in.

Appendix B

Here you will find quick reference overviews of key concepts, frameworks, and questions to support you as you cultivate the healing power of the Sacred Witness.

SACRED WITNESS TRAITS AND STAGES

The Sacred Witness is the rich and capable aspect of us that can interact with all the various Parts and aspects of our complex inner being—Body, Mind, Heart, and Soul.

The Sacred Witness not only notices and tracks our system, but it does so with unconditional compassion, care, and attunement. Thus, the Sacred Witness allows us to honor and work with aspects of us we would normally judge, dismiss, or reject. When we are being held by a Sacred Witness, we have a visceral sense of being deeply heard, seen, felt, and understood. In this presence, all healing becomes possible.

The Sacred Witness:
- Sees the wisdom held in our survival and trauma adaptations.
- Trusts our inner healing power.
- Connects us to the unconditional love emanating from our Heart and Soul Beings, no matter how far away from that connection we have wandered.
- Is unattached to outcome and allows exiled aspects of us to organically come forward and welcomes them with curiosity and acceptance.

- Knows that we are whole, powerful, and worthy of health, wellness, and joy—just as we are.
- Is comfortable sitting in the discomfort our system often wants us to avoid.
- Offers us compassion without an agenda.
- Seeks to empower the ever-present light inside us that seeks to share its warmth and support within and with others.
- Helps us take what we discover in the witnessing process and move into aligned action from our True Selves, which helps us move from love instead of fear.

OUR FOUR INNER ASPECTS AND THEIR TRAITS

Body Being: Our Body Being is more than our physical body and its components of bones, tissues, cells, and organs. It serves as our "home" for this lifetime and carries an intelligence that helps us maintain overall balance, safety, enjoyment, and interaction with what is within and around us. It has an innate healing wisdom that can automatically assess and tend to the physical aspects of us in need of support.

The Body Being serves as a conscious Sacred Messenger for ALL aspects of us, including what is happening within other Beings. Our Body Being talks with us through the language of somatic, meaning physical sensations, or the felt sense.

Mental Being: Our Mental Being is associated with our mind, beliefs, and automatic programs that run our body from both a survival-level consciousness and a cognitive-level consciousness. On the latter level, it handles problem-solving and executive functioning, such as learning language and muscle memory of sequencing and other repetitive motions. It is often called our *psyche* or the *ego* *mind.* However, it is beyond a personal image of Self. Our Mental Being contains a consciousness that includes both our own personal experiences, memories, and thoughts, and the collective's. It contains survival programs and experiences of ALL life—our families of origin, communities, and all Beings through time and space. Our Mental Being's main language is our thoughts. Like the Body Being, the Mental Being has very real rules of engagement to help us stay safe—designed to help us survive first at all costs, then if those needs are met move to the personal needs and preferences, and eventually open to meeting the needs of the Soul.

Heart Being: Our Heart Being is often only associated with our emotions, yet is way more than that. It serves as the organizing nucleus for our whole system. The Heart holds our needs, wants, desires, dreams, and inspirations that come from our Soul. The Heart Being speaks to us through symbolism, archetypal patterns, and emotions to help us connect with all it is sensing. The Heart Being can hold true to our inner guidance, where the Mental Being feels shadow fears and doubt. It shepherds the creative inspirations from the Soul that our Mental Being often struggles to connect with. It also is the messenger for wounded Parts of us the Mental Being has exiled because it didn't believe we had the support or stability to process and tend them. The Heart Being is an incredible aspect of us that has a capacity beyond the survival levels of us to believe in ourselves and to take leaps of faith to follow the guidance of the Soul Being. This aspect of our being is associated with the four survival archetypes, which I call the Guardians of the Heart.

Soul Being: The Soul Being is not a static, externally-dwelling aspect of us, watching us work our way through life. Our Soul Being is active, internal, and an integral part of what makes us, well, *us.* Each Being's Soul has its own unique frequency, traits, and gifts. The Soul Being is the part of us not bound by the different labels or filters of our ego-self, which is often taught to desperately cling to outside validation for a sense of worthiness. The Soul Being knows our intrinsic worth. Our Soul Being can transcend the limits of our personal consciousness or ego mind and connect us to the wisdom and knowledge of the collective, the inner wisdom we have accumulated from ALL our experiences beyond this lifetime, and allows us to access the cosmic mind. Our Soul also links us to the Cosmic Heart, limitless radical love, and the Medicines of the Soul.

Basics of the Check-In

Check in by noticing (via your felt sense not your Mental Being):

- What can I see right now?
- What can I smell right now?
- What can I hear right now?
- What can I taste right now?
- What can my body feel or sense right now from the external world?

Next, shift to an Internal Check-In:

Sense and notice what your body is "doing" with each one of the questions above, again, without changing or altering it.

For example, *when I check in with what I am seeing right now, I notice . . .*

. . . my breath and what it is doing,

. . . my body posture,

. . . my heart rate,

and so on.

Bridge of Connection™

Outer Bridge

The Outer Bridge facilitates access to Self through the Safety of Others and is the first Bridge of Connection we require as a young child. If all five pillars are in place and functioning, our little system gives us a green light to access and show up as our True Self. If one of the questions our system asks at a pillar comes back with a no, then our Mental Being kicks into gear with its protective programs and takes us into the safety of our survival programs and adaptations, trying to help us survive the best we can, while keeping our Heart safe.

Main Questions Asked at Each Pillar of the Outer Bridge of Connection:

Trust—Can I predict you? If I can predict you, my nervous system feels that it knows what to do to meet those conditions and gives us an inner sense of "calm."

Respect—Do I feel you have regards for me in a predictable way? If I feel that you care about my feelings and needs as a sentient being (that I'm allowed to have my own thoughts, ideas, emotions, and ways of being), I feel a sense of acceptance and connection between us.

Willingness and Choice—Do I feel I have the right to say yes, no, or maybe to a request from you without our connection suffering? If not, I do not continue on the Bridge of Connection with you or with myself, and instead default into the protective versions of myself: flight, fight, people-pleasing, appeasement, fawning, folding, and even freezing.

Connection—Do I feel that you respect, model, and help hold healthy boundaries for me and you in our dance of connection?

Purpose and Values—Do you honor my own unique values and inner knowing, or do you require me to meet and adopt yours? If you do, I feel free to be and act in alignment with my True Self, sharing the ideas, musings, and insights I gain from my Heart and Soul, inviting you into my world and seeking to understand and be a part of yours in kind.

Inner Bridge

The Inner Bridge facilitates access to Self through the Safety of our own connection and Faith in our True Self and is the second bridge that develops as we become adults with increasing degrees of freedom and power to provide for our own safety and survival relatively free from the influence or authority of another. Our Inner Bridge helps us dismantle any protective and survival adaptations we had to make early in life so we can feel secure in our own ability to show up for life in alignment with our Heart and Soul's guidance.

Main Questions Asked at Each Pillar
of the Inner Bridge of Connection:

Inner Trust—Can I predict myself to stay true to my guidance and inner Code of Conduct? When I am out of alignment with my Heart and Soul, can I predict that I will lovingly and compassionately help myself and the Parts of me that are scared, concerned, or resistant to release their unresolved needs or wounds so I can re-align with my True Self?
Self-Respect—Do I have regards for my own self evidenced by how I treat myself—internally as well as externally, in relationships and exchanges?

Willingness and Choice—Do I give myself permission to say yes, no, and maybe? Do I honor my own working edges and honor myself through my thoughts and actions?

Connection—Do I stay true to my inner guidance when I'm in the dance of connection? Can I engage in healthy compromise? Do I remember that boundaries are in an inside job and the responsibility for holding and setting them belongs to me?

Purpose and Values—Do I seek my Heart and Soul's guidance and council to help me understand and connect with choices that will bring myself and others greater balance, freedom, healing, and wellness? Do I follow and act in alignment with that guidance the best I can?

Repair Work for Your Bridges: Our system doesn't demand perfection, or that we remain aligned with each pillar's invitations all the time. That would be incredibly unkind and outside of the laws of wholeness. Instead, it asks us to be willing to receive guidance and insight from the Sacred Witness when we are driving off course and acting or thinking in ways that weaken or shake each pillar's themes in our life.

The repair process has a simple framework, a willingness to run through the questions above and receive feedback and insights from the Sacred Witness on where Parts of you need your attention and care so they can heal their unmet needs and unresolved wounds. The act of Sacred Witnessing allows you the opportunity to then dismantle your old protective programs and reconnect with your Heart and Soul's true operating system through the fifth pillar of Purpose and Values as the new orientation for how you can both stay true to yourself and meet your survival and personal needs.

The Four Guardians of the Heart
Key Traits and Gifts Held within Each Guardian

Child, the Guardian of Innocence

- A Child, by its nature, needs a caregiver.
- A Child, by its nature, has no real power and requires adults to honor their voice.
- A Child is in the moment, they do not have the same orientation to time as adults do.
- A Child can see, hear, feel, and interact with different dimensions and innately sees all types of Beings as the same, value-wise.
- A Child perceives differences as beauty.
- A Child has no Inner Critic.
- A Child is free to imagine, laugh, play, and enjoy the sweetness of life—free from the burdens of meeting their own survival needs.

Victim, the Guardian of Truth and Choice

- The Victim, by its nature, is not personal. It helps us shift from "why me?" to "why not me?" Honoring that harm, sickness, and adverse events will happen to all life.
- The Victim engages us with acts of Care: Because we will experience moments of harm, confusion, and pain, the Victim in the Light can compassionately and willingly witness and take us into action around tending our wounds and others' wounds.
- The Victim provides us with Choice. Once we can see that care is needed, this Guardian helps us move into motion—seeking, receiving, and taking actions to address, support, and behave in ways that would support overall healing.

Prostitute, the Guardian of Worth and Integrity
- The Prostitute engages us in the Dance of Relationship. Every connection we make internally and externally comes with requests, giving, receiving, yielding, leading, and compromising.
- The Prostitute invites into understanding what has Authority within us.
- The Prostitute asks us to look at the choices we are making and why.

Saboteur, the Guardian of Empowerment
- The Saboteur is an archetypal signal we are close to empowerment and only comes forward in our system when we are ready to shift into a new stage of power, consciousness, and self-agency.
- We often don't believe we are ready to leap, and the Guardian of Power helps us remember to have faith in our innate power to follow our Heart and Soul Beings.
- This Guardian asks the Mental Being to pass the baton and trust that our survival can be met through our Heart and Soul's guidance and support.
  It asks three main questions:
- Are you ready for the impact that your committed powerful action will have on your world and the people in it?
- Are you okay if it doesn't go well or as planned? Are you going to lose power if that happens?
- Are you willing to hold your power and stay true to it, or are you going to abandon it if someone challenges you?

About the Author

Over the past twenty-five years, Michelle has served as a full-time Healing and Wellness Practitioner to a diverse range of clients seeking to find themselves and reengage fully with their life after complex trapped trauma in their body disconnected them from themselves and their ability to live, love, and lead their authentic life.

Michelle's devotion to supporting others' healing and spiritual journeys back to their Heart and Soul is seeded in her own seeker's journey. She knows from personal experience that one of the main blocks to healing and wellness for trauma survivors is the ability to feel safe and worthy enough to connect back to their Heart and Soul's love. Through both client work and her personal journey, she realized that any type of healing journey required building an internal secure attachment with all aspects of yourself: body, mind, heart, and soul. She developed her proven Bridge of Connection™ process, showcased in *Trauma Informed Enlightenment* among other key teachings, that helps clients feel safe and held as they rediscover their own innate inner healing ability to connect to their True Self.

Michelle's work is integrative and visionary in nature. Pulling together the healing toolbox she developed over the past two decades has significantly contributed to greater trauma informed practices within both equine-assisted professions and wider healing and spiritual practice circles. A few of the trainings Michelle has completed that have influenced her unique methods include:
- Archetypal Consultant Certification through Caroline Myss
- Eden Energy Medicine Practitioner
- Usui Reiki Master and Teacher
- Somatic Internal Family Systems Informed Certification

- Extensive trauma and attachment theory trainings/ certifications
- Equine Partnered Psychotherapy and Coaching™
- Training and Certifications in Energy and Wellness Coaching, Spiritual Coaching, Mindfulness and Meditation Coaching, and indigenous shamanic practices facilitation

Through these trainings and beyond, Michelle has spent thousands of hours supporting clients to rediscover and establish a connection with their True Self after complex trauma and attachment wounds through the work she offers in *Trauma Informed Enlightenment*. She is the founder of the non-profit Unbridled Change, which you can find at unbridledchange.org.

Continued Work with Michelle

If you are looking for ways to continue and deepen your journey with the Sacred Witness within, you can find more information about the different workshops, programs, offerings, and resources at unbridledchange.org.

The Sacred Witness Oracle Suite

Sacred Witness
Oracle
Guidebook

AWAKENING
YOUR INNER
HEALING
POWER

Michelle Holling-Brooks

ILLUSTRATIONS BY Kimberly Ganley

Trauma
Informed
Enlightenment

AWAKENING TO THE HEALING
POWER OF THE SACRED
WITNESS

Michelle Holling-Brooks

FOREWORD BY Mary O'Malley

31. Inspiration

23. Mental Being

15. Talk with